CHRISTIANITY
in the
21ST CENTURY

CHRISTIANITY
in the
21ST CENTURY

Edited by
Deborah A. Brown, Ph.D.

A Crossroad Classic Book
The Crossroad Publishing Company
New York

Permission is gratefully acknowledged to quote from
George Herbert: The Country Parson, The Temple,
ed. John N. Wall, Jr., copyright © 1981 by Paulist Press.

Royalties from the sale of this book will be donated to charity.

The Crossroad Publishing Company
370 Lexington Avenue, New York, NY 10017

Copyright © 2000 by Deborah A. Brown

Cover design by Troy B. Scarlott

Printed in the United States of America

Library of Congress Catalog Card Number: 99-068423
ISBN 0-8245-1842-X

2   3   4   5   6   7   8   9   10   05   04   03   02   01   00

CONTENTS

ACKNOWLEDGMENTS

Several people worked with me on this book, and to them I offer thanks for their advice, hard work, and enthusiasm. A colleague, James A. Robinson, political scientist and president emeritus of the University of West Florida, provided valuable review that greatly enhanced this work. I also am very grateful to three staff members of the Episcopal Diocese of Newark. Lyn Conrad and Gail Deckenbach spent hours proofreading, helping to shape the final manuscript. Many books have a heroine; Margaret Giammarino is the heroine of this work. She wholeheartedly devoted her entire summer to producing version after version of the manuscript with both precision and speed. Her help on this volume was enormous, and I will remain deeply indebted to her many talents. Finally, I express my deep love and appreciation to my husband, Chuck, without whose unending support this volume could not have been undertaken.

INTRODUCTION

Deborah A. Brown

IN PRAISE OF JOHN SHELBY SPONG, eighth bishop of the Episcopal Diocese of Newark in northern New Jersey (1976–2000). During his controversial episcopacy — in which he presided over 124 churches and their some forty thousand members — Bishop Spong was characterized in vivid terms by both his supporters and critics. The large number of his admirers recognize his defense of the rights of African-Americans in the church during the 1960s, his leadership in support of women's equality and ordination in the 1970s, his courage in tackling another contentious civil rights battle by supporting the ordination of homosexuals, and in 1987, his urging the national church to acknowledge gay and lesbian marriages. Loyalists say the bishop reflected the mind of Christ in his faithful support of those who are marginalized as he struggled to keep his church relevant to all social segments in a complex modern age.

This favorable view is hardly the last word on the bishop, however. Vehement detractors point to the provocative twelve theses, drawn from his book *Why Christianity Must Change or Die: A Bishop Speaks to Believers in Exile,* as proof that he has utterly and publicly abandoned Christianity. The bishop published his theses in Luther style in the diocesan paper and on the Internet in May 1998 to initiate the debate he was seeking. By portraying him as undermining the faith and even as demonic, some adversaries have swept the bishop into the "once a Christian, but now an atheist" dustbin of church history. At best, he is dismissed by his fiery opponents as a wayward secular humanist who long ago should have exercised self-censorship or removed himself from the pulpit and the episcopate.

On both sides of the "Spong aisle," there is cause and emotion, as well as ironic crossover. His supporters have sometimes wearied of his limelight and embattlements, while his critics have acknowl-

1

edged more than once that his episcopacy has caused almost everyone, conservative or liberal, not to take the faith casually.

Jack Spong, as he is called by friends, is one of the church's best-known and most widely published liberals, who — frequently in combative style and always unflinchingly — presses progressive causes. In his books and in his lectures across the world, he has proclaimed his version of Christianity, which is open to new possibilities and compelling for many. Bishop Spong invites his audiences to abandon biblical literalism and to enter a radical theological debate. To the admiration of some and the consternation of others, he has supported racial diversity, access to birth control, legal abortion, and the morality of physician-assisted suicide under certain circumstances. He has campaigned for justice for all, including women, gays, and lesbians. These efforts have deeply troubled many traditionalists. Yet, while traditionalists dispute what they call the bishop's ultraliberal positions, their overarching charge is that he violates the boundaries of orthodox Christianity. Faultfinders say the bishop denies the Virgin Birth, the Resurrection, and the Ascension of Jesus, and because he opposes theism, he no longer believes in God. Behind each of these criticisms lie differences in definitions, however. Bishop Spong counters that traditionalists must separate the Virgin Birth from biology, the Resurrection from the idea of physical resuscitation, the Ascension from principles of gravity, and the concept of God from theistic categories of antiquity. Conventional definitions, he maintains, became inadequate in the twentieth century.

This volume, however, written by nine of today's preeminent scholars and theologians, does not celebrate Bishop Spong's theological or social positions. Rather, it commemorates an often overlooked but powerful feature of his episcopacy: the desire to investigate and scrutinize the religious status quo, with the aim of keeping the minds of the church — clerical and lay — open to seeking new ways to carry forward Christian beliefs and affairs in modes that will protect the interests of civilized society, stimulate human prosperity and healthy growth, and advance creative fulfillment of individuals.[1] This work honors Bishop Spong's conscience and commitment concerning the destiny of the Christian Church. He has urged open debate and called

---

1. For a discussion of prophetic considerations in contemporary thought, see Neal Riemer, *The Future of the Democratic Revolution: Toward a More Prophetic Politics* (New York: Praeger, 1984).

the faithful to be true to the spirit of the scriptures and to seek ways toward greater interrelatedness among society's members.

In Bishop Spong's charge to both the Episcopal and other Christian churches, there is the recognition of inevitable conflict but also an underlying appreciation of the necessity for ultimate accommodation. His challenge does not assume debate without dispute and even antagonism, but holds out hope for honest discussion and resolutions to certain and understandable disagreements. Perhaps most importantly, the call for debate affirms that, in many matters of religion, there must be acts of faith. At the core of the Protestant tradition, however, is awareness that knowledge processed by humans is always subject to fallibility. In the 1500s and other times, new approaches shook, and sometimes overturned, what previously had seemed like solid ground. Nevertheless, Christianity grew as a result; it was not diminished. And today Christianity claims more followers than any other religion.

Christians view themselves as brothers and sisters in Christ; therefore, in keeping with their understanding, reconciliation must be anticipated in existing and future discussions. So it is essential to the influence and growth of Christianity in the twenty-first century that creative tension does not die, but continues to guard against complacency as Christian communities consider how they will better respond to human needs and views in a world in which people of different religious, cultural, and political persuasions interact regularly via Internet, airplanes, leisure visits, and business transactions.

The Buddha cautioned his followers that change is inevitable, and if they insisted on clinging to what they knew to protect themselves, they were seeking refuge in a false security. We also might add, as Neal Riemer, a Jewish-American political scientist, has cautioned, that change "is safest in an open, self-correcting system modeled on our openness to God and redemption."[2] Bishop Spong's concern about the church's contemporary performance in an age of acute individualism does not demand agreement with his views but militates against limiting the church's vision to former understandings and sometimes weak, irresolute, or even prejudicial policies and practices that may no longer draw support from an increasingly independent-minded, internationally aware, and pluralistically oriented public. Church leaders of the twenty-first century will have to work within the fast-changing

---

2. Ibid., 108.

world as people transform it, even as they struggle to make the church grow in accord with its values, traditions, and beliefs. Thus, members as well as leaders will be challenged in the future, as they have been in the past, to alter the church in the light of changes both in society and in their own vision of new possibilities, whether theological, philosophical, social, ecological, medical, economic, or political. Consistent with the prophetic tradition is the church's capacity for continual winnowing of beliefs, systems, and practices to see if at least some of them have become chaff to be discarded because they are no longer credible, moral, or relevant. Most theologians will agree that religion is not a rigid monument of the past but a fluid, ever-changing entity.

Among his controversial twelve theses, Bishop Spong maintains that literal understandings of the Virgin Birth and the cosmic Ascension run counter to contemporary knowledge about reproduction and the shape of the universe, and that the possibilities of the Atonement cannot be exhausted with the earliest Jewish disciples' interpretation of the crucifixion in terms of the sacrificial lamb of Yom Kippur. Many Christians are outraged by these views, yet in the United States, where some 96 percent of the public expresses belief in God, growing numbers of Christians query and reconsider traditional church positions. And the criticism they level at the church and its leaders is not always subtle. Attacking the Roman Catholic Church, Dr. Elisabeth Schüssler Fiorenza of Harvard Divinity School has called that body "an elite, male dominated, sacred pyramidal order of domination."[3] Sheila Briggs, a professor of religious and social ethics at the University of Southern California, has added, "To ordain women is to give this rotten totalitarian system that the Roman Catholic Church has become the push into the grave."[4]

Even more troubling than the barbs of some academics is knowledge that large numbers of followers skirt church rules in opinion and practice. Many Catholics, for instance, favor abortion rights, and groups such as Catholics for Choice are in place. Some say the abortion debate has become a significant generational issue between younger and older church members. In the mid-1990s, fewer than 21 percent of American Catholics felt bound by church teachings on

---

3. Peter Steinfels, "Women Wary about Aiming to Be Priests," *New York Times*, November 14, 1995, A17.
4. Ibid.

contraception.[5] And a growing contingent of Catholics also questions whether their church's annulment process is honest, fair, or necessary. Estimates are that nine of ten divorcing Catholics ignore the process, and the several million who remarry outside the church and then are denied confession and Holy Communion remain estranged from the church, instead turning to non-Catholic churches — or perhaps to none.[6]

A signal that all is not well in the Roman Catholic Church in the United States is the decline in its number of priests over the last approximate thirty years. The number dropped from about 58,000 in 1965 to about 48,000 in 1997, although America's Catholic population increased some 15 million over the same period. In 1997, there were fewer than 3,200 seminarians studying for the priesthood that serves the nation's more than 60 million Catholics. Required celibacy, competition from other professions, and high-profile publicity of sexual abuse cases involving priests are identified as factors contributing to the decline of the priesthood as a career choice.[7]

The declining number of priests is hardly the last of the church's difficulties. When Pope John Paul II met with 125,000 people in Central Park in Manhattan in October 1995, he exhorted his listeners to spread religious ideals in a world moving toward the third Christian millennium. However, at a Mass in Queens the day before, he had pondered whether, in the midst of a scientific and technological society like the United States, there was room for the mystery of God. This, too, is central to the crisis of the modern Christian Church.

Yet it is still the case, as a senior editor of *Forbes* has pointed out, that "Jesus Draws." Since 1979, more than 1.5 billion people, or about one-quarter of the world's population, have seen the film *Jesus,* part of an outreach program of Campus Crusade for Christ International, a nondenominational evangelical organization.[8] But despite Jesus' impressive contemporary appeal, it remains to be seen whether people will continue to be attracted beyond the year 2000 to main-

---

5. Jeffrey L. Sheler, "Spiritual America," *U.S. News and World Report,* April 4, 1994, 56.

6. Laurie Goodstein, "When a Marriage Never Was," *Washington Post National Weekly Edition,* April 28, 1997, 10.

7. Jon Jeter, "This Is Not Your Father's Catholic Church," *Washington Post National Weekly Edition,* December 21–28, 1998, 33.

8. Susan Lee, "Jesus Draws," *Forbes,* August 10, 1998, 58–59.

line Christian churches as individuals independently consider why the universe came to be, where they came from, why they are here and how they should conduct themselves, the challenges to their quality of life, their spiritual needs, and, at last, where they are going. Because the world has "shrunken in size" with advanced technology, people are exposed daily to alternative views to help them address their greatest wants and worries.

The state of the earth's environment, of course, is one of those urgent contemporary concerns. The world's great religious traditions are in increasing dialogue on such global matters but also in competition as they search for acceptable ways to handle problems. Buddhists, Christians, Confucians, Hindus, Jains, Muslims, Jews, Taoists, believers in Shinto, and followers of tribal religions gathered in the fall of 1998 at the American Museum of Natural History to explore whether their traditions could help reverse the growing human destruction of the planet. Continued investigation of creative possibilities is aimed at furthering conservation of the natural world, while simultaneously religious leaders try to draw their followers' attention to the degradation of the environment.[9]

Like ecology, medicine is another arena in which religious and scientific leaders are increasingly aware that neither group has all the answers. Because much of the knowledge at hand is tentative, open-mindedness and cooperation are assets. Partly in response to changing public attitudes, researchers are finding that science and theology are not separate worlds, but have use for each other. So it is no longer extraordinary that articles and studies explore the effects of religious beliefs and prayer on healing, and that some scientists confess there is much to learn about the interrelatedness of spiritual outlook, biological recovery, and good health.

It is in the "human predicament" that there is much we don't — and likely never will — know. But despite this obstacle, attempts are being made for daily and permanent dialogues among religions' representatives to broaden mutual understanding, recognition, and respect, and to cooperate in addressing the many elements of humankind's suffering. Episcopal Bishop William E. Swing of California aims to develop

---

9. "An Environmental Agenda for the World's Faiths," *New York Times*, October 24, 1998, A15.

a United Religions Organization, whose purpose is to provide at least one such international forum.[10]

It is telling, however, that religious violence was the spur for Swing's idea. More and more, religions are finding themselves developing followings in the same time and place, a fact which should offer hope for common cause. But similar to the erosion of authoritarian political leaders' control because of public access to the Internet, other technical advances, and business and cultural exchanges, the authority of religious leaders and of established church dogma now must grapple with believers' broadening exposure to divergent views. Once, a Christian or Jewish student entering a World Religions class had little or no understanding of Islam, Hinduism, or Buddhism for lack of personal contact with these wisdom traditions. But today's student is apt to sit next to a practicing Muslim, Hindu, or Buddhist and interact with that classmate regularly, both socially and intellectually.

Increased interaction of religious believers with one another can have two simultaneous outcomes: greater mutual respect and cooperation, yet also a growing tendency, at least among traditionalist segments, to view themselves as under siege. Such fear has contributed recently to the attacks by Hindus on Christians in India, the violent response by Muslims against Christians and ethnic Chinese in Indonesia, and the concerns of Iranian religious leaders as they scramble to cope with growing demands — inspired by the predominantly Christian West — for religious and political liberalization. So, while there is improving cooperation and understanding among religions at many levels, concurrently there is movement in some societies to counter the trend toward pluralism by upholding a particular religion as a means of defining culture and boosting nationalism, as is the case in India, Pakistan, Afghanistan, the former Yugoslavia, Russia, Tibet,[11] and elsewhere. Historically, this behavior is familiar.

The thinking of postmodern theologians, therefore, is challenged to overcome some harsh realities. Its nontraditionalism, while seeking broader accommodation and tolerance, is seen by some groups and communities as an attack on their determined and legitimate efforts to preserve their unique heritages, interests, and influences. Non-

---

10. Frederick Quinn, "Metaphors of Motion: Global Initiatives in a New Century," *The Living Church*, July 16, 1998, 8–9.

11. Tibetan Buddhists have been attempting to protect their religious and cultural heritage, which has been under attack by the Chinese Communists since the 1950s.

traditionalism will be resisted (sometimes bitterly) by religious leaders who are intent on protecting what was assumed as theological, moral, and jurisdictional certainty. Of course, prerogative, prestige, power, and matters of loyalty and sovereignty also are involved. A parallel can be drawn in present-day politics. China's sovereignty over Hong Kong was to be governed by the policy of "one country, two systems," itself based on the principles of nonsubordination, noninterference, and mutual respect. But as many observers anticipated, with the intersecting of divergent systems, clear lines of distinction began to blur. This has disturbed persons on both sides of the Hong Kong–China border, who hold their beliefs and ways of life as time-tested, suitable to their histories and societies, and, consequently, worth preserving.

Another consideration of merit as Christianity adapts itself to the twenty-first century is how modifications to it might affect the international political landscape. Over the past two millenniums, there have been far too many examples of Christian institutions and individuals acting in authoritarian, repressive, and even exceedingly cruel ways, which is an unfortunate, humiliating, but very real part of the Christian legacy. Elie Wiesel, for instance, has laid the horrors of the Holocaust on the Christian doorstep. But more recently, Freedom House of Washington, D.C., published figures that deserve attention and investigation: It claims, of the world's 191 countries, 88 are free and afford their inhabitants a broad range of civil liberties, and of these, 79 are majority Christian by tradition or belief. Only 9 of the 50 countries with the poorest records in political rights are majority Christian. Freedom House's researchers maintain that a country with a Christian majority is five times more likely to be free and democratic than it is to be repressive.[12] Certain tenets of Christianity — many of which owe much to Judaism — have had a profound effect in shaping liberal, pluralistic societies. Human equality in the eyes of God, inalienable rights that are prior to the state, and accountability to a higher power are some of the concepts that have advanced the human and civil rights of individuals. Influenced by Judaism, Christians also have embraced the will to closely examine the status quo and to move in collective action toward improvements in society, including broadening social justice and tolerating minority points of

---

12. Adrian Karatnycky, "Freedom and Faith," *Wall Street Journal, Weekend Journal,* January 22, 1999, W13.

view. Obviously, these values are not owned wholly by the Jewish and Christian traditions. But it is almost exclusively in societies that have been heavily influenced by Jewish and Christian heritage where liberal democracies and a passion for freedom and justice have flourished. So, as Christians modify their understandings of themselves during the twenty-first century, which promises to be a period of broader cultural integration, they will have to reflect carefully on what they believe their contributions to the world should be. Indeed, the majority of Americans see a creator God as the guiding force of America's democracy.

But it is also the case that people in the United States, Great Britain, and other politically liberal societies find tension between their spiritual needs and their secular impulses. In the closing decades of the twentieth century, people asserted individual freedoms regarding their faith and resisted conventional religious constrictions. And as exchange between diverse cultures increased, many people became more uncertain about how they should approach religion in secular, pluralistic societies. Parents and grandparents, perhaps still parochial in their religious outlooks, had children and grandchildren who were less committed to their churches or even to their denominations, thus showing their willingness to be more universal in their religious beliefs. In a country like the United States, where inclusiveness is now a watchword, it is not surprising that postwar and younger generations take a more generalist and tolerant approach in their religious views. Indeed, it is in keeping with the moral imperative to be more accepting of people of other faiths. Consequently, not only Bishop Spong but also many other church leaders envision future generations becoming less theologically and institutionally fixed and moving toward greater flexibility, experimentation, and perhaps even deep mysticism in their personal spiritual journeys.

For some, including Bishop Spong, this dynamic also includes a desire to shift away from a premodern theistic concept of the divine to a more abstract understanding of Perfection. They find the perception of one God who is "out there" as deliberate creator, ultimate ruler of the universe, known through revelation, and bringer of rewards and punishment to be a premodern understanding that no longer is compatible with where they today find themselves intellectually, emotionally, or spiritually. As the bishop explains, he and similarly minded people are seeking the profound spiritual experience of antiquity, but recast in a mode that is inspirational and relevant in a postmodern world. This new way of experiencing spirituality, freed from conventional Christian theological entrapments, is meant to allow the transcendent holy in each individual to be fully realized: thus, exercise of this new understanding of Christianity is expected to arrive ultimately at the answer to how Jane Doe can be wholly Jane Doe.

But at a minimum two hurdles appear: (1) Will theistic Christianity easily accommodate a nontheistic path which has a decided flavoring of the East? (2) Will the huge number of the nearly two billion Christians in the world who approach God through the heart with love and emotion and who seek a personal God with attributes — often including face and form — accommodate themselves to an abstract, transpersonal understanding of the divine? And if they don't, will these two groups, who both view themselves as followers of Christ, be willing to eschew fundamentalism so that the two distinct approaches to the Truth can gracefully coexist? Because many in the postwar generations are independent-minded and willing to experiment, a growing nontheistic form of Christianity becomes a possibility. In many avenues of life, from sexual expression to occupational choice and from parenting to selection of food and more, people have been breaking with traditions and exploring alternatives.

Regardless of one's position on these theological views, the existence of the tension between perspectives shows that the church, indeed, is not stagnant and that we live in a time of spiritual ferment. Immigration, once predominantly from European nations, now brings a broader mix of cultures and their religions into our midst. So, we grow more eclectic, even as immigrants seek acculturation. And while the most impressive growth among Christians, at least in the United States, has been in evangelical churches, mainline Protestant and Roman Catholic churches slowly have been losing ground.[13] Ironically, while evangelicals present a vision of certainty to their followers, it is often argued that for mainline churches, the days are numbered for their leaders to realistically expect orthodoxy from their members, since now they are freely challenging many traditions of their faith.

---

13. Among numerous sources, see "Belief by the Numbers," compiled by Russell Shorto, *New York Times Magazine*, December 7, 1997, 60.

Inevitable change in patterns of believing leads us to contemplate new directions of Christian thinking as we engage the future. Acknowledging the need for a forum to study and discuss emerging ideas, Bishop Spong established the New Dimensions and the John Elbridge Hines Lectures in the Diocese of Newark to bring some of the world's most esteemed theological and scientific minds into conversation with church members. Since 1976, some sixty renowned intellectuals have addressed new visions of religion and science in this forum. Among them, the authors of this volume presented conceptual breakthroughs that were so thought-provoking it seemed advantageous for Christians and others to enter the next century with the insights of their most recent views.

Bishop Spong's ministry, especially his episcopacy, has reached out alike to faithful and to those who would pray to be faithful. For those with overbelief, as William James called people of faith, as well as those with other searchlights for truth as God gives them to see truth, these essays combine to inspire readers in the post-Spong era, whatever their aisle, whatever their pew.

DEBORAH A. BROWN is a member of the Asian Studies Faculty at Seton Hall University and an Associate Scholar at the Foreign Policy Research Institute in Philadelphia. Her writings on religious issues and on China, Hong Kong, and Taiwan affairs have appeared in many publications including the *Asian Wall Street Journal, Freedom Review, The Free China Journal, China Perspectives, Christian Century,* and *Asian Survey.* Her research has centered on political developments in Hong Kong, Taiwan, and China, with special emphasis on matters of democratization in these societies, including the positive and negative roles of religious institutions, leaders, and beliefs in that process. As Managing Editor of the *American Asian Review,* in 1998 she edited a special edition on Hong Kong following the July 1, 1997, handover, which included consideration of the future of religious freedom in China's new Special Administrative Region. She contributed "The Role of Religion in Promoting Democracy in the People's Republic of China and Hong Kong" to *Church State Relations in 21st Century Asia* and authored *Turmoil in Hong Kong on the Eve of Communist Rule,* which considers the fate of the territory and its Anglican Church.

Chapter 1

THE FUTURE OF GOD

Karen Armstrong

KAREN ARMSTRONG has been a Roman Catholic nun, a university lecturer, and schoolteacher. Since 1982, she has been a freelance writer and broadcaster and is also a part-time lecturer at the Leo Baeck College for the Study of Judaism and the Training of Rabbis and Teachers. Her books include *Through the Narrow Gate,* an account of her life in the convent; *The Gospel according to Woman; Holy-War: The Crusades and Their Impact on Today's World; Muhammad: A Biography of the Prophet;* the international best-seller *A History of God; A History of Jerusalem;* and *In the Beginning: A New Reading of Genesis.* Her books have been translated into thirty languages. She is currently writing a history of fundamentalism in Judaism, Christianity, and Islam. Karen Armstrong holds a degree from Oxford University and is one of the world's most prominent spokespersons on religious matters.

W E CAN NO LONGER be religious in the same way as our ancestors. The world has been irrevocably transformed and so have our patterns of thought and experience. During the twentieth century, human beings initiated change to an unprecedented degree. We achieved a greater control over our environment than any previous generation; our technology created the global culture that links hitherto distant parts of the world together in close electronic proximity. We traveled around the world with astonishing speed and facility; we saw our planet from outer space. Our perspectives radically altered, and, if we are not to reduce religion to an archaic, interesting, but obsolete museum-piece, our theological beliefs and practices must change, too. This is a matter of great urgency, because during the troubled twentieth century, we were deluged with the spectacle of human suffering as never before. Every evening, news of disasters that we would never have heard about before the advent of the mass media penetrated our homes. The twentieth century was one of genocide: our technological efficiency enabled us to slaughter our fellow humans on a scale that would have been impossible for a regime circumscribed by the more traditional methods of slaughter. In the Armenian massacres of 1917, the Nazi Holocaust, the Gulag, Bosnia, Rwanda, and Kosovo, we had dark epiphanies of human depravity and evil. Without the deliberate cultivation of a faith that, despite the unpromising evidence to the contrary, our lives have ultimate meaning and value, men and women are liable to fall into despair. But because of our utterly changed circumstances, the old religious doctrines, which helped to give us such faith in the past, no longer work for an increasing number of people.

Jack Spong has long recognized this, and his courageous and insistent warning that "Christianity must either change or die" has been the great gift of his episcopate. Freelancers such as myself or individual scholars who have issued a similar message can be dismissed by the conventional and the timorous, but when a bishop, a member of the establishment, speaks out, the faithful are compelled to take his words more seriously. The venom that Jack's books, articles, and pronouncements have inspired, among both clergy and laity, reveals a deep resistance to such a revisionist view of religion, but it also springs from a denial rooted in fear. Change is always painful, especially when it is as accelerated as in our own day. People not unnaturally fear that if they can no longer think about God or Jesus in the same way as their grandparents, all hell will be let loose, and that, as W. B. Yeats predicted earlier in the century:

> Things fall apart; the centre cannot hold;
> Mere anarchy is loosed upon the world.[1]

But change, development, and evolution are fundamental laws of life and cannot be resisted indefinitely. As in any other field of human endeavor, our ideas about religion in general and God in particular have been in constant flux, and they will be transformed in the twenty-first century whether people like it or not. The only intelligent, responsible, and creative response is to meet the challenge, as Jack has done throughout his episcopate, and save the human race from the devastating consequences of the loss of any sense of sacred-

---

1. W. B. Yeats, "The Second Coming," 3–4.

ness — consequences that were revealed so horrifically in Auschwitz and Kosovo.

One of the most crucial periods of change and transition in world history began in about the seventh century B.C.E. Because the pace of life was slower, the transformation was less dramatic than that which is taking place in our own time, but its effects are still with us. Historians have called this era "the Axial Age," because it proved pivotal to the spiritual experience of humanity. During this Axial Age, all the major societies of the Oikumene, the civilized world, developed a culture based on a surplus of agricultural produce, which revolutionized their social, economic, and moral conditions. They evolved a market economy, and merchants and money-men became more influential than before. As a result of their changed circumstances, people found that the old pagan faith which had served their ancestors so well no longer spoke to their condition. In each corner of the Oikumene, sages, teachers, prophets, and philosophers reformed the old paganism to make it accessible to their modernity, and the great confessional faiths that have continued to nourish human beings emerged: Taoism and Confucianism in China; Buddhism and Hinduism in the Indian subcontinent; monotheism in the Middle East; and rationalism in Europe. Confucius, Buddha, Zoroaster, Isaiah, and Plato were men of their time. They saw the need for radical change to save their fellows from anomie and their societies from crippling injustice. They were often reviled by their contemporaries because their ideas seemed shocking or even blasphemous, but because they spoke to the conditions of the Axial Age, their visions prevailed and have enlightened billions of men and women.

The religions that evolved during the Axial Age each had their own special genius and were, in many respects, very different from one another. But, operating as they were within an agrarian-based culture, they shared basic conceptions. All posited, in various ways, a single source of sacredness, which utterly transcended any human system and could be glimpsed only partially by our limited minds. All agreed that it was impossible to "define" (a word that literally means "to set limits upon") God, nirvana, or Brahman, because it lay beyond any words, concepts, or categories that were familiar. It could not be reached by the rational, logical discourse (*logos*) that was essential for the more practical affairs of life, but could be experienced only by means of the more intuitive disciplines of mythology, mysticism, contemplation, and ritual, and by such ethical practices as compassion, a virtue which all declared to be cardinal. The sacred was not simply a transcendent value "out there" but was inseparable from humanity and present in each individual.

In Axial Age spirituality, therefore, reason (*logos*) did not reign supreme. We could not survive or function adequately without it. *Logos* was indispensable for mathematics, medicine, science, technology, and politics. But when confronted with the ultimate questions about the nature of God or the sacred, which lay beyond the reach of sense perception, reason had nothing to say. Similarly, when human beings experienced tragedy, rational thought could not assuage their sorrow nor prevent them from succumbing to despair. They turned instead to *mythos,* the intuitive discourse of spirituality, which gave them access to the inner reaches of what we would call the unconscious mind and helped them to perceive those deeper currents of existence that have always been part of the human experience, even if they cannot be expressed logically or proved scientifically. The myths of religion were not meant to be taken literally. A primitive form of psychology, they spoke of the mysteries and dynamics of the interior life and tried to express insights about mundane conditions that were too elusive to be expressed in a more prosaic way. They were not capable of logical demonstration, but worked upon human beings, in conjunction with ritual and contemplative practices, in rather the same way as a great piece of music, which lifts us momentarily beyond ourselves, touches something deeply buried within us, and gives us a conviction that all will ultimately be well. Reason and intuition — *logos* and *mythos* — were complementary modes of knowledge in the Axial Age religions. Both were necessary for human beings, but each had its particular sphere of competence, and they were not meant to be confused with one another. *Mythos* could not solve a mathematical or political problem, and *logos* could not help men and women to find God.[2]

Today we are in the throes of a new Axial Age. In the sixteenth century, the people of Europe and — later — its American colonies began to develop a wholly new type of culture, one based not on a surplus of agriculture but on technology. The spectacular achieve-

---

2. Johannes Sloek, *Devotional Language,* trans. Henrik Mossin (Berlin and New York: W. de Gruyter, 1996), 53–96.

ments of scientific rationalism in the West at this time gave *logos* unprecedented stature, so that by the mid-nineteenth century, it had begun to displace and discredit *mythos,* and an increasing number of people started to see it as the sole source of truth and knowledge. Only those propositions and facts which could be demonstrated rationally and shown to be effective in the physical world were held to be valid. Science and reason were held to be acceptable sources of information, and myth, in popular parlance, became something that was not true; to describe an event as "mythical" was tantamount to saying that it had never occurred. Western people also developed a new scientific view of history. Instead of seeing incidents in this world as mundane reflections of timeless laws and realities (as in Axial Age historiography), history was seen as a succession of unique events. Instead of trying to describe what an occurrence had meant, historians concentrated on what had actually happened. The purveyors of modern rationalism mounted a principled assault on religion, attacking the old *mythoi* of the Judaeo-Christian tradition as vehemently as the prophets of Israel had inveighed against the pagan deities. These old symbols, which had once given men and women intimations of transcendent significance, had now become meaningless and, consequently, were seen as false, as mere idols. Marx declared religion to be the opiate of the people; Feuerbach argued that a supernatural God alienated humanity from itself; Freud believed that faith was the most dangerous enemy of the scientific *logos,* which alone could save men and women.[3]

Where *logos* and *mythos* had once been seen as complementary, scientific rationalism became inimical to faith. In premodern spirituality, myth had been inseparable from cult, so much so that it is a matter of scholarly debate as to which came first: the mythical narrative or the rite attached to it. By means of rituals and ceremonies, men and women appropriated a myth and made it part of their interior lives. The Passover meal, which symbolically represented the liberation of the Israelites from Egypt, made that ancient myth a living reality in the lives of generations of Jews. The Mass, a symbolic reenactment of Jesus' sacrifice on Calvary, did the same for the Cru-

3. Karl Marx, *Karl Marx: Early Writings,* trans. T. B. Bottomore (London: Watts, 1963), 166–67; Ludwig Feuerbach, *The Essence of Christianity,* trans. George Eliot (New York: F. Ungar, 1957), 33; Peter Gay, *A Godless Jew: Freud, Atheism, and the Making of Psychoanalysis* (New Haven and London: Yale University Press, 1987), 6–7.

cifixion for generations of Catholics. Without such ritual, myths have no spiritual potency and become incredible. This is what happened to God. Without cultic, meditative, or ethical practices, such propositions as "I believe in God" are meaningless. But because *logos* alone was regarded as the sole means of arriving at truth, people felt that they had to prove God's existence rationally *before* they embarked on such spiritual disciplines. But reason was not capable of revealing the sacred. All it could do was produce the attenuated religion of Deism or such logical conundrums as the so-called proof of the seventeenth-century mathematician René Descartes. Descartes held that the only reality of which we could be certain was the experience of doubt, which showed us the limitations of our minds. But the very notion of "limitation" presupposed the idea of "perfection." A perfection which did not exist was a contradiction in terms. *Ergo,* God must exist. This is not an argument that would convince a modern skeptic. When faced with the ultimate, reason can only stutter in fundamentally unsatisfactory ways.

Descartes was a devout Catholic. It was not simply unbelievers who saw reason as the sole source of truth. By the end of the nineteenth century, many religious people in the West also felt that if their doctrines were not rationally demonstrable they could not be taken seriously. The Protestant fundamentalism that emerged in America at the beginning of the twentieth century took this to an extreme. In their way, fundamentalists were ardent modernists. In 1922, A. C. Dixon, one of the early fundamentalist leaders, explained that he was a Christian "because I am a Thinker, a Rationalist, a Scientist." Faith was no leap in the dark but depended upon "exact observation and correct thinking."[4] Fundamentalists were strict literalists. Instead of seeing allegorical, mystical, or symbolic meaning in the Bible, alongside its plain sense (as was common practice in premodern religion), fundamentalists read their scriptures like moderns: for information and hard facts. If the Bible said that God created the world in six days, this discounted the views of such scientists as Lyell or Darwin, who had suggested that the earth and the species evolved over many millennia. If the Bible foretold that Jesus would fight a battle with Satan outside Jerusalem in the Last Days of human history, this was not a symbolic utterance but was an accurate prediction that would come to pass

---

4. A. C. Dixon in *The King's Business*, 1922.

exactly as the inspired text said. If St. Paul promised that before the tribulation of the End Time, true believers would be "taken up into the clouds . . . to meet the Lord in the air" (1 Thess. 4:17), born-again Christians could confidently expect Rapture. Religion was a matter of fact; it was *logos* and not *mythos*.

Most Christians would not go so far. But in our modern Western culture, we have so lost a sense of the mythological that many find it hard not to interpret the truths of religion rationally. They are disturbed to hear that the events of the Bible may not be "historical" in our modern scientific sense. We expect a truth — such as the existence of God — to be convincing independently of emotive ritual. God is regarded by many as an objective fact, which is experienced by everybody in an identical manner. Christians may not see Genesis as scientifically accurate in every detail (as the fundamentalist Creationists do), but they often believe in "a God" who created the world and supervises events here below rather as human beings make things and organize their affairs. But this literal interpretation of classical Western theism has become increasingly problematic. If God is responsible for all that happens and is the source of all that is, how do we account for evil? If God is all-powerful and all-compassionate, as official theology has it, how do we explain such atrocities as the Nazi death camps? In the light of what we have learned about the depth and richness of other religious traditions, can we believe Christianity to be the one true faith? Is Jesus, as he claimed, the only way to the Father? And, if so, what does this say about a God who has left the vast majority of human beings in error (or, at best, with an inferior form of faith) for the whole of human history?

A factual and rational interpretation of theism is increasingly distressing to large numbers of people. In Britain, it has become so distasteful that the bulk of the population wants nothing more to do with Christianity. In London, the churches are emptying and being converted into warehouses, theaters, and restaurants. Only 35 percent of Britons claim to believe in God, and only 10 percent attend a religious service regularly (as opposed to the 90 percent of Americans who believe in God, 60 percent of whom are churchgoers). But, as I have found during my travels in the United States, the ostensibly orthodox Americans are often disenchanted with establishment theism and are hungry for something new. This is hardly surprising. Monotheism was one of the spiritualities which evolved

during the first Axial Age; as such, the symbol of the one God is not
accessible to *logos,* but can be apprehended only intuitively and imaginatively as a *mythos.* Considered rationally, the conventional theism
has worrying *lacunae,* as I have tried to indicate above. The doctrine
of the Trinity, for example, makes no sense. The formula: "Three
in one and one in three" becomes — like Descartes "proof" — an
empty conundrum. Western Christians are often embarrassed by the
apparent irrationality of the Trinity and do not realize that the doctrine was devised by Greek Orthodox theologians during the fourth
century precisely as *mythos.* As Gregory of Nyssa explained, "Father," "Son," and "Spirit" were not objective facts but simply "terms
that we use" to evoke the process whereby the "unnameable and
unspeakable" Godhead becomes known to mere mortals.[5] Like any
mythos, Trinitarianism makes no sense without a cult, liturgy, and
contemplation.

When reason tries to address religious truth, it is attempting a task
that it is not equipped for. When it endeavors to explain or prove
a *mythos,* it can only become a caricature of itself — neither good
science nor good religion. If we are to recover a sense of the sacred,
we have to liberate God from the prison of the literal and purely
rational. Instead of seeing God as a fact that can be demonstrated
in the same way as the invisible atom, Christians must be helped to
realize that the sacred lies beyond our doctrines, words, and concepts.
To attempt to satisfy ourselves intellectually about the divine *before*
engaging in the cultic, contemplative, and ethical practices of religion
is to put the cart before the horse. Before we can reinstate God, we
have to create rituals that truly speak to the condition of men and
women in the twenty-first century. This will demand the same kind of
aesthetic discipline and genius as a great work of art. Liturgy is, after
all, a form of theater. Extricating God from the toils of reason does
not mean the abdication of intellect. Quite the contrary, the evolution
of cult and dogma demands creative intelligence of a very high order.
We should expend as much thought and sensibility on the weekly
service as a director gives to the interpretation of *Hamlet.* And when
a theologian tries to express the inexpressible nature of the sacred, he
or she needs the poetic gifts of Shakespeare when he wrote *Hamlet.*

But as the prophets of Israel made so abundantly clear, a decorous

---

5. Gregory of Nyssa, Letter "To Alybius; That There Are Not Three Gods."

and inspiring liturgy is pointless without the discipline of compassion. This was one of the chief insights of the first Axial Age, though the churches today often seem to have lost sight of it. Compassion is also crucial to the New Testament vision. As St. Paul said, a faith that moves mountains but which is without love is "worth nothing at all" (1 Cor. 13:2). One of the earliest biblical stories, expressing a primitive Hebrew theology, makes the point clearly. The tale of Abraham and the three strangers at Mamre shows that compassion is not the effect but the cause of faith (Gen. 18:1–15). Sitting outside his tent in the hottest part of the day, Abraham saw three strangers on the horizon. Strangers then — as in our own world — were potentially lethal. Few of us would invite three total strangers off the streets into our own homes as Abraham did that day. He brought them into his encampment and ordered an elaborate meal, pouring out on these unknown people all the refreshment and comfort in his power to sustain them on their journey. In the course of the ensuing conversation, it transpired quite naturally that one of these strangers was none other than Abraham's God. An act of practical charity had led to a divine encounter; it had created an experience of the divine. All the great traditions insist that egotism and selfishness hold us back from true religious vision. Compassion, which demands that we displace ourselves from the center of our concern and put others there instead, enables us to transcend ego in a disciplined, unsensational way. Recognizing the sacred in the other thus yields an ecstasy which is not a hysterical rapture but *ex-tasis* in the true sense: a going beyond the self which enables us to glimpse what we call "God," an experience that is more authentic (according to long tradition) than any amount of theological reasoning.

If the churches concentrated less on castigating the faithful about their beliefs or sexual habits and more on the discipline of charity, they would help Christians to recover a sense of the divine that many have lost during the unfolding of our rational modernity. Many church-persons, unlike Jack Spong, however, prefer to be "right" rather than compassionate. One of the most instructive points in the Abraham story is that the patriarch glimpsed the divine in a stranger who did not belong to his ethnic, religious, or ideological camp. One of the great religious advances of the twentieth century was our wholly new knowledge and appreciation of other traditions. If God has to be liberated from our narrow *logos,* God also has to be freed from our parochial denominational confines. Wilfred Cantwell Smith, the former professor of comparative religion at Harvard, once suggested that, in the light of what we now know about the profundity of other peoples' faith, it could now be blasphemous to insist that any one tradition has the monopoly of truth.[6] We shall never be able to see either our own or other people's religion in the same way again.

Anybody who has honestly opened him- or herself to the insights of Judaism, Islam, Buddhism, or Taoism (to name only a few faiths) will find it increasingly difficult to believe that Christianity alone gives human beings full access to God. That is not to say that we must all work to create a giant conglomerate religion but that we should develop a form of Christianity that treasures the insights of Jesus, Paul, and the saints but that is also open to a vision of sacredness in the stranger, in faiths that were formerly considered "false" and alien. This will be the test for Christians in the third Christian millennium. The second began with the Crusades, when Western Christians slaughtered thousands of Jews and Muslims in the name of God. This was succeeded by a thousand years of intolerance in which Christians not only killed "infidels" but also butchered one another. Any God who commands us to persecute and harry others in his name is an idol that we have created in our own image, a travesty of religion that gives a seal of absolute approval to our most ignoble hatred and prejudice. In the twenty-first century, Christians must show that they have learned this lesson if we are to be true to the compassionate spirit of the gospels.

We cannot return to the spirituality of the premodern world, but moving forward to a less exclusive, absolute, and objective conception of God will also bring theology more closely in line with the dynamic of our time. Modern thought has moved on from its old certainties. What is, perhaps offputtingly, called "postmodern thought" advocates a more open-ended attitude to truth. It is characterized by the determination to deconstruct established interpretations, to undermine absolute claims, and points out that all our knowledge can only be interpretive and that we can never attain absolute certainty. Instead of sticking to a literal interpretation of a text, a critic such as Jacques Derrida calls attention to the layers of meaning that

6. Wilfred Cantwell Smith, *Towards a World Theology* (London: Macmillan, 1981), 126.

exist beneath the surface and argues that there is no such thing as a secure or safe meaning. These new currents of thought also favor pluralism, the deprivileging of our "own" discourse, and a new appreciation of perspectives that were hitherto deemed heretical. This fresh appreciation of complexity and ambiguity will certainly characterize the thought of the twenty-first century, and, if utilized creatively by monotheists, could restore us to an enhanced realization of the sacred as a dimension that can never be wholly contained in any single human creed.

Chapter 2

THE INCREDIBLE CANON

Robert W. Funk

ROBERT W. FUNK is director of the Westar Institute in Santa Rosa, California, and founder of the Jesus Seminar. The field of religion has been enriched by his scholarship in teaching, writing, translating, and publishing. A Guggenheim Fellow and Senior Fulbright Scholar, he has served as Annual Professor of the American School of Oriental Research in Jerusalem and as chair of the Graduate Department of Religion at Vanderbilt University. He also has been a faculty member of the Religion departments of the University of Montana, Drew University, Emory University, and Texas Christian University. His large body of writing includes *Language, Hermeneutic, and Word of God: The Problem of Language in the New Testament and in Contemporary Theology; Parables and Presence: Forms of the New Testament Tradition;* two volumes of *New Gospel Parallels: The Synoptic Gospels* and *John and the Other Gospels; The Five Gospels: The Search for the Authentic Words of Jesus* (with Roy W. Hoover and the Jesus Seminar); *Jesus as Precursor;* and most recently with the Jesus Seminar *The Acts of Jesus: The Search for the Authentic Deeds of Jesus.*

> What you are liable to read in the Bible —
> It ain't necessarily so.
> — *Porgy and Bess*

> I haven't read the Bible,
> but I know that it's true.
> — *Les Misérables*

It is always a fortunate moment in the literary life of a country when masterpieces from the past thaw out and once again become matters of urgent contemporary interest, for they then produce on us a completely fresh effect. — GOETHE

T HE AIM OF THE WESTAR INSTITUTE and its research seminars, particularly the Jesus Seminar and the Paul Seminar, has been to awaken renewed and informed interest in the Bible. To that end, we have attempted to thaw out the scriptures — to return them to a vibrant liquid state — so they will have "a completely fresh effect." The thawing process has involved fresh translations into current idioms and a sustained effort to distinguish fact from fiction at a time when the two continue to be hopelessly confused.

As a further step in the thawing process, we intend to issue a revised New Testament that will have the effect of breaking through the protective crust of "revealed truth" provided by the boundaries of the canon. Moreover, the addition of one or more new gospels, along with other early Christian documents, will whisk away the cloak of familiarity and stereotypical interpretation that has functioned to insulate the modern reader from the intent of all these ancient Christian texts. The additional step of revising the canon was, in fact, suggested to us by the course of modern biblical criticism, which, since the late eighteenth century, has eroded confidence in the claims made for the historical reliability and theological dependability of the texts included in the New Testament, claims that are directly linked to the concept of a biblical canon of sacred scriptures.

We already have embarked on this additional step by producing *The Gospel of Jesus,* which is a collection of all the authentic sayings of and anecdotes about Jesus molded into a new gospel.[1] A second volume, *The Gospel of Paul,* will contain the authentic letters and letter fragments of Paul. Together, they will constitute what might be called *The Essential New Testament.*

It was the initial distinction between fact and fiction which prompted those of us in the Jesus Seminar to reconsider the boundaries and status of gospels assigned historically to the canon. The quest of the historical Jesus has had the effect of making the canonical gospels incredible.

What prompted the further step of revising the canon is not difficult to discern, once the impact of the quest on the New Testament gospels becomes clear. On the one hand, by isolating sayings and anecdotes that capture the image of the historical figure of Jesus from the rest

---

1. Robert W. Funk and the Jesus Seminar, *The Gospel of Jesus* (Santa Rosa, Calif.: Polebridge Press, 1999).

of the gospels, we appear to be reducing the boundaries of the canon. (Fictional materials are assumed by literalists and others to have less than canonical status.) Among scholars, that process is sometimes referred to as identifying a canon within the canon. On the other hand, we have treated extracanonical gospels, such as the Gospel of Thomas and the hypothetical Sayings Gospel Q, with seeming canonical respect, which suggests that we have expanded the boundaries of the canon. At the same time, our growing conviction that much of the gospel narrative consists of fictions has tended to challenge the theological validity of the canonical gospels: For many believers, historical reliability and theological validity are inseparably linked. The argument goes: If Christian faith is faith in Jesus of Nazareth, and if the canonical gospels cannot be trusted with historical information about Jesus, then they cannot be the basis of faith. And yet, for the Bible Party, as we may term this group, the New Testament is assumed to be the basis of faith. A counterargument advanced by what may be termed the Apostolic Party runs thus: The Christian faith is not faith in Jesus of Nazareth; it is faith in the faith of the "apostles," and their faith is best represented by the canonical document — acts, letters, and apocalypse included. The Apostolic Party holds that the canonical scriptures are those writings that represent "the faith once for all delivered to the saints," that is, to the first apostles and believers. For this reason, all extracanonical writings are considered the work of heretics and, thus, derivative. Accordingly, they should not be used to determine the content of the faith.

The decision to reconsider the canon follows from the conviction that the quest of the historical Jesus (and modern critical scholarship, generally) has made the New Testament incredible. Our first order of business is, therefore, to expand on this notion. That is the topic of the first section of this essay. The prospect of a revised canon brought with it the urge to review the history of the process that produced the canon in the first place. That review produced some surprises. Those surprises are the subject of the second part of this essay. In a third section, I outline my own proposals for altering the boundaries of the New Testament. To anticipate, those proposals focus on three different forms of "scripture": an essential New Testament, as suggested above; an intermediate selection of writings, representative of the full spectrum of early Christian opinion; and, finally, a complete collection of all primary Christian writings that originated in the first three centuries of the Common Era. These three forms of scripture give all interested persons access to the full range of Christian perspectives, from the founding voices of Jesus and Paul to all the writings claiming to represent either of those initiating voices.

By implication, I also address the question whether the canonical documents — and only the canonical documents — contain a privileged form of information. A revision of the canon implies that the ecclesiastical councils and Bible publishers made decisions that are not infallible. Other voices and perspectives may contain aspects of the truth. In his own way, Bishop Spong has contributed significantly to rescuing the Bible from literalism and fundamentalism by demonstrating that the biblical documents were produced by persons belonging to another time and place and so are limited in their access to ultimate truth. A reconsideration of the boundaries of the New Testament is another part of the strategy to thwart the arrogant claim that Christians have some special knowledge denied to everyone else.

Canon as Untrustworthy

Historical scholarship has made the canonical gospels incredible, as remarked earlier. By incredible, I mean historically untrustworthy. To be more precise, scholars have shown the gospels to be statements of faith mixed with some historical reminiscences. But the presence of fiction — of the free play of the storyteller's imagination — in stories about Jesus has cast the shadow of disbelief across the New Testament gospels. The gospels can no longer be regarded as reports of historical events to be taken at face value. In addition, the New Testament documents turn out not to be what the early fathers of the church claimed them to be: very early reports based on the testimony of "apostles," who were eyewitnesses of the events depicted. The gospels do not contain eyewitness reports. This second deficiency will require us subsequently to review two of the criteria for canonicity: apostolic authorship and ancient origin — which are not faith claims; they are historical claims and, therefore, subject to historical verification.

The steady erosion of confidence in the literal accuracy of reports in the gospels over the last two centuries has prompted many scholars, including the Fellows of the Jesus Seminar, to attempt systematically to discriminate fact from fiction. Critical scholars go behind, around, and beyond the canonical gospels in their search for the historical truth. They go behind the canon in order to reconstruct the history of the tradition that precedes and underlies the gospels as received texts. They go around the canonical gospels in order to check those reports against other contemporary sources of information, both inside and outside the New Testament. And they review the history of scholarship since the Enlightenment in order to compare their own conclusions with the data compiled by other competent scholars. In other words, we who are Fellows of the Jesus Seminar regard ourselves as responsible to a community of scholars and a steadily unfolding tradition of research. Those of us with respect for our discipline prefer to stand on the shoulders of our predecessors and mentors rather than trample on their corpses.

The justification for the procedures of historical scholarship does not depend on the validity of any or all of the details of its results. In any case, those results will change over time as new sources, new methods, and new perspectives emerge. What is not at issue is the process itself: We will never return to precritical naiveté in which the gospels are taken to be straightforward reports of actual historical events. The discrepancy between the historical Jesus and the picture painted of him in the narrative gospels is a permanent feature of critical scholarship and theology. Critical scholars are those whose historical judgments are not dictated by dogmatic considerations.[2]

In our fourteen years together, the Fellows of the Jesus Seminar have concluded that only 18 percent of the words attributed to Jesus in the gospels were actually spoken by him, and then not in the precise form, or even in the same language, in which they are preserved. We also are reporting that only 17 percent of the 392 reports of 172 events have some basis in actual fact. Our efforts to distinguish fact from fiction in the gospels were sketched into the two color-coded reports of the Jesus Seminar: *The Five Gospels: The Search for the Authentic Words of Jesus* (New York: Macmillan, 1993) and *The Acts of Jesus: The Search for the Authentic Deeds of Jesus* (San Francisco: HarperSanFrancisco, 1998).

I am aware that Bishop Spong, an Honorary Fellow of the Jesus Seminar, does not have much confidence in our ability to isolate the

---

2. On the present scene, because of academic dissembling, it is often difficult to tell who is a critical scholar and who is not.

words and deeds of the historical figure of Jesus in the gospels. Yet, his paper on Judas persuaded a majority of Fellows that Judas is a fiction of the author of the passion narrative. Moreover, in his most recent book, *Why Christianity Must Change or Die*,[3] he goes in quest of the real Jesus by drawing on the experiences of the first believers. When he spells out the disposition of that Jesus, he comes up with many of the same characteristics identified by the Seminar. For example, Bishop Spong is certain that the Kingdom of God as Jesus viewed it had no social or ethnic boundaries. He believes that Jesus accepted both women and children in his retinue. Moreover, he seems not to trust the historical reliability of the gospels any more than other critical scholars. His present concern to reinterpret Jesus without reference to the traditional mythical theistic frame of reference deserves extended applause.

Our first task is to explain to those who still regard the gospels as historically trustworthy how and why the Jesus Seminar came to such startling conclusions about the fidelity of the gospels in reporting the words and deeds of Jesus. We share these reasons with most critical scholars. A brief review will demonstrate why, for most of us, the gospels have become incredible.

In concert with most critical scholars, we took the view that Mark is the earliest of the narrative gospels and that Matthew and Luke made direct use of Mark's narrative in the construction of their gospels. In the work of the Seminar, and in the work of countless other scholars, when Matthew and Luke retell and alter the stories they take from Mark, they are not adding new or better historical information to their source; for the most part, they are freely inventing in accordance with their own theological proclivities and the requirements of good storytelling. As a result, stories reported only by Mark and copied by Matthew and Luke have a single basis in the tradition; we are not comparing the independent memories of more than one storyteller when reviewing the changes Matthew and Luke make to the text of Mark. Therefore, we must assess these so-called triple-tradition reports on the basis of their intrinsic merits.

We think that Matthew and Luke also made use of another written document, the Sayings Gospel Q. Yet, Matthew and Luke often diverge in reporting what they probably found in Q, without either of

---

3. San Francisco: HarperSanFrancisco, 1998.

them having independent confirmation of those Q materials. A reconstructed Q would presumably differ from both the Q versions found in Matthew and Luke. In assessing the Q materials taken over by Matthew and Luke, we are dependent on our ability to reconstruct the history of those traditions. Because the Gospel of Thomas overlaps to such a large extent with Q, Thomas has been an important factor in our ability to recreate the history of these so-called double traditions.

It was just remarked that Matthew and Luke made use of the Gospel of Mark. Which edition of Mark did they use? We have reason to believe that Mark went through at least two editions, and it is possible that the later rather than the earlier edition was canonized. It is unclear whether Matthew and Luke made use of the same version we now have in our Greek New Testament.

Matthew and Luke also seem to have made use of special traditions, which may have reached them in oral form, or perhaps have come from some document now lost. Scholars refer to these stray traditions as special Matthew and special Luke. Among these stray traditions are a number of the major parables of Jesus. It seems that Matthew and Luke made use of three sources each: the Sayings Gospel Q, the Gospel of Mark, and their special source.

In the opinion of many scholars, Raymond E. Brown[4] included, the Fourth Gospel has had a checkered history. Critical scholars think chapter 21 was added to an earlier version that ended with chapter 20. Robert Fortna[5] and others believe there was an earlier edition of John that is known as the Signs Gospel. Other scholars think that John shares a miracles source with the Gospel of Mark, which both evangelists freely edited. To put matters bluntly, the Fourth Gospel apparently went through three or four stages, perhaps more.

Behind the written gospels lie two or more decades of oral tradition. The first storytellers repeated the words of Jesus they could remember and told anecdotes about him. Those anecdotes take the form of pronouncement stories, exorcisms, cures and resuscitations, call and commissioning stories, nature wonders, legends, and myths — story forms known to all storytellers in that age. Since these stories were formulated and transmitted orally, their content varied

---

4. *The Gospel according to John (I–XII)*, Anchor Bible (Garden City, N.Y.: Doubleday, 1996).

5. *The Fourth Gospel and Its Predecessors: From Narrative Source to Present Gospel* (Philadelphia: Fortress Press, 1988).

from telling to telling. As folklore, much of this lore is wrapped in memories that edited, deleted, augmented, and combined elements many times over many years. As a consequence, it is very difficult to sort out fact from fiction. Nevertheless, those of us engaged in the quest think there is some modicum of reliable historical data embedded in these stories.

When the author of Mark — whoever he or she was — decided to compose the first narrative gospel, the author gathered sayings and anecdotes from the oral tradition and arranged them in a continuous narrative without knowledge of the actual order of events. We know this because Mark groups anecdotes and sayings by type of story, by form, or by content, often employing catchwords to join independent sayings. To make the narrative cohesive, the author provided the story with framing events: John the Baptist and the baptism of Jesus as the beginning; the transfiguration and the predictions of the passion in the middle; and the passion and empty tomb story as the climax. It was that narrative frame that eventually became the basis of the Apostles' Creed.

These are just a few of the reasons the canonical gospels have become incredible as sources of history. They have covered over much about the real origins of Christianity, particularly about the role played by Jesus of Nazareth, not because they deliberately intended to do so, but because they had neither the interests nor the tools to do otherwise. In effect, they have effaced the actual story with their own evangelical convictions.

Canon as Process

The Quest and the Canon

Our critics correctly perceive that *The Five Gospels,* with its symbolic color-coding, undermines the historical trustworthiness of the New Testament gospels. *The Five Gospels* distinguishes words Jesus is alleged to have said from the words he really said, in all probability. The integrity of the gospels — for the literalistic mind — is being compromised in the process. *The Acts of Jesus* similarly calls into question the historical reliability of the anecdotes told about Jesus.

At the same time, our critics fail to note that we have made a large claim for the historical reliability of some data found in the gospels. We believe that there is some dependable information to be isolated in those ancient texts, provided care is taken with method and provided the results are not overwhelmed by prior theological commitments. Our critics have discerned that we have been identifying a "canon" within the canon. Our "canon" of scripture is larger than the four canonical gospels, but our database of historical information is considerably smaller than any one of the gospels.

For traditionalists, it was inevitable that our work would be regarded as subversive of the integrity of the canon. That is how David Friedrich Strauss's *Life of Jesus* was perceived when it was first published in 1835–36, and how Johannes Weiss's rediscovery of eschatology first struck his liberal critics in 1892.[6] That is also how Rudolf Bultmann's *History of the Synoptic Tradition*[7] was regarded by many of his critics on both sides of the Atlantic in 1921. That is certainly how Bultmann's demythologizing essay of 1941[8] was viewed as it exploded into controversy in Europe and North America following World War II.

In spite of its obvious implications, many of our critics misunderstand the purport of the work of the Jesus Seminar. They believe that because we treat the Gospel of Thomas with respect, our intention is to elevate Thomas to canonical status — to the status of absolute trustworthiness, to the level of specially revealed truth, which they assume for the New Testament gospels. They fail to realize that most scholars have actually demoted the New Testament gospels — assigned them to the same level of reliability as Thomas and other extracanonical texts. The leveling that has taken place permits us to give equal credence to texts both inside and outside the New Testament, depending on the assessment of their position in the development of the gospel tradition. Since the Sayings Gospel Q and some hypothetical first stratum of the Gospel of Thomas probably come early in that development and represent independent witnesses to the Jesus tradition, a recognition of that fact would be to include them in the same collection of sacred writings as the four New Testament gospels.

---

6. Johannes Weiss, *Jesus' Proclamation of the Kingdom of God*, trans., ed., and with an introduction by R. H. Hiers and D. L. Larrimore (Philadelphia: Fortress Press, 1971 [1892]).

7. Revised edition, trans. John Marsh (New York: Harper & Row, 1963).

8. The original essay is available in translation in *Kerygma and Myth: A Theological Debate*, ed. H. W. Bartsch and Reginald H. Fuller (New York: Harper & Row, 1961).

The Meaning of the Term "Canon"

I use the term "canon" in its broad, secular sense to refer to any collection of literature produced during the formative or golden age of a cultural tradition. In this extended definition, a canon need not be concerned with either "orthodoxy" or "heresy," only with the quality and variety of the emerging tradition. Reference is frequently made to the Classical Canon or the canon of literature in English. Classical scholars do not talk about either orthodox or heretical works produced during the classical age of Greece; they speak only of works of higher or lesser quality, works that are more or less representative of the genius of the golden age of Greece. The twenty-six works Harold Bloom includes in his canon of great Western prose and poetry have nothing to do with what might be considered by some to be orthodox or heretical in great literature.[9] This is the sense in which I use the "canon" of the literature of primitive Christianity.

The canon of Christian literature should, I assume, have some connection, however remote, with Jesus of Nazareth, the alleged precipitator of the tradition that stems from him. This is the only absolute requisite for documents to be thought of as Christian. Beyond this fundamental criterion, selection should be based on the quality and variety of the voices that come to expression in written documents.

The formation of the Christian canon took place over a long period of time and in a variety of contexts. The process has not, in fact, been brought to a final resolution, except in rare instances, and even then, practice has tended to override formal restrictions. The process may be thought of as taking place in two stages.

STAGE ONE

The production and identification of a canonical collection of scriptures was a process that began quite early but has not been consummated even at this late date. As we all know: the gospels were created in stages; the four narrative gospels and Thomas went through editions; later works revised and incorporated earlier gospels; the assembling of the fourfold gospel took place over two centuries and more; the original text of the gospels has not yet been established; and the complete history of the gospels is not known and probably never will be known. The evolution of the gospels is paradigmatic of

---

9. *The Western Canon: The Books of the Ages* (New York: Riverhead Books, 1994).

the larger process by which early Christians assembled and utilized
other types of sacred writings. That process includes a number of
other aspects that I can only briefly sketch.

Jewish scriptures. The Jesus movement began at a very early date
to search the "scriptures" — principally the Prophets and Psalms —
to look for evidence that Jesus was the expected messiah and had
fulfilled ancient prophecies. It is unclear how widely Christian scribes
cast their nets among ancient documents available to them, but it is
certain that the texts they canvassed do not correspond to any form
of the present Old Testament.

In addition, their scriptures were the Greek translation (the Sep-
tuagint, usually referred to as the LXX) of the Hebrew Bible, rather
than the Hebrew Bible itself. Because modern scholars know that the
original language was Hebrew, we have blithely substituted the Hebrew text for the Greek in preparing translations of the Christian
"Old Testament." Thus, the canon of most modern churches em-
braces a different set of texts in a different language than was the
case for Jesus and the "apostles." We seem ready enough to ignore
the historical facts about the canon when it is convenient to do so.

To put the matter succinctly: The Christian movement purloined
a set of scriptures not its own, in a secondary language, and then
created a "canon" of proof texts within that "canon" to support its
own claims. In view of the history of this process, I think it is time
we return the Hebrew Bible to the Jews whose Bible it is and confine
ourselves to scriptures that were historically employed by the first
Christians. If we need a collection of ancient documents that function
as "background" to the rise of Christianity, we should readopt the
Greek Old Testament (LXX) and translate it into English as our "First
Testament."

Letters: particularity. When Christians began to define themselves
and deal with issues that arose in their daily and institutional lives,
they wrote letters to each other. The primary letters in the church's
canonical collection are the letters of Paul. The authentic letters of
Paul were written to specific churches with reference to particular
problems. The question always arises in this connection: Are the particular solutions proposed by Paul of Tarsus to particular problems of
Christians living in the first century binding for all time on Christian
communities? The answer nearly all theologians give to that question
is negative. Paul's responses, they reason, were relative to his time

and place and to the range and purity of his vision. His responses in several important respects require modification.

In addition, there are many competing voices in the letters of Paul — he does not always say the same thing. What are we to make of his manifold perspectives? This problem has led some scholars to attempt to find the real voice of Paul among that chorus of voices — again, to find a canon within the canon.

The "canonization" of the letters is, thus, an ongoing process — an effort to locate and articulate the normative witness they are assumed to represent and to adapt that witness to present circumstance.

Gospels: plurality. Why are there four gospels rather than one? Irenaeus's reply that there are four because there are four winds and four cardinal directions is scarcely convincing. The plurality of the tradition, like its particularity, is an issue concerning the authority of the canonical writings. Historical criticism has called the unity of the New Testament writings into question. Indeed, it may be safely said that, today, the New Testament is viewed by critical scholars as a babel of competing voices; scholars specialize in pointing out the divergences, in making distinctions between this point of view and that.

There is irony in this dilemma. If the tradition were not particular and plural, it would not be historical either. This is precisely what makes the creeds an anomaly in the history of Christianity: The creeds pretend to be universal in their scope — not subject to the relative point of view of the time and place in which they were created. For that reason, to regard the New Testament writings as authoritative guides for Christian belief and behavior in all times and places has become an acute problem as we have moved farther and farther away from the world in which that tradition was conceived. To retain the New Testament as canon in its ancient sense is to condemn it to progressive irrelevance with each passing century.

Tradition as oral and written. The Christian movement, contrary to popular opinion, was not a religion of the book from the beginning. It was, in fact, a movement of the spirit. Jesus is represented as asserting his freedom over against the law and the prophets and the religious practices of his day. He spoke with immediacy, directness, spontaneity, as Amos Wilder used to say.[10] He did not mimic

---

10. For example, in *Early Christian Rhetoric: The Language of the Gospel* (Cambridge, Mass.: Harvard University Press, 1971).

the scribes and the Purity Party in the close exegesis of the law or the strict interpretations of purity codes. He had a strong preference, perhaps an exclusive preference, for the oral word.

The aversion to writing persisted in the early movement well into the second century. Although Paul writes to his churches, he promises in letter after letter to assert his real authority when he comes to them in person. It has frequently been pointed out that several of the fathers preferred oral tradition to written as late as the middle of the second century C.E.

But there is a tendency in the New Testament gospels to move in the direction of a written tradition. The shift to writing goes together with the tendency to create something that is stable, crystallized, definitive — that can be handed around and on with ease. The very notion of canon presupposes tradition that is written. The transition from oral to written goes together with the move away from the free expression of the spirit to the controlled expression of bishops in an institution. It marks the transition from word *of* God to word *about* God. As Gerhard Ebeling once remarked, a word about God is a human word; only a word from God is a divine word. Lee McDonald is entirely correct in stating that a fixed canon imposes a limit on the Holy Spirit.

This observation brings me to usage in the ancient churches as a criterion for canonicity. The usage criterion tells us how the bishops began to understand their own tradition: If the tradition had passed into the public domain and could be considered the opinion of the average communicant, then it was canonical. That indicates that the tradition has now been leveled, flattened, as it were, so that it can be readily grasped by the average believer. Canonization, in fact, was an integral part of the bureaucratization and politicization of the tradition.

The canonical process itself functioned to flatten and crystallize the tradition. It was for that reason that the institutional church insisted on the right to interpret the written text. That held open the possibility of a revision of what stood written. However, the institution was not willing as a rule to endorse deviant interpretive behavior, which means that Jesus of Nazareth would have been no more welcome among the church fathers than he was among members of the Purity Party in his own day.

The canonical writings as "apostolic." The early fathers of the church argued that the canonical writings were produced by the "apostles," who were presumed to be either among the first followers of the historical Jesus or amanuenses (secretaries) to those followers. We now know that most if not all of those claims are inaccurate. This is another point at which the tradition has become historically untrustworthy.

This same deficiency applies to the claim that the New Testament documents are ancient, that they belong to the formative stages of the tradition, and not to its hardening phase. We now believe that much of the New Testament was not written until late in the first century or early in the second. We think that the reports of the gospels and acts are often derivative and unreliable. Thus, the councils were in error in making the claims they did about the age of the documents they canonized.

The canon as orthodox and inspired. To claim that the New Testament documents were both orthodox and inspired is to say the same thing. A book was thought to be inspired if it were orthodox, and orthodox if it were inspired. The employment of these two criteria is a tactical ploy: define as canonical what the bishops have decided is orthodox and declare it to be inspired at the same time; eliminate everything that does not fit the orthodox mold and you produce an impregnable circle.

The canon of the early Christian movement is a spectrum of tradition and interpretation. The only question is whether the ancient councils and bishops narrowed the spectrum too much. They certainly did not expand it prodigally; yet they were wise enough to include a variety of documents in their lists of works recommended to be read in the churches; it was not a monolithic collection. It now appears that they were so exercised about heresy — read, their own authority and power — that they narrowed the spectrum too much both laterally and vertically. With respect to the lateral dimension, they failed to include a fully representative spectrum of memory and interpretation in their definition of "orthodoxy." As a consequence, the tradition soon became too incestuous and brittle to adapt itself to new contexts and problems. With regard to the vertical dimension, the tradition was cut off at an early date from some of its roots — the vision of Jesus was obscured by interpretive overlay and the authentic voice of Paul smothered by Pauline imitators. These deficiencies, unfortunately, cannot be entirely remedied since some of the founding documents have been destroyed.

STAGE TWO

Adoptions: lists, codices, lectionaries. Evidence for the content of the canon consists of one of three kinds of data, prior to the Council of Trent in 1545: lists of books; documents published in a single codex; and books included in lectionary cycles.

In *Honest to Jesus,* I attempted to demonstrate that the twenty-seven books in the New Testament, and only those twenty-seven books, were never included in a single codex prior to the invention of the printing press.[11] The New Testament did not exist as a physical book until the sixteenth century. When it did appear, it was the product of publishers, not of the church.

Eusebius of Caesarea was the first to make a list of accepted, rejected, and disputed books. Eusebius made that list in the fourth century. When we quote Athanasius's festal letter of 367 C.E. as a definitive canonical list of New Testament books, we are elevating the judgment of a single ancient church theologian to the status of orthodox dogma, when, in fact, the contours of the New Testament had not yet been settled.

The only other physical basis we have for determining which documents were regarded as sacred are the lectionaries — manuscripts of readings arranged for the liturgical year. Our knowledge of the lectionaries is incomplete, but we know that the Book of Revelation, for example, was never included in the ancient lectionary cycle.

Canonical languages: Latin, Greek, Aramaic, and Hebrew. When the Roman Catholic Church got around to canonizing its scripture in the sixteenth century — April 8, 1546, to be exact! — it canonized the Latin Vulgate. The canonical gospels for that church are thus the Latin translations of Jerome and others. In the Fourth Gospel, the Latin text included the pericope of the woman caught in the act of adultery (usually versified as 7:53–8:11). As a consequence, commentaries on John by Catholic scholars must address that pericope. Protestant scholars, who prefer for the most part to think of the Greek text as canonical, skip that pericope in their commentaries because they think that it did not belong to the original text of John. This is a minor example of an unresolved canonical problem.

So far as I know, no one has ever canonized the Greek text of the

---

11. San Francisco: HarperSanFrancisco, 1996, chap. 6.

New Testament; the United Bible Societies have copyrighted it, but they have not canonized it. Both Protestant and Catholic scholars simply buy each new edition of Nestle's critical edition of the Greek New Testament as it appears and use it as though it were the real New Testament. There have now been twenty-six editions of Nestle. Which edition, with its catalogue of more than seventy thousand significant variants, is canonical?

Earlier, I mentioned the problem of the scriptures of the early Jesus movement. They made almost exclusive use of the Greek translation of the Torah, Prophets, and Psalms. Should Christians not regard the Greek scriptures as their canon?

The original language of the gospels, so far as we know, was Greek. However, many of our colleagues think Jesus spoke only Aramaic. Were we to discover a text of Jesus' teachings in Aramaic, would that displace the Greek translations we have in our Greek New Testament?

Conclusion

These meager facts suggest that the process of canonization is a continuing one. It has never reached a final, fixed stage, except perhaps in the case of the Latin Vulgate. But even here, Catholic scholars take liberties with the dictates of their own councils and work with an ever-changing Greek text.

A *New* New Testament

During the half century that separates us from World War II, we have come to the end of the Christian era. By that I do not mean that Christianity has come to an end; I mean rather that the hegemony of the Christianized, industrialized West over the rest of the globe has come to an end. We are passing through a radical cultural transition which marks the close of the Christian era and the beginning of a global society.

In addition, the symbolic universe, with his layered heavens above and a fiery Sheol beneath, is no longer tenable. A geocentric universe has been replaced with one of almost infinite dimensions: The observable universe is 30 billion light years across and 15 billion years old. The earth itself is 4.2 billion years old. The magnitude of the physical

universe boggles the mind. The earth is scarcely more than a speck
of dust in that frame of reference.[12]

The myth of the redeemer who descends from earth-related heavens, performs some salvific function for humankind, then returns to
the heavens to sit at the right hand of God, awaiting the signal to
make a second entrance, is no longer plausible to many Christians.
Yet, even they continue to repeat the words of the creed, with mental
reservations, to be sure, without realizing that the creed itself em-
bodies perspectives and values they are no longer willing to endorse.
With his telescope, Galileo changed our perceptions of space and time
forever; Einstein and Hubble only made matters worse. However, the
churches continue to pretend that nothing really has changed with respect to the mythic framework of the gospel. The old world is gone,
and all the church's horses and all the church's men cannot put that
world together again.

As we make the transition to the new age, the scriptures once
thought to be the epitome of Christianity will look increasingly
quaint, like a lacquered icon that has survived from some long lost
world. Nevertheless, buried in the pages of those ancient documents
is a vision of the world as God's domain that once turned the whole
of the Western world in a new direction. Those who treasure that
vision must ask themselves whether they can retain that vision while
shedding the remnants of a worldview whose archaic values and
mythology are no longer viable. It is a formidable challenge to the
church and all the members of the church alumni association, as
Bishop Spong calls them. And it is a labor of love to everyone —
church-connected or not — who has caught a glimpse of what Jesus
of Nazareth was all about.

The development of biblical scholarship in the last fifty years,
prompted by the cultural transition mentioned above, has opened the
door to a reconsideration of what the Christian scriptures ought to
contain. It will be a great tragedy if we do not seize the opportunity to
revamp and revise. The vitality of the Christianity movement and the
future of the church may well depend on the courage we can muster to

12. Roger S. Jones, professor of physics at the University of Minnesota, has an interesting
discussion of the relation of physics to theology in *Physics for the Rest of Us* (Chicago:
Contemporary Books, 1992). He assumes that the old mythical world of the creed is gone,
yet he argues that physics also operates largely with metaphorical language and, therefore,
does not really describe some metaphysical reality completely external to our perceptions
of it.

meet the challenge. We require a new New Testament, indeed, a new Bible, that will find its way into bookstores and on the Internet into a section clearly marked "Bibles." There, readers will stumble across it and be surprised at its contents. They will make use of copies in their study and discussion groups and carry them into their churches, where pastors and teachers will have to respond to the issues raised by a revised collection of scriptures. The effect will be electric.

As the way to get to a new New Testament, I have three very different agendas to propose. The first is the most practical. I believe we must resume the process of canonization as though it were not consummated and bravely undertake the modification of the New Testament in some important respects. In this context, I am able only to sketch my suggestions without developing them in detail. The second agenda is typical of the academic: include all ancient texts in a library of early Christian writings, in modern, idiomatic translations, so that those really interested can sample the full spectrum of documents. The third agenda is more radical: excavate to the foundations and retain only those glimpses of the Kingdom of God that can survive in the rarefied atmosphere of the third millennium.

Canon One

In the most practical approach, I suggest we begin by making certain modifications in our translations that go beyond, but do not contradict, the Greek text of the gospels. It has often been pointed out, for example, that the Romans are identified in the passion narrative only when they are viewed in a positive Christian light. In Mark 15:39, the Roman officer is made to say, "This man really was God's son!" Why not identify the Romans wherever they appear in the text, in both positive and negative contexts? When Mark writes, "And the soldiers led him away," we should translate, "And the Roman soldiers led him away" (15:16). When Mark says, "And they kept striking him on the head with a staff, and spitting on him," translate, "And the Roman soldiers kept striking him on the head with a staff, and spitting on him" (15:19). There are dozens of places where a simple identification of the subject would give the reader an entirely different impression of the roles of the various parties in the passion of Jesus.

Similarly, the term "Pharisee" should be dropped from our translations and the phrase "the Purity Party" substituted. Rather than read, "Whenever the Pharisees' scholars saw him eating with sinners..."

in Mark 2:16, the translation should read, "Whenever some scholars who belonged to the Purity Party..." The poor Pharisees have suffered long enough for their concern for the applicability of the Levitical codes to all areas of life.

Of even more significance would be the decision to adopt the term "Judeans" as a substitute for the term "Jews," especially in the Fourth Gospel. In the Hebrew Bible, the people of the covenant are Israelites. In the period of the Second Temple, they should be referred to as "Judeans." Only with the advent of rabbinic Judaism and the synagogue should the people of this faith be called "Jews." While this simple modification would not erase the anti-Judaism that remains in many Christian texts, it would be a small step in that direction.

An additional minor step would be to reorder the books of the New Testament. For example, in *The Five Gospels,* the Fellows of the Jesus Seminar placed Mark first among the four gospels since, in the judgment of the majority of modern scholars, Mark was the earliest to be written. We could move Acts to a position after the Gospel of Luke in order to indicate that Luke-Acts is a two-volume work. And we could arrange the Pauline letters in the order in which we think they were written. These simple steps would shatter the patina of familiarity that tends to inhibit engagement with the content of the texts. Of course, for those who rarely look into their New Testaments — and that may be most of us — such maneuvers would not help.

As a minimal step toward a new collection of gospels, I suggest that we preface the four New Testament gospels with a reconstructed version of the Sayings Gospel Q, along with the Gospel of Thomas, to indicate that the first gospels were collections of the words of Jesus without a mythical narrative framework. There would then be six gospels rather than four in our New Testament. For those who wish to be even bolder, we might preface the six gospels with a compendium of the authentic sayings of Jesus, making use of the findings of the Jesus Seminar or creating an entirely new compendium.

Finally, honesty requires that we identify those passages that espouse perspectives and values that we, most of us, find inadequate, primarily self-serving, archaic, or just plain immoral! — values like slavery, anti-Judaism, the patriarchal suppression of women, and Christian arrogance and exclusivism, to mention only the most egregious. Readers should be warned by some device in the text that these features are no longer considered God-sanctioned and, consequently, not acceptable to Christians.

In my view, it is also necessary to delete one or more books from the traditional New Testament in order to signal our seriousness in modifying the scriptures. This, along with the other steps mentioned above, would serve to destabilize the canon and simultaneously open it up to new horizons of understanding.

Canon Two

My second suggestion is to offset the negative reaction to the creation of a new New Testament by publishing an entire library of early Christian texts. The Jesus Seminar has retranslated twenty-one gospels and included them under one cover in *The Complete Gospels*. The Fellows of the Seminar are currently working on *The Complete Letters* to go with the gospels. *The Complete Acts* and *The Complete Apocalypses* will follow. Even more volumes will be needed to complete the library.

Canon Three

My third proposal was suggested to me by Harold Bloom in his work *The Western Canon*. The twenty-six works he includes in his canon of great Western prose and poetry consist of what he calls strong poets, poets who appeared on the stage of history as intrusions into their time and place, as seers born out of season. In a canonical work, Bloom writes, "you encounter a stranger, an uncanny startlement rather than a fulfillment of expectations."[13] Strong poets startle and frighten because they invoke visions of worlds aborning, of vistas not accessible to the habituated perspectives of the everyday and ordinary. Their words cannot be assimilated to the received tradition, to what everybody already knows, because they have chosen them with such great care so as to offend, to disrupt, to bewitch, to charm, to enchant. Strong poets mark the turbulent transition to new worlds.

Bloom reminded me of what we learned about the parables and aphorisms of Jesus thirty years ago in the parables movement. When one encounters the authentic words of Jesus — when they are freed from the surrounding flattening prosaic terrain — one is as surprised as the victim in the ditch in the parable of the Samaritan, as those

---

13. *The Western Canon*, 1–11.

hired at the eleventh hour when paid a denarius, as the street people ushered into the great banquet, as the prodigal upon returning home. Our surprise is triggered by their surprise.

The followers of Jesus began to forget their surprise, their startlement, almost immediately. Or, rather, they began to transpose it into a new key. They found the vision of Jesus difficult to remember and transmit in its original form. In addition, they willed to forget what was not practical and useful in their struggle to conquer the empire. Nevertheless, that surprise is preserved in incidental traces here and there in the gospels and in the letters of Paul, but everywhere else began to fade almost immediately, lost in the practical concerns of the everyday.

Jesus and Paul are the only strong poets in the New Testament, the only authoritative voices, and they are the precipitators of the vision that produced the Christian movement. Yet, they have both been muffled by an oppressive overlay of mythic iconography and tables of received virtue. The process occurred in three stages. In the first stage, the community of the Jesus movement made the transition from orality to scribalism as a way to fix and thus hang on to the unruly initiating vision. (By way of reminder, the oral may be written and not lose its orality, which is to say that orality is here a metaphor.) In the second stage, the redactors, the evangelists, who were editors of the Jesus tradition, and the editors of letters, came along and encased Jesus and Paul in suffocating prose enclosures, again in an effort to preserve the original vision. Finally, in the third stage, the startling expressions of Jesus and Paul (they are now verbal expressions and not ineffable glimpses of worlds aborning) are assimilated to what everybody already knows, to the received myths widely embraced in the secular world, to proverbial lore, and their genius thereby effaced. The canon is now what is read at the behest of the bishop, who has decided what it is safe for his parishioners to read. Heresy is now possible since there is a fixed norm by which to measure deviation. The original deviations of Jesus and Paul have been brought to heel. The tradition now awaits its new prophets, who will speak in the spirit and disrupt the steadying control of the ecclesiastical bureaucracy. If and when that happens, the tradition will rediscover its initiating vision and be born anew.

This process has been repeated over and over again in the history of the Christian tradition — partial rediscovery, eruption of the spirit, suppression by the Creedal Party, or the Canon Party. The Creedal Party prefers its own formulation of what Jesus and Paul were all about and is willing to suppress unruly views. The Canon Party wishes to endorse the ancient formulations but prefers the overlay that tames Jesus and Paul. The church bureaucracy and scholarship beholden to the church obediently prefer order to the chaos produced by the spirit.

The preferences of biblical scholarship for order and control are evident in the way its agenda has unfolded in its modern history. A recital of developments will reveal how scholars have moved from the uncontrollable to the staid, steady, safe. First, form criticism was designed to go behind the written gospels to recover the Jesus tradition in its fluid, wild state. Form criticism came under fire as the subversion of what stands written: We were admonished by the pedants to study the gospels and letters as they appear in our reconstructed Greek texts and not in some prior hypothetical oral state. Then came redaction criticism with its penchant for ignoring the underlying soul of the tradition and its call to concentrate on how the individual evangelists interpreted Jesus and Paul. Under its tutelage, Mark, Matthew, and Luke displaced Jesus as the source of the primary vision. Finally, reader response criticism reared its egalitarian head to produce the final flattening: Jesus and Paul mean whatever readers take them to mean; as reader, I am the final authority of what they meant.

In spite of scholarly efforts to control the tradition, the old New Testament has long since ceased to be a canon: It lacks real authority in our society, even among, or perhaps especially among, scholars, despite protestations to the contrary. The common reader hears only what study Bibles permit him or her to hear. And scholars devise hermeneutics to support the party line: redaction criticism, reader response criticism, an eschatological Jesus positioned outside of space and time, who is now weightless and timeless, available for whatever service his worshipers need. That Jesus is no longer a threat to anyone or anything. Paul has suffered a similar fate. The Pastoral epistles have all but obscured the historical Paul; the Pauline school has turned Paul into a manual of church order.

The Creedal Party much prefers the framework stories of the Gospel of Mark, where the myth of the Apostles' Creed is vested. One can draw a straight line from those framework stories in Mark to the original second-century version of the Apostles' Creed and thence to Nicea and the final abstraction away from the vision of Jesus to the predominant myth and metaphysics of the Byzantine world. It is perfectly clear that many critics of the Jesus Seminar have no use for the Jesus of the parables and aphorisms. That Jesus cannot be managed by the Creedal Party. They prefer to ignore Jesus' admonition "love your enemies," the most radical, demanding ethic ever devised. The love of enemies simply erases the lines separating believers from heresies and heretics. Such a radical ethic does not fall within the purview of the Creedal Party. The new New Testament, suitable for the third millennium, should include whatever traces of the original strangeness of Jesus and Paul we can isolate or reconstruct. As Bultmann once suggested, excavate to the foundations. Save nothing that does not preserve fragments of the initiating, unsettling, disruptive dreams. Admit that Jesus died precisely for a few provocative witticisms and a handful of subversive short stories that leave us gasping for breath at every reading. Applaud Paul for the agonizing struggle with his own Pharisaic past, the Paul who caught sight of the boundaryless community with no social barriers separating female from male, Gentile from Jew, slave from free, black from white, homosexual from heterosexual. Reinstate the prophetic insight that Satan has been cast out of heaven and the demonic powers subdued. Recover the shocking notion that access to the divine does not require brokers, that life is to be celebrated, that trust is nectar of the gods. These are the provocative features of those who caught a glimpse of God's domain once upon a time.

Chapter 3

CONVERGENT SPIRITUALITY

Keith Ward

KEITH WARD is Regius Professor of Divinity at the University of Oxford. An ordained priest in the Church of England, he also is canon of Christ Church, Oxford. Prior to his current post at Oxford, Professor Ward was fellow, dean, and director of studies in philosophy and in theology at Trinity Hall, Cambridge, where he remains an Honorary Fellow. He also has served as professor and head of the Department of the History and Philosophy of Religion at the University of London. Professor Ward is a member of the Governing Council of the Royal Institute of Philosophy, the Academic Advisory Board of the Oxford Centre for Islamic Studies, and the Editorial Boards of *Religious Studies, Journal of Contemporary Religion, Studies in Inter-Religious Dialogue,* and *World Faiths Encounter*. He additionally serves as joint president of the World Congress of Faiths, the world's oldest interfaith organization. Professor Ward has given the Edward Cadbury Lectures at the University of Birmingham (1980), the Teape Lectures in Delhi, Bangalore, and Calcutta (1989), the Selwyn Lectures in Auckland and Wellington, New Zealand (1993), and the prestigious Gifford Lectures at the University of Glasgow (1993–94). He has taught frequently in the United States as a visiting professor (at Drake University, Iowa, Claremont Graduate School, California, and the University of Tulsa, Oklahoma) and as an invited lecturer (at the Bornblum Jewish Studies Department in Memphis and the Divinity Schools of Harvard, Yale, and the University of Chicago). His publications in the last six years include *Defending the Soul; Images of Eternity; God, Chance, Necessity; God, Faith and the New Millennium,* and three books of a four-volume "comparative theology," published by Clarendon Press: *Religion and Revelation, Religion and Creation,* and *Religion and Human Nature.*

"GLOBALIZATION" IS A CONCEPT that became increasingly used as the world approached the twenty-first century. It is expressed visually by the picture of Earthrise, taken from the moon, which for the first time in human history allows us to see the planet Earth from another world. In the twentieth century, it became possible for the first time to travel around the earth in days, rather than in months or years, to communicate instantly with any part of the planet, and to manufacture goods with parts from many different continents, for a worldwide market.

What these things have made possible is a way of thinking which takes the whole earth into consideration, and which is freed from limitations of local culture to a very great extent. That new way of thinking has both positive and negative aspects. Positively, the availability of vastly increased markets makes goods cheaper to produce, and thus makes them available to greater numbers of people. One can be released from the narrow perspectives of a particular society or culture and learn to see things from a more multicultural and international viewpoint. One can easily experience at first hand many different cultures and ways of life, and thus understand the diversity of human life much more fully.

However, there are negative features of this process which lead some people to oppose globalization as an almost evil force. The growth of multinational industries puts immense wealth and power in the hands of companies which may not have the interests of any particular nation at heart. This may give rise to extremes of wealth distribution, as firms go to the poorest countries to manufacture goods, which are then sold in the richer countries. Whole areas of the world may become industrial fodder to preserve the lifestyle of the developed parts of the world, and a justifiable sense of injustice becomes widespread, with the attendant consequences of unrest and instability.

Even the experience of other cultures can easily degenerate into a sort of "tourist attitude," for which cultures become quaint objects of entertainment, rather than seriously considered claimants to insight, truth, and moral excellence. Moreover, sometimes globalization is associated with homogenization, whereby all cultural differences are leveled down to one bland cultural hegemony. In the modern world, this is the hegemony of Hollywood, of fast foods and pop music, which some believe obliterates complex traditions of local culture with a superficial "instant fix" which keeps people occupied, even overloaded, with entertainment, but undermines powers of discrimination and reflection.

So, there are those who enthusiastically support the process of globalization, looking for it to raise living standards and eradicate old national hostilities. But there are also those who oppose the process as undermining traditional cultural values and reducing vast populations to being little more than commodity consumers.

The world's religious traditions share in this ambiguity of attitude. In the early history of humanity, what we now call religions were tribal folkways, sustaining a relationship to localized gods and spirits which was almost entirely confined to the tribe and had little concern to extend more widely. Such tribes had little opportunity to encounter or little reason to think about people living great distances away. Their relations were with adjoining tribal groups and were largely concerned with moderating hostilities. In such a context, religious practice was more concerned with sustaining the values of the local group against hostile invasion than with seeking any form of wider perspective. It is entirely natural that the earliest social function of religion should have been one of sustaining intense group loyalty, together with guarded hostility to all outsiders.

With the spread of trade and military expansion, some of these tribal traditions took on more imperialistic ambitions. They annexed the gods and sacred powers of other tribes and imposed their own sacred narratives and symbols on conquered populations. Now religions did seek to extend their range, but this was seen largely in terms of conquest and expansion, not in terms of any sort of joint exploration with other traditions. Beginning with tribalism, and quickly annexed to imperialism, religious traditions have always been closely associated with the drive to ethnic superiority and the overt symbolization of power.

Naturally, the conquered often sought to preserve their own traditions as bastions against invading empires. For them, religion became a bond of social cohesion when confronted by superior forces and a statement of local, often ethnic, identity. Complexes of law, custom, ceremony, and story bound together particular social groups and helped to preserve them in the face of surrounding hostility.

So, in the first two major phases of religious life on this planet, there was little concern to seek a truth in matters of religious faith about which there was universal agreement. Tribal religion remains particular and local. It has little concern with what outsiders believe and sees religion as a set of customs, symbols, and rites to which one belongs by birth and which relates the tribe to sacred powers. Imperial religion is concerned with social domination or — by reaction — with defense against hostile invaders. The power of the cult is the power of the imperium, or the last defense against the imperium, and religious life becomes associated with broad ethnic and cultural alliances and conflicts.

It would be quite wrong to hold, as some do, that religion somehow causes conflict and intolerance. "Religion" is not some sort of autonomous power, which can cause things to happen to human beings, whether they like it or not. It is more plausible to suppose that particular rites, customs, and symbols are used to define the tribe and extend or resist the empire, without express reference to any specially "religious" beliefs that may be involved. Even an avowedly secular empire will adopt its own symbols, rites, and myths of origin as expressions of its own preferred forms of life. It is pretty clear that the secular empires of the Mongols, of Rome, and of modern Russia and China have caused a degree of human suffering which dwarfs any efforts that religious organizations may have made in that direction.

Nevertheless, if religious beliefs are beliefs about the ultimate powers and values which govern human existence, one might well see the symbols of secular empires as verging on the religious and easily moving into the territory of religious belief. It is natural for a society to see its own chief values as values which are somehow rooted in reality itself and to see its own power as validated by the powers of the cosmic order, which it successfully manifests. Such values and powers are often expressed in images of gods or ancestral spirits, and the contemplation of and cultivation of relationships with such gods is a natural human activity, which will carry all the main characteristics of the culture of which it is part. Religious forms of life will be good or bad, deep or superficial, beautiful or repellent, insofar as the cultures which express their own values and aspirations in such forms of life exhibit such qualities.

This may sound like a Durkheimian account of religion, for which religious traditions are in fact expressions of the social will, with the function of making a society cohesive and strong. Indeed, I think Durkheim was very largely right; that is how religion is typically used. The inadequacy of Durkheim's analysis appears only when it is taken as an explanation of what religion really is — which involves the claim that the typical function of religion in society is to be identified with its inner character and meaning.

It seems obvious, however, that once anyone begins to believe that his or her religious practice is a worship of the collective mind of a group, the practice will self-destruct. The collective mind is just not worth worshiping in the end. Unless it reflects some higher cosmic or moral principle, the collective soul is an abstraction which bears all the fallibility and imperfection of its individual human members. If I would not worship my neighbors or colleagues, I am hardly likely consciously to worship a whole collection of neighbors and colleagues, most of whom I would probably disagree with completely.

So, though religion is often used to affirm and legitimate the values and power of social groups, it is important to their successfully playing such a role that the values of the group can plausibly be seen as reflecting and expressing some value and power which exist beyond the group. In other words, the question of truth, of the adequacy of symbols and rites to a suprahuman reality, is of fundamental importance to religious belief and cannot be wholly denied.

The question of truth introduces an important dimension to the analysis of religion, and when it is taken seriously, it throws into sharp relief the problems of the tribal and imperial phases of religious life. Of course, tribal cults are concerned with truth. Their adherents suppose that the spirits really exist and have causal effects on the environment. But as tribes come into contact with one another, it can hardly fail to become clear that different tribes have different ways of naming and relating to spiritual realities.

At first, it may seem enough to say that each tribe has its own god, and its own way of relating to God, mediated through the shamans or prophets of the tribe. But sooner or later the question must be faced: Do the spirits exist as individual entities, or is talk of spirits a metaphorical discourse which partly cloaks a deeper and more mysterious spiritual reality? Are religious symbols to be given a realist interpretation or a metaphorical one? This problem probably does not occur in this form in primal traditions, but it is one which is bound to surface in a world for which local tribalism has been superseded by more national and international social frameworks.

It may seem that when the question of truth is put to tribal traditions, they must wither and die, since they are usually committed to prescientific (and false) worldviews, and to ineffective causal practices, like trying to cause rain by dancing. Primal religion, however, has not been outmoded by globalization. On the contrary, as one considers the religious traditions which exist in the world today, one cannot fail to be struck by their apparently increasing variety and internal complexity. Many tribal traditions — usually now called primal traditions — are experiencing a revitalization, and this is partly due to the wish to stress the distinctiveness of local culture in the face of the perceived cultural hegemony of the West. However, this also often involves a rejection of a scientifically informed view of reality.

One way of countering the dominance of a foreign culture is to rediscover some superior resources in one's own culture. So the scientifically founded atheism of the West is said to be inferior in many ways to the spiritual perceptions of the shamans and teachers of primal traditions. It probably is true that what is called Western culture lacks spiritual depth in some respects. One only has to think of Nietzsche's proclamation that "God is dead" or note the commercialism and exploitation by which the Western powers have utilized the Eastern and Southern nations, wherever they could, to realize that the West is not generally noted for its self-renouncing spiritual teachings.

Christianity itself has been shaped by four great imperial systems — Byzantium, Rome, Europe, and the United States of America — all of which have seen themselves as, and sought to be, leading military powers, with the will to divide and control the whole world. For most of those who encountered Christianity through missionaries belonging to these powers, the Christian faith was from the first usually seen as imperialist, alien, and subordinate in practice to economic and military aims and objectives.

In this context, tribal faiths in the modern world are the faiths of the dispossessed. They are assertions of ancient rights and wisdom, however newly invented these are in fact. They affirm the dignity of ancient cultures, which are unable to compete economically or militarily in the modern world. They tend to be deeply suspicious of the scientific approach, which seems to have led to the collapse of religious faith in Europe and to its fragmentation into a thousand competing sects in America.

In a world in which it is impossible for most people to understand the equations of quantum physics and computer algebra, there seems little to choose between the fantasies of physicists who talk of time going backward, or humans evolving from pieces of primitive jelly over generations, and the rich mythical worlds of tribal tradition, where the gods and spirits walk the earth no more strangely than the quarks and probability waves of quantum theory.

To most people in the modern world, science may be totally ir-
rational, for all they know. Its theorems are discussed by small elite
groups, which bar admission to all who cannot pass the initiation
test of solving differential equations. Its view of a world of ten-
dimensional warped space-time and tiny whirling invisible particles
seems wholly opposed to the commonsense perception of solid objects
lying alongside one another in three-dimensional space. Paradoxically, science, by its difficulty and surprisingness, has opened the door
to a new age of irrationality, where reality is very different than it
seems, and where only a small elite have access to the truth about
how things are.

Where quantum theory cannot be connected coherently with general relativity even by the most brilliant physicists in the world, who
cares if tribal faiths, sponsored by the shamanistic elite and revealing
the world to be much stranger than it seems, cannot be coherently
connected with the theories of science? So, it is not unusual to find
pseudoscientific terminology being used by many modern religious
movements, together with claims that a small group of initiates has
special access, by special training, to realms of reality hidden to ordinary mortals. The counterculture of new religion apes the elite
vocabulary of new science, but it uses that vocabulary to reject the
atheistic and exploitative dominant culture that the new science has
brought.

Globalization has been made possible by scientific discovery, and
one of its symptoms is that scientific technology is now present
everywhere throughout the globe. Yet, it produces by reaction a
many-headed counterculture, which refuses the methods of critical
inquiry and dispassionate experimental observation which gave birth
to modern science. Instead, it asks for participation in tradition, and
as its reward it offers access to depths of reality with which the sciences do not deal — depths of the human mind and personality, in
their relation to spiritual depths beneath the material warp and woof
of the universe.

Globalization does not necessarily produce a globalized form of
religion. On the contrary, it can evoke a fierce localization of religious tradition, which is simply not concerned with relating to other
perspectives on human life and faith. This is what has been called the
postmodern condition. If modernity is closely associated with the sciences, with claims to achieve a knowledge of universal and objective

truth by dispassionate critical inquiry, then postmodernity rejects the possibility of universal truth and dispassionate inquiry and disputes the value of critical inquiry, which may cut one off from one's roots in a particular tradition.

Postmodernity is largely born of fear of science. It may be asked, where has this concentration on pure reason and experiment led? It has led to Auschwitz, to experimentation on animals and humans, to wars of utterly inhumane technological sophistication, to the end of belief in God and in objective morality, to the rule of the heartless technocrat. Well did Marx cry that religion was the heart of a heartless world, though he himself was so influenced by materialistic science that he thought religion was only an opiate, a drug without inner truth. In the postmodern world, the reaction against the dispassionate heartlessness of science can be expressed by a return to tribalism, to the alleged self-sufficiency and finality of one's own religious tradition, whatever it is.

It might even be said that as the world moves into the third millennium, it is in the grip of two massive fundamentalisms: the fundamentalism of science and the fundamentalism of religion. The former says that all knowledge comes from experimental observation and by techniques of critical public inquiry. By that standard, the only knowable world is the material world, the world of particles in motion. The scientific fundamentalist says that is the only world there is. All else is illusion, to be consigned to the flames. The latter says that some sort of revelation provides complete and inerrant truth, in every literal detail. To doubt it is to imperil eternal life. To criticize it is to oppose God himself. The religious fundamentalist says that only revelation contains truth worth considering. It must be guarded jealously, even fiercely, against any change or deviation, for truth lies in the past, and the future can only bring decay, deviation, and ultimately death.

Religious fundamentalists are antimodern. They reject the fundamentalism of science, which claims the authority of universal reason and so defines modernity. There can, the religious fundamentalists say, be no claim to a universally accessible, rationally establishable truth in religion, for religion is clearly disputed in almost every one of its claims by intelligent and informed people. Therefore, religious fundamentalism has to claim that religious truth is restricted to special groups and is a matter of revelation and tradition, rather than of critical investigation.

Scientific fundamentalists, by contrast, can claim a growing body of knowledge and a method which brings virtually universal agreement among the informed. In what sense, then, are they fundamentalists? Precisely insofar as they make the claim that such knowledge and such a method of acquiring it are the only worthwhile human epistemic activities. It is important that there are dispassionate methods of inquiry, that the material universe can be understood by the human mind. But the mind deals not only with information and analysis. It is also, and equally importantly, concerned with meaning and evaluation. Religion claims that there are forms of knowledge which essentially involve personal commitment and which do not involve the accumulation of information so much as growth of moral and personal insight.

The reason for religious fundamentalism lies in the fact that it is, paradoxically, too much influenced by the model of modernity. It sees religious truths as being of the same sort as scientific truths. They are accessible in principle to all, but sin or attachment to desire obscures the truth. They are matters of additional information, but only the few are given access to this information through revelation. In that sense, religious fundamentalism could only exist after and in reaction to modernity, after the growth and success of scientific method. It sees religion as a sort of mirror image of that which it most fears, and so it comes to advocate a sort of occult science, whose truths are known only to initiates chosen by God.

It is anachronistic to think of primal religious traditions as fundamentalist. But the revival of such forms of religious life in the scientific age becomes fundamentalist, precisely because it must consciously turn its back on the scientific worldview and at the same time model itself on a perverse view that religion exists to provide arcane information and magical techniques for influencing the natural world. This is a perverse view because it subtly but profoundly distorts the motives and goals of religious practice.

Religion is concerned with knowledge — knowledge of a being or state of wisdom, compassion, and bliss, which can be realized only as one prepares oneself for positive relationship with such a reality. Religion is concerned with influencing the world by spiritual means — one's relationship to spiritual reality enables one to become a channel of wisdom, compassion, and bliss to the human world, and thereby influence it for good.

Religious knowledge is not, however, dispassionate and universal. It requires a form of practical commitment, and it values particular creative imagination as well as dispassionate investigation. Religious causality is not predictable and quantifiable. It arises out of a quasi-personal relationship which depends upon trust, compassion, and forgiveness as much as upon efficiency and technical expertise.

If one looks at primal traditions in this light, one can see them as providing ways of coming to apprehend beings or states of compassion and bliss, symbolized in many ways, and empowerment to live more fully, through ritualized practices and customs which relate members of the tribe to established traditions in positive ways. This is not, as Tylor and Frazer thought, an attempt at primitive science. Rather, it is an attempt to see and experience human life in relation to ideal values which in some way have objective existence and define a human goal of enduring significance.

What we think of as the great religious traditions are developments of such a primal vision of the world as interpenetrated by a higher spiritual reality which gives human existence a particular significance and purpose. There is no fear of science, as such, in primal traditions. There is no reason why investigation of the physical world should endanger the primal religious vision. It will, however, conflict with many particular assertions which will be found in all pre-scientific worldviews, including religious ones. Knowledge advances by the discovery of error and inadequacy. Thus, certain aspects of all religious traditions will stand in need of revision, as the quest for truth advances.

It is not only new scientific discoveries which will bring this about. Both moral reflection (disentangling unreasoned traditions from reflective principles for human flourishing) and considerations of intellectual economy and coherence (seeking to place the millions of imaginatively conceived gods in some sort of coherent and systematic framework) have important parts to play in the development of religious traditions.

So, in the Hebrew Bible, one can trace a development from the cult of a tribal warrior and storm god, who favors his own tribe above all others, to the postulation of one controlling Lord of all history, who enjoins justice and mercy on all people. In the *Upanishads*, one can trace a development from chants and esoteric formulae with magical power to bring fertility and success, to the postulation of one Intelligence present in all beings, which can be known only by the practice of nonattachment. Christian, Muslim, and Buddhist paths build on these traditions to develop further distinctive specifications of the reality or value which is the true goal of human endeavor and which promises the ultimate elimination of suffering from existence.

The developed concepts are different. The utterly transcendent and sovereign God of Islam presents a different image from the suffering God of Christianity, who unites creation to his own being through Incarnation. The Vedantic all-including Self of all, of whom all finite selves are part, is a different image again. And the Buddhist notion of nirvana, whose nature is bliss and compassion, but of which little can be positively said, is yet another very different way of conceiving the ultimate value toward which religious practice is directed.

One might consider that these different images belong to different cultures — the Middle East, the West, India, and South East Asia, respectively — and they should just be left as badges of cultural identity, rather as tribal traditions could live alongside one another without troubling too much about their relationship. There are forces in the modern world which would welcome such a model, but they can be all too closely associated with the forces of nationalism and reaction, of the imperialist attitude which in practice, if not in theory, asserts the superiority of my culture over others.

The situation is further complicated by two main factors. First, at least two major religions, Christianity and Islam, are overtly missionary faiths, and followers wish to proclaim their faith in all parts of the world without exception. They do not want to be confined to one geographical area. In a world in which travel and communication are so easy, the other faiths, too, have copied these missionary ambitions; one finds Hindu temples in California as well as Christian churches in Kerala. Today, every faith is to some extent a missionary faith with global ambitions.

Second, there are diaspora communities virtually all over the world, so that the ethnic and cultural faiths can be found as minorities in almost every country. Faiths cannot be simply confined to one part of the world. To the extent that ethnic cultures are diluted, or that they expand, they even cannot be confined in principle to ethnic subgroups within a majority culture. In a world in which travel and interaction have been fully globalized, religious faiths obtain new ways of existing outside their originating cultures. So, at the same time as globalization is opposed by religious forces reasserting local cultures, it is reinforced by religious forces moving into dynamic interaction with one another in all parts of the world.

That tension, between strongly linking religion and culture and disconnecting truth-claims from cultural practices, is one that exists in every modern religious tradition. Religious diversity takes a new form in the modern world. It was always obvious that there were many local cults and forms of religious belief. But as the great traditions developed, they did so in close association with particular cultures, imperial or counterimperial. Insofar as those cultures were happy to develop on their own terms, their relation to other cultures was largely oppositional. A policy of the coexistence of national or supernational religious blocks came into being. One could think of "the Christian world" or "the Muslim world," and, in many ways, that is still the way things are seen on the world stage.

Yet, that model is already outdated. With the foundation of the United Nations in 1948, many people began to view the world as a human totality, and ethnic or national groups as subsets of the wider class of simple humanity. Wilfred Cantwell Smith argued, in *The Meaning and End of Religion*, that the term "religion" was itself a product of the imperial strategy of the Western powers. It may be that his claim was overstated, but the underlying point was that faiths have become associated with cultural/national groupings, and can be used as symbols of identity and confrontation in a fiercely competitive world. However, such an association is logically contingent and now largely occurs as a defensive reaction against historical processes which are moving the world into a more multicultural unity.

Insofar as religions are identified with particular cultures, their tendency is to divide and oppose. This is a particular problem for traditions which make such a link central to their worldview, as Judaism does. Many Orthodox Jews see the role of their faith as precisely to make them different and to affirm a quite distinctive Jewish cultural identity. For some of them, relations with *goyim* should be kept to a minimum, and their aim is to be a completely self-contained community.

Such views will always exist — there are Christians, too, like the Amish, who share a restrictive conception of their faith. They will almost certainly be minority views, however, and their reflective adherents cannot be satisfied with a complete indifference to the rest of the world. The most Orthodox form of Judaism, for example, is committed to universal truth-claims, claims which hold for all people everywhere. If Orthodox Judaism is correct, it is true that there is a creator God who wills justice and mercy and who makes a covenant with Israel. An outgrowth of this belief is that Orthodox Jews have an interest in seeing that all people concede the truth that Israel has a covenant with God and accede to the existence of the creator. This may not take an overtly missionary form, but it is certainly a truth which it would be good if everyone accepted. The most Orthodox and introverted of Jews have an interest in seeing that *goyim* accept the existence of God and worship God. This is a religious truth-claim which is separable from the cultural practice of Judaism, but which arises from that cultural practice.

Therefore, a distinction can be made between the religious practices of a particular group and the universal claims implicit in those practices, which presumably all people should accept. Most religious traditions, however tribal, are committed to the existence of a supernatural reality, and to the correctness of their own set of descriptions of it, in some sense, however subtle. It may seem that, in the existence of a supernatural reality, there is at least a basis for religious unity, which can coexist with or even encourage a diversity of particular religious practices, in accordance with diverse revealed traditions.

Unfortunately, one thing that has become obvious in the modern world is that the existence of any supernatural reality is itself a matter of fundamental dispute. The existence of God, for example, cannot be demonstrated by reason. Even if one thinks that it can, one has to admit that many very rational people are not convinced by such demonstrations. They do not carry conviction, even if to some they seem reasonable. I myself think the existence of a creator God has quite a high probability, on the grounds that it provides an elegant and simple hypothesis for the existence of the universe. But I am aware that some of my colleagues think it has a rather low probability, while others think it has no probability at all, being completely indemonstrable. That is not what one would call a demonstration in any other area of thought, so one has to conclude, whether reluctantly or not, that the existence of God is not demonstrable by reason (or at least that it has never been demonstrated).

Not only is the existence of God not demonstrable, but many

people find belief in God offensive and immoral. They point to the intolerance of some believers, the reactionary and infantile nature of some religious ethical codes, and the repressive effects of some religious practices; they hold that we would all be better off without any religious beliefs. Religious belief is, it seems, inherently disputable. For anyone who believes in a free society, it follows that religious belief should not be made compulsory in any society, that it should be a matter of conscientious choice.

Such conclusions about the limits of reason in matters of religion are conclusions of modernity and are associated with the development of critical thought in the European Enlightenment. Similarly, belief in freedom of conscience, that people should be free to follow their consciences in rationally disputable matters, arose as a somewhat unintended consequence of the European Protestant Reformation, which reacted against the authority of the Roman Catholic Church. The acceptance of critical inquiry and of freedom of conscience are closely linked and have their roots in the culture of modernity. They mark a decisive advance in the understanding of religion, moving from the tribal and imperial toward a view of religions as offering competing visions of truth, which can be individually chosen.

This is an advance, because it draws out of the phenomenon of religion the element of truth-seeking and rational inquiry which is always implicit in and essential to it, though it is often overlaid by a stress on its ethnic, tribal, and imperial functions. The modern attitude may suggest a view of many religions offering their views in the marketplace of free inquiry and people choosing to accept or reject such views, in accordance with where their consciences lead them. At that point, a conflict may well emerge between insisting that people are born into a religious heritage and a belief that it is treason for them to leave it, and an insistence on freedom of conscience for each individual.

It is, of course, unrealistic to suppose that every individual will carefully consider a range of religious views and choose among them. Everyone is born into a tradition of practice and belief, and he or she will seek to live within it, unless strong reasons emerge which seem to compel change. So, the modern insistence might be that individuals typically are educated in a religious tradition and encouraged to find an individual path within that tradition, while they should not be prevented from leaving if that seems right to them. The age of diverse religious traditions is not dead, though they will have to be seen in a nontribal and nonimperial light in a post-critical age.

How is it possible to see traditions in such a light? Usually, a religious tradition is defined by an accepted text or body of texts, held to embody or amplify the teaching of an original founder or group of founders. To reject the authority of the text is to leave the tradition — as Buddhism became non-Hindu by rejecting the authority of the Veda. Also, there are usually rites of initiation, by which one explicitly joins a community, using such a text as a source of authoritative teaching. In sum, tradition is normally defined by an authoritative text and an interpretative community.

It has seemed for a great deal of history that religious belief is a matter of accepting an authoritative text as the final truth and, therefore, of rejecting other texts as deficient in various ways. But in the last two hundred years, a number of factors have changed this perception. The most important is the rise of critical methodology, both historical and literary. This brings one to see the sacred text not as a direct utterance of God, but rather as a set of diverse human responses to discernments of the divine presence, in a less propositional and more experiential way. Traditional interpretations of religion have been basically propositional. They have taken it that revelation consists in the provision of propositions by God. God can speak only in one tradition. How, then, can one interpret other traditions? Either they are just false, or in some way people make various mistakes in interpretation, even though they truly apprehend God.

Thus, even conventional views have a way of interpreting religious traditions other than one's own which is not either wholly dismissive or wholly accepting. One can see such traditions as containing human errors but also as containing genuine apprehensions of a spiritual reality, however inadequately (from the point of view of one's own tradition) perceived. This, for example, is the traditional attitude of Christianity toward Judaism and of Islam toward Christianity. Add to this the growing recognition, at least in the Christian case, that there are many errors of fact and quite a number of morally unacceptable views in the Bible, and one can see how easy it becomes to hold one's own tradition and others as on a par — as all fallible and partly mistaken interpretations of originative understandings of the divine.

It is, then, the ascent of critical and historical method which has given rise to the possibility of seeing all religious traditions as

containing fallible and partial comprehensions of spiritual reality.
Increasingly sensitive knowledge of how traditions have developed
over the years also contributes to the sense of the historical and cultural situations of all religious traditions and, thus, to a lessening of
plausibility of claims to absolute and unrevisable truth in any such
tradition.

Insofar as propositional views of revelation are weakened, another account of revelation is required, one that is founded on the
occurrence of specific experiences. One might see the founders of religious traditions as people who had particularly intense and vivid
experiences of spiritual reality and whose lives displayed a wisdom,
compassion, sensitivity, and power which seemed to derive from their
experience. Nevertheless, their teachings would be influenced by what
they had learned from their culture, with all its historical partialities,
and their experiences would be interpreted with the aid of concepts
drawn from that culture.

In the case of Jesus, for example, one might claim that he indeed
had an intense awareness of a God of loving-kindness and a sense
of vocation to proclaim the rule of God as an urgent and imminent
reality. But he learned his faith from his Jewish teachers, and he interpreted his experience in terms of the God of Abraham, Isaac, and
Jacob and of the covenant to keep the law of God and establish a
community of justice and peace.

It also could be fairly said that Gautama the Buddha had an intense
awareness of a state of compassion and bliss which gave liberation
from suffering and selfish desire. But the concepts he used to interpret his liberative experience were derived from the ascetic traditions
of Indian spirituality — concepts of *karma, moksha,* and *samsara* —
even though he modified those concepts in quite radical ways in the
light of his own experience (as Jesus did).

Could one reasonably claim that Jesus and Gautama had the same
sort of experience, differently interpreted in their different contexts?
Or perhaps that they had different experiences of the same thing? In
order to say that two people experienced the same thing, there would
need to be some common descriptive content in the way their experience was described, together with an explanation of such differences
as existed. These descriptions might be rather vague or metaphorical, and, if they were, it would be harder to say whether Jesus and
the Buddha really experienced the same thing, rather than two quite

similar things. But at that point, other considerations might enter as to the sort of thing they claimed to experience and what it would be like for there to be two or more such experiences.

Naturally enough, we have no records of the nature of Jesus' experiences of God. But it would be absurd to say Jesus was never aware of God the Father — and there are plenty of sayings attributed to Jesus which ascribe many properties to God. For example, God is described in the recorded teachings of Jesus as Father — *abba* — and as one who, while scrupulously just, seeks to save the lost with the utmost endeavor. Allowing for the presence of metaphor, one has a clear notion of a personal loving creator, in whose presence there is joy, whose wisdom surpasses all human wisdom, and who acts with compassion as well as with justice.

Gautama refused to describe the liberated state but was quite clear that there is one and that it has the character of limpidity, freedom from passion, equanimity, and joyfulness. There is no idea of a personal creator. But joy, wisdom, and compassion are all characteristics of the liberated state, and it is fairly clear that this state is not merely a psychological state of mind, since it is a state which is beyond the cycle of death and rebirth. It is also not a purely material state, since it has the character of awareness (joy and wisdom cannot exist without some sort of awareness). It may be thought to be a rather inactive or changeless state; immutability is said to be one of its characteristics.

One can build a contrast between a personal Lord who relates as one personal being to other persons and a changeless state of joyful awareness into which one enters at liberation. Yet, there is good reason not to make such a contrast too definitive. When Catholic theology comes to describe God, the object of Jesus' experience, it describes an immutable, eternal being, who is totally different in kind from any finite person. Indeed, for Aquinas, God is *esse suum subsistens,* the pure act of being, rather than a finite instantiation of being. It would be wholly true to say of Aquinas's God that he is "a changeless state of joyful awareness."

One might say that the Catholic tradition just has it wrong. But the tradition is aware of the Fatherhood of God and is able to construe God as three persons in one substance. So, from the Catholic perspective, it might be better to say that there is a difference between the philosophical analysis of the concept of God, which shows God to be simple and eternal, and the practice of devotion, which leads to eternal life and regards God as personalized as Father, Son, and Holy Spirit. These are not two different beings but two appropriate ways of speaking of a God whose reality transcends the literal understanding of terms in any human language.

If Gautama experiences a changeless state of joy and wisdom, it is quite possible to hold that he experiences what is in fact God, as philosophical analysis of the concept makes clear. He does not experience God as Trinity and as a person, but there is no reason why some human experience of God should make one aware of every property of the divine being. He does not experience God as a separate reality but seems to enter a nondual state in which subject and object are not distinguished. Christian mysticism is quite familiar with unitive experience of God, in which one cannot distinguish God and oneself as separate. That is like a close experience of loving another person, when one may feel that the two have become one. Theologically, of course, the two never become ontologically merged. But as far as experience goes, one might be unable to distinguish duality in such experience. Consequently, a Catholic should have no difficulty in supposing that Gautama's experience of nonduality is an authentic spiritual experience of God, even if it does not discern the duality between infinite and finite which, for a theist, always remains.

This is all said from a Christian perspective. But the same sort of thing might be said from a Buddhist perspective. Buddhist tradition is complex and varied, but within it there are major strands of devotion to Buddhas and Bodhisattvas, who may be seen as helps and supports in the practice of the spiritual life and, in some traditions, as personal expressions of the primal Buddha-nature, which pervades all things. What is important here is not that all Buddhists believe such things but that they are not alien imports into Buddhism from outside. They are strands of Buddhist thought which allow a rich devotional relationship to enlightened beings and which can even speak of personal aspects of the primal Buddha-nature (the *Dharmakaya*) by which it attains personal expression.

In this case, Buddhists will often say that there is a distinction between the pure Buddhism of the monks, whose aim is the cessation of desire, and the helpful Buddhism of the laity, who aim at better forms of existence and at helpful relations with beings in many spiritual realms, including Buddhas of the past and the future. True, there is no doctrine of a personal creator. But one can experience higher spiritual realities in a personal form, and such experiences are valid for beings at a certain stage in their development. Theistic experience of a personal God could be regarded as authentic religious experience, though at a less exalted level than the unitive experience of the nondual state.

There is no difficulty in each tradition granting to the other a partial but authentic experience of the supreme spiritual reality which is their ultimate concern. If one forces the question of which experience is more adequate, it is doubtful whether that can be answered simply from the occurrence of some experience itself. Both experiences may be of the same reality, which, though in itself possessing a certain form of simplicity, has many complex facets in relation to finite beings. But to rank those experiences in terms of their adequacy to how ultimate reality truly is will require general philosophical arguments rather than deeper introspection.

Religions do have authoritative texts and interpretative communities. But the authority of the text may be seen to lie in its witness to a liberating human experience of the divine, and the community may be seen to contain many possibilities of diverse interpretation. Not only that, but the texts do not typically contain propositional information about the nature of ultimate reality. They very often contain sets of poetic metaphors for evoking or expressing paradigmatic religious experiences. The interpretative level of theoretical formulation comes at a third remove, after experience and metaphorical expression. Although theoretical systemization is essential for a fully reflective worldview, it is not foundational for a religious tradition. What is foundational is the metaphorical expression of forms of experience which are paradigmatic for that tradition.

So, in the case of Jesus and Gautama, the concepts of God's kingdom, of resurrection, and of the great judgment day, on the one hand, and of nirvana, rebirth, and karma, on the other, are primarily metaphors expressive of the liberative experience of Jesus, Gautama, and their first disciples. They are not in the first instance literal doctrines — although some systemizations interpret them as such.

It is possible to interpret the Kingdom of God as a future period of political rule in which Jesus literally will be a King, the resurrection as the resuscitation of our present bodies on a future earth, and the judgment day as a specific time when all the dead will be assembled before the throne of God. The trouble with such an interpretation is that it turns religion into a series of factual predictions, which are bound to be seen as very poorly evidenced. They could be accepted only on authority, and the infallibility of that sort of authority is exactly what has been put in question by critical inquiry.

There is another interpretation available, however. The Kingdom is the rule of God in the heart, the resurrection is the raising of the whole person (but not in anything like our present physical bodies) to the presence of God, and the judgment is a symbol for the fact that our present deeds determine our eternal standing before God (or would, if it were not for divine mercy). In this interpretation, the symbols primarily stand for presently experienced realities. They are given on authority — on the authority of one who experienced the rule of God in the heart, new life in God's presence, and an intense sense of divine command and forgiveness. They do involve beliefs about the future — about a fuller expression of these experienced realities which, on faith, one accepts as implicit in a belief in a supreme spiritual power who wills good for creatures. But such future states are only metaphorically expressed. The eschatological future is not a continuation of the present world forever. It is a radically new creation, far beyond what we can literally imagine.

The strength of such an interpretation is that it is based on experience, and it gives religious language the function of evoking such experience, leading to the faith that such experiences can be extended and fulfilled for all created persons. What is paramount and primary is not that one accepts certain predictions as true but that one's present life is transformed by the presence and power of God, a reality of unique and supreme value. One follows a teacher who is believed to have been so transformed. The symbols of the Kingdom, of resurrection, and of judgment evoke and express such inner experiences and create a hope for a form of existence in which they are fulfilled in unimaginable ways, beyond the realm of suffering and death.

Such an interpretation of the key symbols of faith has become common in Christianity since the early nineteenth century. It is a reorientation of religious faith around the focal notion of transformative experience, based on an exemplary experient, instead of around theoretical propositions about supernatural and future facts, based on supposedly infallible teaching dictated by God.

Similarly, in the Buddhist case, there is an interpretation which would take nirvana to be the entrance into (or realization that one always in reality has been) a nondual reality, rebirth to be the repeated entrance of the personal stream of consciousness into many different bodies of animals and humans, and karma to be an inexorable law of moral cause and effect. There has always been a strong strand of thought in Buddhism, however, which is skeptical of any such theoretical views, and which considers such doctrines as skillful means to help liberation rather than as literal descriptions of scientifically unknown facts.

One would then say that nirvana is not literally describable, not even as a "nondual reality." In speaking of nonduality, one would simply be negating the thought that things will continue in the liberated state much as they are now. The image of the limpid pool contrasts with the busyness and stress of much of life, but it does not imply that liberated existence is wet. Rebirth can be interpreted to mean that one's acts will cause consequences for good and ill for future sentient beings, so that one is connected to all sentient life in morally important ways. It does not mean that there is a continuous self or soul which actually gets reborn. And karma is not a quasiphysical law. It states the principle that one's acts shape one into the sort of person who will naturally tend to have good or bad experiences, that one will, in some unspecific and certainly unquantifiable sense, reap the rewards of one's actions.

Thus, the important teaching of Buddhism would be that an existence liberated from egoistic desire is even now possible, that attaining it will be for the good of all sentient beings, and that there is a future in which such liberated existence can be wholly fulfilled beyond the realm of suffering and grasping desire. The teaching is based on the exemplary experience of Gautama, the liberated one, whose life was interpenetrated by a state of wisdom, compassion, and bliss, and who was released from hatred, greed, and grasping.

As in the case of Christianity, there is here a focal notion of transformative experience, expressed in the symbols of a sacred cosmology (of karma and rebirth, the seven heavens and hells, and that which lies beyond), which have the primary function of leading individuals to freedom from sorrow. It is possible to take these symbols literally, but it is not necessary to do so.

I suggest that nonliteral interpretations have always been possible in religious traditions, and that they form the true core of religious belief and practice. In much religious thought, the distinction is simply not made between literal and symbolic thought, so it would be misleading to say that religious thought was once literal and later became symbolic. When the literal/symbolic question was raised, it was at first natural to take a literal view, where there was no reason to doubt it (with regard to the age of the earth, in early medieval Christianity, for example). But the symbolic (allegorical, anagogical, and moral) senses were always the most important in practice.

However, because the major religions became associated with empires, it was natural for them to stress the literal differences between their (superior) imperium and the (mistaken) alien and competing empires. This attitude remains in those who speak of the Christian West, the Muslim world, and Oriental religions. The world divides into competing religio-political power blocks, all striving, at least culturally but sometimes militarily, for dominance. This is the thought-world in which the Samuel Huntington thesis, of a war between world cultures and religions, is at home.

But there is another, more positive, possibility for the modern world. The rise of the natural sciences has clarified the difference between literal and metaphorical. And it has laid down the conditions for literal truth in terms of public observation and experiment and the rigorous mathematical formulation of results, wherever possible. The consequence is that religion is more firmly rooted in its own true ground, the ground of the personal, experiential, and liberative. There is also a growing feeling that there is no future for the politics of opposition in a globalized and integrated planet. Instead, one must look for the unities, the common aims and purposes, which bind humans together and encourage the pursuit of those unitary aims in many locally diverse ways. One can encourage diversity, as long as one feels that there is an underlying unity of long-term aim. One can strive for truth, by criticism and encounter, as long as one feels all are genuinely striving for the same sort of thing.

In religion, as in all other spheres of human knowledge, truth must be one, though access to it, and perspectives on it, may be diverse. One reason religions cannot be content to be simply opposed to one another, as competing sets of doctrines, is that it is important to seek the truth, and one can never rest content with contradictory views of truth. Another reason is that intellectual opposition, in any case, misses the heart of religious life and focuses on argument rather than on the search for liberation or salvation. The many religions of the world are not simply or primarily competing philosophical systems. They are metaphorical or symbolic systems encoding paradigmatic forms of spiritual experience, experience leading to liberation. Each system can be interpreted systematically in a number of different ways, although each systematic interpretation will seek to make its originative experience, and symbols for expressing it, central to its vision of how things are.

If one can sensibly speak of such paradigm experiences as of the same spiritual reality — and I have suggested that one can — then one might well begin to feel that, whereas religious doctrines generate infinite differences and arguments, an emphasis on evoking paradigm liberative experiences might lead to a convergent spirituality. Differences would still remain. Muslims would remain committed to the inerrancy of the Qur'an, whereas Christians would demur from that commitment. But what Christians could do is to revere the Qur'an as indeed an inspired teaching, arising from the Prophet Muhammad's intense experience of God. There would be respect, although not agreement. And what Muslims could do is to see how much of the Qur'an is verbal symbolism for realities which defy straightforward literal translation. Its teaching would be a teaching of the way to true devotion to God, expressed in dramatic narratives and symbols, not primarily a set of factual statements about what happened in ancient history, for example.

Convergent spirituality does not seek to bring about intellectual agreements among believers, even of one tradition, let alone of many different traditions. It accepts such disagreement as part of our limited, finite human condition, and even as a salutary fact, insofar as it prevents uncritical dogmatism from repressing human creativity and inquiry. It is concerned with spirituality, with ways of prayer and contemplation, of relating human lives consciously and liberatively to a source of supreme value and power beyond all human lives. It is concerned to place that at the core of religious life, to which all else must be subordinated. It is concerned with convergence, because it is important that all religious believers, whatever their tradition, are directing their efforts toward the same unitary goal, the goal of liberation from greed, hatred, and ignorance by conscious relation to a reality of supreme wisdom, compassion, and bliss. Such a reality will have many aspects and can be approached by many paths. To say that those paths converge on one and the same reality and goal is not to say that they are the same, or that they are all equally direct and sure, or that there is little to choose among them.

What has become possible in modern times is a recognition of the convergent spirituality underlying the religious diversity of the world. In the past, this has been disguised by the limitations of tribal or localized outlooks, or by the imperial ambitions of the cultures with which the major world faiths were associated. Now, when there is an urgent need to find roots of human unity, without eliminating cultural diversity, religions must overcome their past tendencies to mutual incomprehension, indifference, or hostility. They must learn to distinguish the cultural from the truth-claiming, to distinguish the literal from the symbolic, and to discern the object and goal of spiritual convergence and the ways in which that object can be more fully known and understood.

Growth in knowledge requires two main things: first, a preparedness to face criticisms of one's own views as fearlessly and openly as possible; second, an effort to extend the range of understanding as widely as possible, and so to learn from other paths toward the spiritual goal, however strange they may at first seem. One can stand firmly rooted in one's own tradition of liberative experience of the Supreme. But the pursuit of spiritual truth requires that, standing there, one learns from many other traditions the plurality of ways to the goal and the ultimate convergence which underlies the diversity of those ways. Religion is about spirituality, not doctrine. Spirituality is about convergence to unity in that which is of supreme value, not about an uninformed confidence in one's own opinions.

I am aware that the word "spirituality" can give rise to misunderstanding, partly because of the semantic width of the Atlantic Ocean, whereby words are apt to change their meanings as they cross. So, I want to make clear that by "spirituality" I do not mean paganism, tree-hugging, "new age" forms of faith and horoscope-gazing. I do mean the practices of prayer, contemplation, and meditation which are aimed at liberative experience of a spiritual reality and which, if I am right, form the heart of the world's religious traditions.

Many people in our world claim to have spirituality without religion. In saying that, perhaps they are concerned to disentangle the ethnic and narrowly tribal features of religion from the heart of religious experience and action for the sake of human flourishing. It should be clear that is a concern I fully endorse. Nevertheless, traditions of prayer cannot be maintained without symbolic and ritual practices within which individual lives can be shaped to a deeper understanding of spiritual reality. Just as persons cannot flourish without community, so spiritual faith cannot flourish without a spiritual community. The social dimension — for Christians, the church — is essential to the flourishing of the spiritual dimension. Spirituality cannot exist without organized religion. And if religions are to be preserved from their potential for encouraging exclusive hostilities, it is vital that they should be led by those whose primary concern is with spirituality. Spirituality should not, then, be opposed to religion. But it is still spirituality which is convergent, in aiming at a common reality and goal, while specific religious traditions can properly remain diverse, both in the sets of symbols they use, and in the doctrines they propagate.

Perhaps to the scientific icon of Earthrise we might add the ancient Buddhist icon of Indra's net, wherein each tradition of faith is a jewel bound in a net to thousands of others, and wherein each will show its true beauty only when it reflects in itself, in its own unique way, the beauty of the others. The spiritually rising earth is embedded in Indra's net, and the earth's incipient spiritual beauty will be realized only when earth's religions rise from the darkness of dogmatic disputation to appreciate through the common practice of spirituality the fact not only of their rich diversity but also of their convergent unity.

Chapter 4

ECOLOGICAL CONSCIOUSNESS AND THE SYMBOL "GOD"

Gordon D. Kaufman

GORDON D. KAUFMAN is a General Conference Mennonite Church minister and the Edward Mallinchkrodt, Jr., Professor of Divinity, Emeritus, at the Harvard Divinity School. During his distinguished academic career, he has held visiting professorships and lecturerships in politically and theologically diverse areas of the globe, including the Institute for Teachers of Systematic Theology in Bangalore, India; Doshisha University in Kyoto, Japan; the University of South Africa, Pretoria; the University of Oxford, England; Chung Chi College, Chinese University, Hong Kong; and Fudan University, Shanghai. Professor Kaufman is a past president of the American Academy of Religion and the American Theological Society and is an active member of the Society for Buddhist-Christian Studies. His extensive writings include *Relativism, Knowledge and Faith; Systematic Theology: A Historicist Perspective; God the Problem; Nonresistance and Responsibility, and Other Mennonite Essays; The Theological Imagination: Constructing the Concept of God; Theology for a Nuclear Age; In Face of Mystery: A Constructive Theology,* which won a 1995 American Academy of Religion Award for "Excellence"; and *God — Mystery — Diversity: Christian Theology in a Pluralistic World.*

BISHOP SPONG has devoted much of his life and ministry to addressing ways and respects in which traditional Christian beliefs and practices have interfered with — even blocked — efforts of Christian people and the Christian churches from effectively coming to grips with major contemporary problems. He is to be respected and honored for the courage with which he has taken up some of the most controversial issues Christians today face. In this essay, I seek to so honor him by examining traditional Christian understandings of the symbol "God," in light of our growing contemporary ecological consciousness, and by proposing a theological reconception of

72

God — and of humanity in relation to God — more in keeping with that ecological consciousness.

The task of the Christian theologians, as I understand it, is to scrutinize carefully, critically evaluate, and *reconstruct* (in whatever ways seem appropriate and necessary) the central Christian symbols, so they will encourage and support a faith and life appropriate for today.[1] In our time, it is no longer sufficient for theologians simply to take for granted that the basic structure and commitments of traditional Christian faith are — in all of their main lines — right and proper, and to proceed, then, to expound and reinterpret them in whatever ways seem intelligible and persuasive. Whatever may have been the value and justification of this sort of theologizing in the past, the crises of the end of the twentieth century and the beginning of the twenty-first (to many of which Christian symbols, institutions, and practices have themselves contributed) have made it clear that thorough reassessment of the traditional Christian symbol-system is required, with an eye to its (possibly drastic) reconstruction. It is with this critical and open understanding of the task of Christian theologians today that this chapter has been written, in the hope that such reconstruction will help enable Christianity to continue to contribute to human well-being, and to the well-being of the rest of life on planet Earth.

Throughout my professional life, I have been concerned with the problem of the continuing viability (or lack of viability) in our contemporary world of the symbol "God," as that symbol has been understood through most of Western history not only by Christians and Jews, but also by many humanists and secularists. And for the last thirty years or so, I have been reflecting on the issues which our growing ecological consciousness poses for our understanding of — and our ordering of life in terms of — this symbol. In an early paper,[2] I attempted to show that there is a fundamental tension — indeed, a

---

1. I have spelled out this understanding of Christian theology in some detail in *In Face of Mystery: A Constructive Theology* (Cambridge: Harvard University Press, 1993). A discussion of the methodological concerns that underlie it is found in *An Essay on Theological Method*, 3d ed. (Atlanta: Scholars Press, 1995). A considerably briefer version of these matters, with special attention to their import for the issue of religious and cultural pluralism, is presented in *God — Mystery — Diversity: Christian Theology in a Pluralistic World* (Minneapolis: Fortress Press, 1996).

2. "The Concept of Nature: A Problem for Theology," *Harvard Theological Review* 65 (1972): 337–66; later reprinted (with some alterations) under the title, "Theology and the Concept of Nature," in *The Theological Imagination: Constructing the Concept of God*

conceptual and logical incompatibility — between, on the one hand, the understanding of God, and of the intimate relation of humanity to God (as seen in our Western religious and philosophical traditions), and on the other hand, our growing awareness that human existence is essentially constituted by, and could not exist apart from, the complex ecological ordering of life that has evolved on Earth over many millennia.[3] The main emphasis in that paper remains largely correct in my view, and I shall begin my presentation here by summarizing some portions of its argument. This will set the stage for the remainder of the chapter which will be devoted to sketching briefly the (perhaps somewhat drastic) reconception of the symbol "God," and of the human relation to God, that appears to me to be required now, if Christians (as well as others who seek to order their lives in relation to God) are to come to terms with our current ecological consciousness and knowledge.

I

In this paper of twenty-five years ago, my intention was not to develop a Christian ecological theology, but rather to examine carefully the

---

(Philadelphia: Westminster Press, 1981), chap. 8. All references to this paper in the present text refer to the version published in *The Theological Imagination*.

3. Most Christian theologians appear not to regard the theological problems posed by modern ecological and evolutionary understandings of human beings to be as serious as do I. Therefore, they continue to work within the traditional framework that pictures God as creator / lord / father of the universe and all within it. A path-breaking writer on ecological issues, working with this view, was Joseph Sittler, "A Theology for Earth," *The Christian Scholar* 37 (1954): 367–74. Others that deserve mention for their early theological work on ecological issues are Conrad Bonifazi, *A Theology of Things* (Philadelphia: Lippincott, 1967); Philip Hefner, "Towards a New Doctrine of Man: The Relationship of Man and Nature," in *The Future of Empirical Theology*, Bernard E. Meland, ed. (Chicago: University of Chicago Press, 1969); Frederick Elder, *Crisis in Eden: A Religious Study of Man and Environment* (Nashville: Abingdon Press, 1970); and H. Paul Santmire, *Brother Earth: Nature, God and Ecology in Time of Crisis* (Thomas Nelson & Sons, 1970). About the same time, Lynn White, Jr., published a widely influential article strongly criticizing what he regarded as Christian theological sources of modern ecological problems: "The Historical Roots of Our Ecologic Crisis," *Science* 155 (1967): 1203–7. A good many important theologically oriented writings on ecological matters have appeared over subsequent years, some of them calling for fairly radical theological reconstruction. Three recent ones are: John Cobb and Hermann Daly, *For the Common Good*, 2d ed. (Boston: Beacon Press, 1994); Sallie McFague, *The Body of God: An Ecological Theology* (Minneapolis: Fortress Press, 1993); and Rosemary Ruether, *Gaia and God: An Ecofeminist Theology of Earth Healing* (San Francisco: Harper, 1992). In my view, perhaps the most important study of the biblical material bearing on ecological questions is to be found in the recent work by Theodore Hiebert, *The Yahwist's Landscape* (New York: Oxford University Press, 1996).

concept of *nature* that had emerged in the course of Western history and had — particularly with the growing importance of the natural sciences in modernity — become central to our Western understanding of ourselves and of the world in which we live. A major conclusion to which the article came was the following:

> The very ideas of God and humanity, as they have gradually been worked out over millennia [in the West], are so framed as to blur or even conceal our *embeddedness* in the natural order as we now are increasingly conceiving it. The great religious struggle between Israel and Canaan was over the question of the metaphysical importance of *natural power and process* on the one hand and *personal moral will* on the other. When Yahweh won that struggle it meant that the object of ultimate loyalty and devotion for humans in the West would be conceived increasingly in terms of models rooted in our *moral and personal* experience, not in our sense of dependence upon and unity with the orders and processes of nature. Thus the very concept of God itself — as that concept has developed in the West — has built into it a depreciation of the metaphysical, and certainly the religious, significance of nature (226; emphasis added).

Let me sketch briefly the argument supporting this claim.

The symbol "God" — not "nature" — functioned during most of Western history as the ultimate point of reference in terms of which all human life, indeed all reality, was to be understood. God was believed to be the creator of the heavens and the earth (as Genesis 1 puts it), the creator of "all things visible and invisible" (as declared in some of the creeds), the lord of the world. It was, therefore, in terms of *God's purposes* and *God's acts* that human existence and life — in point of fact, all of reality — were to be comprehended. The model in terms of which God, from the biblical texts on, was perceived was basically anthropomorphic: God was seen as essentially an agent, an actor, one who was *doing things*, a *God Who Acted*.[4] And human existence was to be oriented most fundamentally on this transworldly reality *God*, not on anything in the world, or on the world (the natural order) itself. For humans to orient themselves and their lives on anything

---

4. As G. Ernest Wright put it in a widely influential book with that title (London: S.C.M. Press, 1952).

other than God was deemed idolatry — a turning away from the very
source and ground of humanity's being and life, and a direct violation
of God's will for humankind. Hence, when the context and ground
of human life becomes increasingly thought of in evolutionary and
ecological terms, as in modernity and postmodernity, *nature* becomes
a direct rival of God for human attention and devotion. Profound
interest in and attention to nature, to the natural orders within which
human life transpires, was not, of course, an invention of modernity;
its roots go back (in the West) to Greek culture. But the reappearance
of this interest in early modernity led to a direct conflict with God's
claims to absolute loyalty.

God was seen as a powerful agent who acted everywhere in the
world in freedom and with intentionality and love. This conception
was based on a model drawn from the human experience of freedom
and creativity, purpose and agency — particularly as experienced by
male members of the patriarchal society within which it became an
important emphasis. And God was from early on thought of almost
exclusively in male-gendered terms. For many centuries, nature and
God were not in any sort of significant tension with each other, since
what we today speak of as "nature" was thought of as God's creation — the finite order — in every respect a product of God's creative
activity and at all points completely at God's sovereign disposal. (The
concept of nature, at least as we today think of it, had no real place
in the biblical story at all.)[5] It is, rather,

> Yahweh and Israel, God and humanity — or even, as in the
> later individualism of much Western Christendom, God and the
> soul (Augustine) — that are the realities of central interest and
> concern [in traditional ways of reading biblical texts]. Though
> humanity may be created out of the "dust from the ground"
> (Gen. 2:7) and could not exist apart from the context provided
> by heaven and earth and the multitude of other living creatures

---

5. The Hebrew vocabulary did not even have a term corresponding to our word "nature" (see H. W. Robinson, *Inspiration and Revelation in the Old Testament* [Oxford:
Clarendon Press, 1946], chap. 1). It was a nineteenth- and twentieth-century mistake, however, for scholars to have reached the conclusion that there is virtually no interest in the
natural environment in the Old Testament, that all attention was focused on *history,* and
God's acts in history. The earliest strands of the Old Testament (attributed to the "J" writer)
present a humanity immersed in and highly dependent on (what we regard as) the natural order round about. For a full discussion of these matters, see Hiebert, *The Yahwist's
Landscape.*

on the earth (Gen. 1), it is clearly the climax of God's creative activity. Created in God's own image (1:27), human beings are the
ones for whom all things were made and to whose will they must
be subject (1:28–29; 2:18–20, 15). Humankind, moreover, is the
(only) creature in which God himself becomes incarnate...the
divine-human relation is clearly the axis around which all else
revolves. In the end when God creates "new heavens and a new
earth" (Isa. 65:17; Rev. 21:1)...this is primarily for the sake
of the "new Jerusalem" where...all human suffering, pain, and
misery will be overcome (Isa. 65:18–24; Rev. 21:2–4)....The
rest of creation, though always recognized and sometimes acknowledged and even reflected upon, simply was not of central
theological interest or importance, and (with the exception of
the angels) never became the subject of any technical theological
vocabulary or doctrines (221f).[6]

With Giordano Bruno and others, nature began to be thought of
as itself *infinite,* and a direct conflict began to emerge with the concept of (the infinite) God — and with God's unique metaphysical and
religious roles. In due course, God and nature were explicitly *identified* with each other (e.g., by Spinoza) — it not being possible to
conceive of two infinites; and it was under the aegis of the concept of
nature (i.e., of natural process) that the identification was made, not
the concept of God (i.e., of a free agent).

What had been two ontologically distinct realities (*God* and
creation) ordered toward each other in a very specific and

---

6. Even Jonathan Edwards, with his systemic holistic thinking and his well-known interest in the natural world, had no doubts that "the last end for which God has made moral
agents must be the last end for which God has made all things: it being evident, that the
moral world is the end of the rest of the world; the inanimate and unintelligible world being
made for the rational and moral world, as much as a house is prepared for the inhabitants"
(*The Nature of True Virtue* [Ann Arbor: University of Michigan Press, 1960], 25). In highly
influential nineteenth–twentieth-century theological texts, we still find such remarks as the
following: "...nature is called into being to serve as a means to God's essential purpose
in creating a world of spirits...the creation of nature by God is...a relative necessity, the
necessity, namely, of serving as a means to God's previously chosen end of calling into being
a multitude of spirits akin to Himself....The whole universe, therefore, considered thus
as the precondition of the moral kingdom of created spirits, is throughout God's creation
for this end" (Albrecht Ritschl, *The Christian Doctrine of Justification and Reconciliation*
[Edinburgh: T. & T. Clark, 1900], 279f.). This general point of view continued on into neo-
orthodoxy: For a thorough examination of Karl Barth's theology on this matter, see Paul
Santmire, "Creation and Nature: A Study of the Doctrine of Nature with Special Attention
to Karl Barth's Doctrine of Creation" (Harvard Ph.D. dissertation, 1966).

distinctive way, so as to preserve the ultimate reality and importance of God, now became one reality (nature) viewed under two
different aspects (*natura naturans* and *natura naturata*). And
God no longer had an unusurpable place in humanity's understanding of itself and of the context within which human life
falls; indeed, it is not clear that God any longer had (could be
conceived to have) any distinctive place at all (219).[7]

The concept of *nature* was becoming the central metaphysical concept; nature was displacing God as the all-encompassing reality.

Thus, in modernity, nature and God have become rivals in the
claims they make on our interest, attention, commitment, and loyalty. Thinking of ultimate reality in largely *ecological* terms, that is,
in terms of the interconnected and interdependent powers and processes of nature — instead of in more traditional religious terms as,
for example, our "heavenly Father" whose children we are, or the
"Lord" of the universe whose loyal subjects we seek to be — leads
to sharply different understandings of who or what we humans are
and how we ought to live. (More will be said about this below.) This
is not to say, of course, that all who today use the word "nature,"
or who are engaged in ecological campaigns, regard themselves as
committed to *naturalism* as a philosophy or religion. Most English
speakers are probably unaware of the metaphysical implications and
tendencies I am pointing out here, and might well disavow them if
they were called to their attention. Yet, they continue to think of
God as in some vague sense "creator and lord of the world" and,
thus, sovereign over the natural order. However, if asked to specify
how this notion can be understood in light of contemporary scientific thinking about nature, they would find themselves hard pressed
to give a clear answer. This continuing use of the traditional symbol "God" in a largely uncritical way tends (as suggested above) to
"blur or even conceal our embeddedness in the natural order as we
now are increasingly conceiving it." To the extent that we, today, take
our experience of "natural" powers and processes as paradigmatic of
ultimate reality — rather than the distinctively *human* activities and
experiences of choosing, setting purposes, willing, thinking, creating,

---

7. As Paul Tillich noted, Spinoza's formula, *"deus sive natura* ... indicates that the name
'God' does not add anything to what is already involved in the name 'nature' "* (*Systematic
Theology* [Chicago: University of Chicago Press, 1951], 1:262).

speaking, making covenants, and the like, which had provided principal models for constructing the traditional symbol "God" — we will inevitably think of the world in which we live, and our human place within it, in terms quite different from those presented by Western religious traditions.

This brings us to the second theme from that early essay which I wish to set out here: the implications, for our human self-understanding, of giving the modern concept of nature the paradigmatic significance it has come to have for most Western life and experience. This concept is very rich and comprehensive but at the same time quite ambiguous, particularly in what it implies about our human place in the natural order — one of the central issues posed by modern ecological consciousness. Are we humans to regard ourselves as simply a *part* of nature, shaped and determined in all important respects by the ecological order within which we have emerged and continue to be sustained? Or, in view of (a) our ability to make nature itself an *object* of our experience and reflection — a reality thus in some sense *over against* us, and (b) our ability to deliberately *transform* in very radical ways (through our technologies) many of the natural patterns and orders found on earth, must we humans be understood as, in certain significant respects, *transcending* these natural orders and patterns? This is a deeper problem than often noted, and unless we find a way to address it, we will set our course in the current ecological crisis in terms of a self-understanding (as human beings) that is thoroughly confused.

Let us sharpen this issue a bit further. On the one hand, so far as nature is thought of as including *all* powers and processes in the world, humans seem to be included entirely within it. Human existence is a moment in a complex ecological balance without which it could not exist and to which it contributes. This understanding of human life within nature often gives rise to an indictment against modern Western civilization:

in our attempts to gain technological mastery of our world and of the ills that afflict humankind, we...have...so polluted our environment and upset the delicate balances which sustain life here on earth as to be destroying ourselves. We must control the population explosion;...clean up our rivers and atmosphere;...stop [using] up resources at exponentially grow-

ing rates;...set aside and preserve those few remaining pieces
of "natural" wilderness...; [and so on;] in short, we must stop
our wanton destruction of nature (214).

On the other hand, this indictment actually stands in a kind of deep
contradiction with the premise (respecting our human immersion in
the natural ecological order) on which it may be thought to be based.
For it straightforwardly declares that

> humans *have* done much to and with the order of nature and,
> second, that they *can* do something now to help restore the bal-
> ance which in their ignorance and rapacity they have disrupted
> ...humans are not [then]...simply a part of nature, one more
> function of the processes and powers that make up the natural
> world[;]...they stand in some sense apart from all these and
> can and do work on them and transform them. It is through
> human artifice, human culture, that the present ecological crisis
> has been brought upon us, and (it is hoped) through a further
> and more sophisticated application of that same artifice the crisis
> may eventually be abated....Nature and culture...[here seem
> to be] set over against each other in polar relation, and humanity
> is somehow in both, as both are in us humans (214f.).

What are the roots of this ambiguity — indeed, contradiction — in
our Western understanding of ourselves within the natural order? We
Westerners (who throughout the modern period have been reorient-
ing our activities and our thinking in increasingly naturalistic terms)
acquired our basic formation and understanding of ourselves as *active creative agents* in a living relation with the God believed to be
creator of the heavens and the earth, a God in whose "image" we
humans had been created. We thought of ourselves as significantly
distinct from and "above" all the other creatures: indeed, God had
given us a mandate to "subdue" the earth and to have "dominion"
over all the other creatures (Gen. 1:28f.; Ps. 8:5–8). Thus, we were
creatures with a measure of active control over our own lives and
destinies, creatures with a relation to the active creator of the heavens and the earth unmatched by any others. As technologies enabling
dramatic transformations of the natural order increasingly appeared
in the modern period, and as a new and much more powerful knowledge of what was believed to be the true order of nature began to

emerge in the science of Galileo, Newton, and their successors, is it so surprising that we in the West came to think of ourselves as "lords of creation," with the possibility of, and a mandate to, expand our powers over nature (as well as over the rest of humankind) in an almost unlimited way?

With the secularization of the West, and the enormous growth of modern technologies and sciences, we today think of ourselves in a double — but incoherent — way. We are products of the natural order here on earth, subject to the ecological balances that have made all life (including our own) possible, and which are necessary for its continuance. But we also are able to understand this in and through our sciences, and we remain free enough of the orders surrounding and sustaining us, and creative enough, to bring into being new possibilities in the way human existence is ordered on earth, and to change our ways of living that have become counterproductive, indeed destructive, of ongoing human life. No other living beings of which we are aware have this double relation to the natural order: being its products, but at the same time transcending it sufficiently to be able to deliberately transform it in significant ways. In the course of history, we have, in fact, brought into the world a whole new order of relationships (and, thus, of reality) — the sociocultural order — which has become for us humans the primary context within which we live and in terms of which we understand ourselves and the cosmos which is our home.

I do not intend in this article to attempt to overcome this doubleness in our modern (secular) human self-understanding. I take it as a given with which theologians and others today must work — a given that demands significantly new formulations of our conceptions of God and of humanity (as well as of our intricate relation to nature), formulations that come to terms with, and can help us more effectively address, the issues discussed in the preceding pages.

II

As we have seen, the anthropocentrism (indeed, *androcentrism*) of the traditional Christian understanding of humanity in relation to God — and the consequent anthropomorphism (more precisely, the andromorphism) of the traditional conception of God itself — tend to obscure and dilute, in Christian theology, ecological ways of thinking about our human place in the world. Is it possible to develop a theological understanding of God and humanity that overcomes these difficulties? I shall introduce three concepts which, taken together, suggest a significantly different understanding of God, humanity, and their relationship to each other. This understanding is coherent with our modern/postmodern evolutionary and ecological conceptions of the appearance and development of life on earth — including the emergence of human historicocultural existence within the ecology of life.

First, I want to spell out briefly what I call a *biohistorical* understanding of human existence. I will argue that the wide modern consensus (at least among many university-educated people) that humankind emerged out of less complex forms of life in the course of evolutionary developments over many millennia — and that we could not exist apart from this living biological web that continues to nourish and sustain us — is too vague and general to provide adequate understanding of the sorts of beings that we humans are. This conception of human being says nothing about the importance of the uniquely *historical* features of our human existence. The natural order is, no doubt, the wider context within which human history has appeared. But it has been especially through our historical sociocultural development over many millennia — not our biological evolution alone — that we humans have acquired many of our most distinctive and significant characteristics.

Second, I want to call attention to what I call the "serendipitous creativity" manifest throughout the universe — that is, the coming into being through time of the new and the novel, whether this leads to what appear (from human and humane perspectives) to be horrifying evils or great goods. I use the conception of "creativity" here — rather than the traditional idea of "God the creator" — because it presents creation of the new as an ongoing activity or process in the world, and does not call forth an image of a kind of "cosmic person" standing outside the cosmos, manipulating it from without. In my view, if we wish to continue using the word "God," we would do well to understand it as referring to this ongoing creativity manifest in the cosmos.[8] Third, since the traditional idea of a

---

8. The issues at stake here are discussed at some length in *In Face of Mystery*, especially chaps. 19 and 22.

powerful teleological movement underlying and ordering all cosmic and historical processes (God's purposive activity) became so problematical in twentieth-century thinking about evolution and history, I propose to replace it with a more modest conception — a conception of what I call "directional movements" or "trajectories" that emerge spontaneously in the course of evolutionary and historical developments.

This more open, even random, notion — of serendipitous creativity manifesting itself in evolutionary and historical trajectories of various sorts — fits in with, but amplifies in important ways, today's thinking about cosmic processes. It is a notion that can be used to describe and interpret the enormous expansion and complexification of the physical universe from the "Big Bang" onward, as well as the evolution of life here on earth and the gradual emergence of human historical existence. This whole vast cosmic process, I suggest, displays (in varying degrees) serendipitous creativity: the coming into being through time of new modes of reality. It is a process that has frequently produced much more than would have been expected or seemed possible, given previously prevailing circumstances, even moving eventually, along one of its lines, into the creation of us human beings with our distinctive history and historicity.

III

Let us consider first the characterization of humans as *biohistorical* beings. It is important to recognize that human *historical* development over many millennia has been as indispensable to the creation of human beings (as we today understand ourselves) as were the biological evolutionary developments that preceded and continued to accompany the emergence of humankind on earth.

As one rather obvious example, consider the impact of the emergence and historical growth of human awareness of, and knowledge about, both the natural world in which we humans live and our own human constitutions and possibilities. Though taking strikingly different forms in the various cultures of humankind, these features — in some form — are present in all. And in all cultures, they have provided women and men with significant powers over their immediate environment as well as over themselves. In the cultures of modernity, human knowledge has become increasingly comprehensive and detailed, giving us considerable control over the physical and biological (as well as sociocultural and psychological) conditions of our existence — control that goes far beyond that of any other animal. Indeed, we can say that we human beings, and the further course of human history, are no longer completely at the disposal of the natural order and the natural powers that brought us into being, in the way we were, say, ten millennia ago. Thus, it has been in the course of human *history* that we humans have gained — especially in and through our various knowledges — some measure of *transcendence* over the nature of which we are part; and with our developing practices and skills, growing in modernity into enormously powerful technologies, we have utterly transformed the face of Earth and are beginning to push on into outer space.

How should we understand these features of our humanity that have emerged largely in human history? It appears to be *qua* our development into beings shaped in many respects by *historicocultural* processes — that is, humanly created, not merely natural biological, processes — that we humans have gained these increasing measures of control over the natural order, as well as over the onward movement of history. Accordingly, in significant respects, our *historicity* (as we may call it) is a distinctive mark of our humanness: We are beings shaped decisively by a history that has given us power ourselves to shape future history in important ways. The concept of historicity gives us a way to clarify and understand the paradox of our being at once a part of nature and yet significantly transcending the natural order. On the one hand, in our transcendence of the natural order within which we emerged (through our creation of complex cultures), we humans, as we know ourselves today, appear to be radically different from any other living beings. On the other hand, in our "utter dependence"[9] on the web of life from which and within which we emerged, we humans are at one with every other species.

Developments in human history have been as indispensable a factor in bringing today's humanity into being as biological evolution, and have resulted in an actual in-building into our human nature itself of culturally informed and shaped dimensions and processes. Even some biological aspects of the organism that finally emerged as human are,

---

9. This is a phrase used (in a somewhat different connection) by the nineteenth-century theologian Schleiermacher.

as the anthropologist Clifford Geertz has pointed out, "both a cultural and a biological product."[10] Our present biological organisms, if left simply to themselves, would be so seriously deficient that they could not function. As Geertz sums up the matter:

> We are...incomplete or unfinished animals who complete or finish ourselves through culture — and not through culture in general but through highly particular forms of it: Dobuan and Javanese, Hopi and Italian, upper-class, academic and commercial.[11]

The development of human enculturedness (and the consequent growth of human symbolic behavior) appears to have had particularly strong effects on the evolution of the brain.[12] So we can say that the growth of cultures — which increasingly came to include flexible and complex languages, a great variety of forms of differentiated social organization, the development of skills of many different sorts, increasingly disciplined powers of imagination, the creation of innumerable kinds of artifacts including especially tools which extend human powers in many new directions, and so on — has affected significantly the actual *biological* development of the predecessors of today's *homo sapiens*. We are, then, all the way down to the deepest layers of our distinctively *human* existence, not simply biological beings, animals; we are *biohistorical* beings.[13] It is, above all, the high development of our human historicity that gives our existence its most distinctively *human* character.

Despite the great powers that our knowledges and technologies have given us, we are all aware that our transcendence of the natural orders within which we have emerged is far from adequate to assure our ongoing human existence. Indeed, the ecological crisis of our time has brought to our attention the fact that precisely through the exercise of our growing power on earth we have been destroying the very conditions that make human life — and all other forms of life as

---

10. *The Interpretation of Cultures* (Basic Books, 1973), 67. The sociobiologists C. J. Lumsden and E. O. Wilson, with their concept of "gene-culture coevolution," appear to concur with this judgment; see *Promethean Fire: Reflections on the Origin of Mind* (Cambridge: Harvard University Press, 1983).

11. Geertz, *Interpretation of Cultures*, 49.

12. See Terrence Deacon, *The Symbolic Species: The Co-evolution of Language and the Brain* (New York: Norton, 1997).

13. This notion is worked out in much greater detail in *In Face of Mystery*, Part Two.

well — possible. We may have brought human existence to the brink of extinction. Paradoxically, then, our understanding of ourselves and of the world in which we live, and our growing power over many of the circumstances on planet Earth that have seemed to us undesirable, may in the end lead to our self-destruction.

What kind of moves is it possible for us humans to make, when confronted with issues of this scope that go well beyond our established knowledges? It may be useful, at this point, to look briefly at certain aspects of the religious standpoint that contributed to the birth of Western culture and science, and which subsequently has continued to nourish our culture (at least to some extent). Our Western religious traditions have long emphasized that it is in and through moves of *faith* that humans address the deep but unavoidable mysteries of life — mysteries often connected with our distinctive human powers as self-conscious agents, beings who must *act,* must take responsibility for ourselves even though the future may be inscrutable, beings with historicity. We are able to *commit* ourselves to this or that construal of the mysteries of life that confront us, and we can live and act in faithfulness to this commitment. All such commitments go beyond the knowledges at our disposal. Human life is able to go on in face of profound bafflements because of our "will to believe" (as William James put it), that is, because of deep-seated attitudes of faith, trust, and loyalty that enable us to continue moving forward into uncertain futures, even though adequate pertinent knowledge is unavailable.

What sort of faith-moves have particularly characterized Western religiousness? In face of the ultimate mysteries of life and the world, how has the human situation been understood? Unlike most other religious standpoints, in the *Hebraic* vision to which the West is heir, human life is construed as falling within a temporal/historical process. Life takes place in a *created* world, a world that began at a particular point in time, a world that has developed in important ways through time because of God's continuing activity within it. This story speaks of both a fall away from God and the emergence of diverse human languages, cultures, and religious practices and beliefs. It culminates in God's expected overcoming of the sin and evil that humanity has brought into the world, thus bringing it to the perfection originally intended. Many details of the modern evolutionary conception of the development of life differ sharply from this biblical story, but the overall *form* of these two accounts is much the same: in both, human life is understood within the context of a larger cosmic temporal / historical / evolutionary development.

The biblical account, however, in contrast with the evolutionary story as usually presented, is able to give this developmental process profound human meaning, through portraying the human dimension of the story (human history) as possessing an overall unity from beginning to end, brought about by God's purposive presence and activity throughout. God is believed to be creatively and redemptively moving humankind toward the full realization of the loving purposes originally expressed in humanity's creation. That is, it was the ongoing presence and humanizing activity of *God* in this story that brought the past, present, and future of the world, and of humankind within the world, together into a coherent and meaningful whole. Basic orientation for women and men was to be found, thus, in relation to God — God's purposes, God's ongoing activity, God's will for humankind. Motivation for humans to orient themselves in accordance with this vision was encouraged by the hope it offered of ultimate human realization and redemption, as God's purposes were consummated. The connection between the nature of things — how things really are in the world — and what is truly of importance to humans was brought about and secured by the central role in the story, and the specific character, of God, whose activity bound the human (and cosmic) past, present, and future together into a single coherent and humanly meaningful account.

We now need to ask whether there is any way, in connection with our modern / postmodern biohistorical evolutionary story, that the past, present, and future of human existence generally — and of our individual lives in particular — can be situated within a similar unity of development. If we can give a positive answer to this question, we may be able to discern significant human meaningfulness in the evolutionary-historical story that would otherwise not be visible. The other two concepts mentioned above, "serendipitous creativity" and "directional movements" or "trajectories," can be of help in exploring this matter.[14]

---

14. A more extensive discussion of "serendipitous creativity" and of evolutionary and historical "trajectories," will be found in ibid., especially chaps. 19–20.

IV

Movement in and through time, as traced today through the long history of the universe and particularly through the evolution of life on earth, appears frequently to eventuate in unprecedented developments, in the appearance of new forms — not simply the repetition of patterns that forever repeat themselves. Moreover, these novel developments — for example, the emergence of new evolutionary lines (new species) — each have specific potentialities for developing further in some directions but not in others. Such tendencies, as biologist Ernst Mayr says, "are the necessary consequence of the unity of the genotype which greatly constrains evolutionary potential."[15] Ever more complex species have emerged along some evolutionary lines, and we can discern *trajectories* of a sort eventuating in these new forms. These trajectories are visible, of course, only to the *retrospective* or backward-looking view that we humans necessarily take up when we survey the past. There is no reason (from a biological standpoint, for example) to suppose that the process of evolution has actually been directed, somehow, toward this or that specific goal, or toward any goal whatsoever. The processes of natural selection, it appears, themselves bring about the directional momentums that emerge along the various lines down which life has evolved.

As noted above, what may be regarded as a new order of reality (*historical* processes and events) has emerged on the line that includes humans. The order of history, with its high development of cultures and modes of social organization, seems to be the only context within which beings with self-consciousness, highly developed imaginative powers, creativity, freedom, and responsible agency have appeared. It is not that the evolution of life has been a sort of straight-line movement, up from the primeval slime to humanity with its historicity and complex histories: evolutionary developments have obviously gone in many directions. Moreover, it is not evident that the human form is as biologically viable as are many other forms. So, from a strictly *biological* point of view (with its emphasis on survival and perpetuation of the species), there is little reason to think that human life is the most successful or important product of the evolutionary process. However, we are not confining ourselves here to strictly bi-

---

15. *Toward a New Philosophy of Biology* (Cambridge: Harvard University Press, 1988), 435.

ological considerations. Our principal concern is to understand our own reality and situation — as bio*historical* beings — in the hope that this will assist us in finding an appropriate way to orient ourselves today in the evolutionary-ecological world.

As we have noted, fully human beings (beings with great symbolic facility, beings with *historicity*) did not appear simply as the last stage of a strictly biological process. It was only after many millennia of *historical* developments (in concert with continuing biological evolution) that human existence as we presently know it came on the scene. Moreover, only with the fairly recent emergence of the *historical standpoint* of late modernity has this biological-historical movement eventuating in contemporary humankind become visible to us humans. However, as we today look back at the gradually cumulating evolutionary, historical, and ecological developments that produced us, outlines of a cosmic trajectory issuing in the creation of beings with historicity become discernible. There are, no doubt, many other cosmic trajectories as well, moving in quite different directions. But, from where we humans stand — with our specifically human needs and interests, and our contemporary human values — the emergence of this particular trajectory is obviously of great importance. This manifestation of the serendipitous creativity in the cosmos has given us men and women our very existence, and, therefore, it quite properly evokes from us both awe and gratitude. Let me make myself clear: I am *not* claiming that we humans are the best, or the highest, or the most important of all species of life. I am claiming that, because of our great knowledge and power — especially our power to destroy so much of life — the extraordinarily complex question of our proper place in the ecological order on Earth is one that demands our address today.

To emphasize, as I have just been doing, the *connection* of what is distinctive about human existence (our humanness, our historicity) with the mystery of creativity in the world, is to take a step of faith, a movement of faith perhaps not as uncommon among intellectuals these days as might at first be supposed. Our speculations about, and search for, intelligent life elsewhere in the universe presuppose that there is some elemental dynamism in the cosmos that can issue in the emergence *in diverse locations* of what we here have been calling historicity — human-like reality. This presupposition, or faith, gives rise to the hope that we may, if we search long enough and carefully enough, eventually uncover signs of similar highly complex forms of life in regions far removed from Earth. Where the particular trajectory that brought human existence into being on our planet will move in the future, we do not, of course, know. Perhaps it will be toward the opening of ever new possibilities for human beings, as we increasingly take responsibility for our lives and our future; perhaps it will go beyond humanity and historicity altogether, however difficult it is to image how that should be understood; perhaps it will move to the total destruction of human life.

Construing the cosmos as constituted by cosmic serendipitous creativity which manifests itself through trajectories of various sorts, working themselves out in longer and shorter stretches of time (a conception consonant with modern evolutionary thinking though not necessary to it), can help us discern our place within the evolutionary-ecological universe that is our home. Our human existence — its purposiveness, its greatly varied complexes of social / moral / cultural / religious values and meanings, its virtually unlimited imaginative powers and glorious creativity, its horrible failures and gross evils, its historicity — has, from this vantage point, a distinctive position within the vast, seemingly impersonal cosmic order. With the emergence of historical modes of being — human being — explicitly purposive (or teleological) patterns appeared in the universe, as human intentions, consciousness, and actions began to become effective. That is, a cosmic trajectory, which had its origins in what seems to have been mere physical movement or vibration, has (in the instance of human existence) gradually developed increasing directionality, ultimately creating a context within which deliberate purposive action could emerge and flourish.[16] With the help of our

---

16. It has recently begun to appear possible, even likely, that the continuous increase in entropy over time in the universe may itself, in the natural course of events, give rise — through the development of so-called "dissipative systems" — to complex forms of organization, eventually including living systems. " ... [T]he picture that is emerging in ... recent thermodynamic analyses ... [suggests that] the movement of the [entropic] stream *itself* inevitably generates, as it were, very large eddies *within* itself in which, far from there being a decrease of order, there is an increase first in complexity and then in something more subtle — functional organization.... There could be no self-consciousness and human creativity without living organization, and there could be no such living dissipative systems unless the entropic stream followed its general, irreversible course in time. Thus does the apparently decaying, randomizing tendency of the universe provide the necessary and essential matrix (*mot juste!*) for the birth of new forms — new life through death and decay of the old" (Arthur Peacocke, "Thermodynamics and Life," *Zygon* 19 [1984]: 430).

three new concepts, we are beginning to gain some *orientation* in the universe as we think of it today.

Let us note five points in this connection. First, this approach provides us with a frame within which we can characterize quite accurately, and can unify into an overall vision, what seems actually to have happened, so far as we know, in the course of cosmic evolution and history. Second, this approach gives a significant, but not dominant, place and meaning to the distinctive *biohistorical* character of human life within this cosmic process. And in so doing, it identifies the ecological niche that humankind occupies within this process as itself, necessarily, a biohistorical one. Such a niche can be properly defined and described (as we have seen) only by specifying carefully not only the physical and biological features required for human life to go on, but also the importance of certain historical features. It is, for example, only in sociocultural contexts in which some measure of justice, freedom, order, and mutual respect sufficiently prevail, and in which distribution of the goods of life (food, shelter, health, education, economic opportunity, and so on) is sufficiently equitable, that children in each new generation can be expected to have a reasonable chance of maturing into responsible and productive adult women and men — that is to say, persons who can take the sort of responsibility for their societies and for planet Earth that is now demanded of human beings worldwide. Third, the biohistorical features of our human ecological niche provide a framework that can assist communities and individuals, as they develop notions of value and meaning, to better understand and assess the adequacy of the biological context of their lives and the import of the historical sociocultural developments through which they are living, thus enabling them to take up more responsible roles within these contexts and developments.[17]

Fourth, because this approach highlights the linkage of serendipitous cosmic creativity with our humanness and the humane values so important to us, as well as with our ecological niche, it can support hope (but not certainty) for the future of our human world. It is a hope about the overall direction of future human history — hope for truly *creative* movement toward ecologically and morally responsible, though still quite pluralistic, human existence. Finally, fifth, a hope of

---

17. A much more elaborated sketch of the ethic implied by the distinctively *biohistorical* character of human existence will be found in *In Face of Mystery,* chaps. 10–15.

this sort, grounded on the mystery of creativity in the world — a creativity that, on our trajectory, evidences itself in part through our own creative powers — can help motivate us to devote our lives to bringing about this more humane and ecologically rightly ordered world to which we aspire. (This hope, of course, carries much less assurance and specificity than traditional religious expectations of the coming of God's Kingdom.) In this way, our human past, present, and future are drawn together in an overall vision of the ongoing biohistorical process in which we are situated — our niche within planet Earth's ecology — a vision, moreover, that will help us identify and address the problems in today's world most urgently demanding our attention.

This frame of orientation or vision of reality is not, in any way, forced upon us. It can be appropriated only by means of our own personal and collective decisions, our own acts of faith in face of the ultimate mystery of life and the world. This is a frame with sufficient richness and specification to provide significant orientation for our time, but it can accomplish this only if we decide to commit ourselves to it, ordering our lives and building our futures in the terms it prescribes. Acceptance of this vision can help women and men in our world — not only those who think of themselves as religious in some more or less traditional sense, but also modern / postmodern women and men of other quite different persuasions — to gain some sense of identity, some sense of who we humans are and what we ought to be doing with our lives. And the hope that the momentum of our biohistorical trajectory will move forward creatively toward a more humane and ecologically well-ordered world can help motivate us to give ourselves in strong commitment to that trajectory's continuing growth and development.

I am proposing that the world can be seen today as a creative process constituted by a variety of trajectories. On one of these, in due course, the historical order emerged. This trajectory (on which we humans find ourselves) represents at least one significant direction in which the cosmic process has been moving in our region of the universe. We humans today are being drawn beyond our present condition and order of life by creative impulses in this trajectory suggesting decisions and movements now required of us. If we respond, in appropriately creative ways, to the historical and ecological forces now impinging upon us on all sides, there is a possibility — though no certainty — that a niche for humankind, better fitted to the wider ecological order on earth than our present niche, may be brought into being. However, if we fail to so respond, it seems likely that we humans may not survive much longer. Are we willing to commit ourselves to live and act in accord with the imperatives laid upon us by the biohistorical situation in which we find ourselves, in the hope that our actions will be supported and enhanced by cosmic serendipitously creative events? In my view, it is this kind of hope, faith, and commitment to which the trajectory that brought us into being now calls us.

V

Thus far, I have deliberately refrained in this chapter from closely connecting the ideas of serendipitous creativity and of evolutionary and historical trajectories with the more traditional notions of God and God's activity to which they correspond. It has seemed to me important that the question about the appropriateness and usefulness of these ideas be considered in their own right, as suggestive interpretations of the evolutionary-ecological universe in which we today take ourselves to be living, whatever may be their specifically theological significance. But I would like to point out now that, without great difficulty, this world-picture can be taken as presenting a way to construe the symbol "God" today — providing one recognizes that the word "God" has always designated a mystery ultimately beyond human comprehension and, thus, does not insist that God be conceived in traditional terms. The full religious potential and significance of the serendipitous creativity to which this world-picture calls our attention will come directly into view, if we decide that it is appropriate today to employ our most comprehensive and profound Western symbol of the ultimate mystery of things — God — as we seek to respond to, and think about, the reality with which we are here presented. It is not difficult to set out the main outlines of this world-picture in theocentric — indeed, in specifically Christian — terms.

It will be obvious to all, I presume, that a world-picture of this sort evokes a significantly different faith and hope than that associated with the Christian symbol-system as traditionally interpreted. There are, however, some important continuities significant enough to warrant considering this picture of the world, and the human place within it, as appropriate for Christian faith today. This world-picture overcomes completely the respects in which (as noted in Part I of this chapter) traditional understandings of the central Christian symbols blur, and must be regarded as partly responsible for, today's ecological crisis.

First and most important, understanding God — the ultimate mystery of things — in terms of the metaphor of *serendipitous creativity* manifesting itself in a variety of *evolutionary and historical trajectories*, facilitates maintaining a decisive qualitative distinction (though not an ontological separation) between God and the created order. This distinction is not entirely clear when God is understood in terms of essentially anthropomorphic creator/lord/father metaphors, and is depicted as working out anthropocentric intentions or purposes in the natural world and in the course of human affairs in history. Such a distinction, perhaps the most important contribution of monotheistic religious orientations to human self-understanding, provides the basis for regarding God (creativity, in the proposed scheme) as the *sole* appropriate focus for human devotion and worship, that which alone can properly orient human life in today's world. All other realities — *created goods* which come into being and pass away rather than the *creative good* from which other goods all come, as H. N. Wieman put it[18] — are finite, transitory, and corruptible, and become dangerous *idols* which, when worshiped and made the focus of human orientation, can easily bring disaster into human affairs. This important distinction between God and the idols is strongly emphasized in the symbolic picture sketched here.

Second, and in keeping with this first point, conceiving humans as *biohistorical* beings who have emerged on one of the countless creative trajectories moving through the cosmos — instead of as the climax of all creation, distinguished from all other creatures as the very "image of God" — makes it clear that we humans are indissolubly a part of the created order, and not in any way to be confused with the serendipitous creativity manifest throughout the entire cosmos, in all its complexity, order, and beauty. So, in the picture I am sketching here, the too-easy-anthropocentrism of traditional Christian thinking is thoroughly undercut. But it is undercut in a nonreductive way. Many antireligious or anti-idealistic interpretations of the human fail to recognize that there is something radically distinctive about human beings, something

---

18. See especially *The Source of Human Good* (Chicago: University of Chicago Press, 1946).

for which we know of no real parallels elsewhere in the created order — namely the freedom, self-consciousness, imagination, and creativity that enable humans to take significant responsibility for ourselves, our future, and our world. That failure is completely avoided in the position here set forth. Although our human creativity, producing in the course of a long history a magnificent spread of quite diverse cultures and societies, may be thought to hark back in some respects to the traditional conception of the *imago Dei,* it is unambiguously clear that our kind of creativity can exist only (so far as we are aware) within the boundaries and conditions of life found on the trajectory within the created order on which it has appeared. Moreover, it is a creativity which is a principal source of *evil* in human affairs as well as of good. This quite dim "image" of the divine creativity should not so easily tempt men and women today (as the traditional doctrine of the *imago Dei* did in past Christian reflection) to think of themselves as the "crown of creation," even (in some versions) nurturing hopes for and expectations of "deification" as the appropriate final destiny for us humans. Such dreams of complete escape from the created ecological order within which we were born, as we are exalted into an ultimate unity with God, have no place in an ecologically responsible conception of human existence.

The understanding of God and of the human presented here, I suggest, is completely open to and in accord with current ecological thinking; moreover, it gives an interpretation of that thinking which renders human life profoundly meaningful. Though strikingly different in important respects from certain traditional Christian emphases, it nevertheless presents a form of *radical monotheism* (to use H. R. Niebuhr's term)[19] that can be developed into a full-orbed Christian interpretation of human faith and life, an interpretation appropriate to the understandings and constraints of modern / postmodern thinking and existence. In view of the problematic character of traditional interpretations of the central Christian themes we have considered here, when examined in light of current ecological concerns, I propose this reconstruction of the conceptions of God and humanity as providing a way for Christian faith — and perhaps some other faiths as well — to reconstitute themselves in keeping with our contemporary evolutionary / ecological sensibility and knowledge.

---

19. See H. Richard Niebuhr, *Radical Monotheism and Western Culture* (New York: Harper & Bros., 1960).

THE MYSTERY OF THE SELF AND THE ENIGMA OF NATURE

Roger L. Shinn

ROGER L. SHINN is Reinhold Niebuhr Professor of Social Ethics, Emeritus, at Union Theological Seminary in New York. His distinguished career in the Academy has been in three fields: religion, ethics, and economics. He has conducted his extensive research on the relations of science and technology to ethics in various social systems in disparate areas of the world: Eastern and Western Europe, Asia, Africa, and the Caribbean. Much of his work has been linked to that of the World Council of Churches, and he has chaired the National Council of Churches' Department of Church and Economic Life and its Task Force on Human Life and New Genetics. In the 1970s, Professor Shinn co-chaired with Margaret Mead the USA Task Force on the Future of Mankind and the Role of the Churches in a World of Science-Based Technology. He is past president of the American Theological Society and the Society of Christian Ethics. Students and faculties at many universities at home and abroad have been inspired by his lectures. Since his retirement from Union, he has continued his teaching at the Pacific School of Religion, Drew University, Le Moyne College, Vanderbilt University, Princeton Theological Seminary, and the Vancouver School of Theology. Author or co-author and editor of eighteen books, his most recent works are the third edition of *Forced Options: Social Decisions for the 21st Century* and *The New Genetics: Challenges for Faith*, *Science, and Politics*. His work has been published in ten languages. Professor Shinn is an ordained minister of the United Church of Christ.

A S CHRISTIANS ENTER THE THIRD MILLENNIUM, we find ourselves rethinking our relation to the realm of nature around us and within us. Like it or not, we have to do this, for two compelling reasons. First, the discoveries of modern science demolish many traditional understandings of nature and confer on humanity new powers, benevolent or threatening. The church has sometimes welcomed, sometimes resisted, the discoveries of Copernicus, Galileo, Newton, Darwin, Einstein, and Heisenberg. Now, new genetic science describes our inmost selves in ways that both exhilarate and jolt us. Second, ecological perils, some local and some planetary, warn us that our present ways of dealing with nature, while destroying much of what we call the environment, are also self-destructive, potentially on a grand scale.

The controversies that rage about these issues often focus on specific political and economic issues. They also reach deeply into our culture, engaging the values and sensitivities that form our thoughts and actions, often unconsciously. In this essay, I resist two broad tendencies of our time: (1) those that neglect nature, depreciate it, or regard it as a warehouse of materials for human exploitation, and (2) those that cultivate pleasant illusions about nature or idealize it as a norm for human living. And I seek some "theological pointers" as guides to responsible living.

As a convenient starting point, think of a phrase heard frequently in contemporary arguments: "human intervention in natural processes." "Intervention" is here a curious word. When a hawk swoops upon a sparrow, we do not call that intervention in nature. It is one natural process clashing with another, as is common in nature. We human beings can talk of intervention only if, in some elusive way, we are more than or other than those processes. Philosophers from Plato to Descartes and after have tried to separate the self from nature, constructing dualisms of mind or soul and body. But that effort, always strained, gets less and less persuasive. The discoveries of science confirm what ancient people, including the Hebrews, knew intuitively. We are bodily beings, in and of nature, of earth, akin to plants and animals, and nature is in us. The processes of physics and chemistry and electronics have more to do with our physical and intellectual activity, our purposes and our spirituality, than we may like to think. We share the universal genetic code — that marvelous four-letter alphabet of A, G, C, and T — with chimpanzees, mice, and bacteria.

Systematic, dogmatic naturalists, of the "nothing but" school, may try to reduce all our activities to natural processes, to those complicated interactions of "chance and necessity"[1] that science investigates with startling results. But when they write books to persuade us of their theories, they engage in acts of imagination, rationality, and

---

1. Jacques Monod, *Chance and Necessity* (New York: Vintage Books, 1972; original French edition, 1970).

will. When they claim truth for their arguments, they rise above the unknowing and unintentional electrochemical processes that they describe. They illustrate a kind of transcendence — controversial word — of the self over nature, the transcendence that impressed Plato and Descartes, even though it misled them to incredible — I'd add harmful — conclusions.

So if we are part of nature, we are a unique part. We can conceive nature as an object, investigate it, talk about it, purposely act upon it, "intervene" in it. We can fleetingly and locally put our "Kilroy was here" upon nature. We may even prate foolishly about "conquering" space, or "managing" the environment, or "controlling" the genetic code. If we are sane enough to avoid such gloating, we, unlike other processes of nature, can write solemn essays about our relation to nature.

Yet, in any such acts, we confront the enigma of nature around us and within us. Out of its evolutionary processes has come human life. It sustains us, inspires us, threatens us, will kill every last one of us, and will outlast our entire species.

Macronature

Nature, when we dare to think of all of it, is an overwhelming reality. According to the currently dominant theory, our universe began with a Big Bang some thirteen or fourteen billion years ago, give or take a few hundred million years. Then a mass, somewhere between the size of a pea and a grapefruit, initiated the explosion that is still going on, shaping and unshaping galaxies. There are dissenters to this theory, and it may be modified in the next century — or month. But alternative theories pose comparable issues, so I use this one, simply as an example.

The Big Bang, it seems, made possible all that followed, including human life: our loves and fears, our artistic imagination, our sciences and intellectual attainments, our wars, our economies, our communities and political organizations, our visions and aspirations, our moral judgments. Yes, the Enlightenment of the Buddha and the Cross of Christ. I do not say that the Big Bang made all these inevitable; that kind of metaphysical determinism, familiar in the seventeenth and eighteenth centuries, gets more incredible year by year. But in the Big Bang were — somehow and in some sense — all these possibilities and many more, yet to be realized or never to be realized. If we love life, we'd better be grateful for the Big Bang.

In this universe, our sun, perhaps five billion years old, is one of billions of stars in this galaxy, which is one of billions of galaxies in this universe. They appear to be rushing outward at tremendous speed. Yet, now and then two of them collide with unimaginable explosions. Our galaxy appears to be moving toward a collision with the Andromeda galaxy, maybe five billion years in the future. With luck, we may only sideswipe it, although nobody on a burnt-out earth will drink a toast to that luck.

Some signs point toward the existence of many universes, rising out of many Big Bangs, "continually being created and destroyed like bubbles on the ocean."[2] But nobody — at least just now — can confirm or refute the theory for certain.

In the vast array of nature, our planet and our sun are minute. Our brief temporality is equally tiny. Hinduism and Pythagoreanism have projected earlier existence of persons, perhaps eternal. Wordsworth put it eloquently:

> ...trailing clouds of glory do we come
> From God, who is our home.[3]

But such visions go far beyond any nature known to science.

A rash of observations, many made possible by the Hubble telescope floating in space, has been inspiring new observations monthly or weekly. As fresh knowledge seems to settle some old arguments, it engenders new ones. This is a bad time for dogmatists, a good time for inquirers.

Some scientists affirm the anthropic principle. In its most modest form, it is a truism: This is the kind of nature in which human life is possible. In the vastness of nature, through eons of time, conscious purposeful beings have emerged on one small plant and in one sliver of time — perhaps elsewhere, also, in times and places of which we have no certain knowledge.

In its stronger, controversial form, the anthropic principle holds

---

2. Nicholas Wade, "The Birth of a Notion," *New York Times Book Review,* September 7, 1997, 30.

3. William Wordsworth, "Ode: Intimations of Immortality from Recollections of Early Childhood," 1897, Stanza 5 (many editions).

that nature points toward the emergence of life. Processes of cosmology are precisely calibrated to make life possible. An extremely slight variation (one part in many millions) in the force of gravity or electromagnetism would have made this universe impossible, as would the most minute variation in the formation of such elements as hydrogen, helium, oxygen, and carbon. The Yale physicist Henry Margenau wrote, to the consternation of many colleagues, "the laws of nature are created by an omnipotent and omniscient God." The eminent astrophysicist Freeman Dyson is a little more reserved: "I do not feel like an alien in this universe. The more I examine the universe and the details of its architecture, the more evidence I find that the universe in some sense must have known that we were coming."[4]

Other scientists just as readily find nature utterly indifferent to human life and purposes. If natural processes temporarily support human life, they likewise support the forces that mutilate and destroy life. This is a universe of cosmic catastrophes, of annihilating events, of "black holes" — collapsed stars so dense that from them nothing, not even light, can escape.

On our plant, more congenial to human life than any other locale that we know about, nature is as perilous as it is supporting. If we formulate an anthropic principle, why not a viral principle? Nature supports viruses that combat human life and health, forces that by all signs have a far greater staying power than we. A microbe, wrote Dean Inge, "had the honor of killing Alexander the Great at the age of thirty-two and so changing the whole course of history."[5] Medical science inflicts many momentary defeats on microbes, but they keep coming back.

Biologists identify five great catastrophes — eruptions of volcanoes or strikes of meteorites — that have brought massive extinctions of earthly species. The most recent if not the greatest, it appears, destroyed the dinosaurs and many other forms of life about sixty-five million years ago. Recovery of biodiversity took twenty million years after that. E. O. Wilson reckons that such a catastrophe is likely every

---

4. Henry Margenau, in *Cosmos, Bios, Theos,* ed. Henry Margenau and Roy Abraham Varghese (LaSalle, Ill.: Open Court, 1992), 61. Freeman Dyson, *Disturbing the Universe* (New York: Harper & Row, 1979), 250.

5. W. R. Inge, *Outspoken Essays,* 2d ser. (London: Longmans Green, 1932; first published in 1920), 166.

ten to one hundred million years.[6] Such an estimate tells us that science is not always a matter of precision. But it explodes any confident and comforting version of the anthropic principle.

"Science," writes Freeman Dyson, "is a mosaic of partial and conflicting visions."[7] When it has done its best, nature is an enigma. The seventeenth-century genius Blaise Pascal, the one person of great eminence in the history of both science and theology, saw the enigma well. Again and again he pointed to the grandeur and the weakness of the self, so frail in the midst of a perilous nature, yet so wonderful. "The eternal silence of these infinite spaces frightens me." "By space the universe encompasses and swallows me up like an atom; by thought I comprehend the world." Yet even our best thought is fragile. "How ludicrous is reason, blown with a breath in every direction!"[8] The enigma of nature meets the mystery of the self.

Micronature

To turn from macronature to micronature is to find more enigmas. From ancient times, the atom was thought to be a tiny, indivisible particle. By the time I got to high school, it was a miniature solar system of protons and electrons. Now, high school students enter that strange world of neutrons, leptons, photons, mesons, quarks and antiquarks, superstrings and quantum foam, and more year by year. (That term "quark" was lifted out of James Joyce's *Finnegan's Wake* — an unusual fertilization of science by the humanities.) Quantum theory tells us that electrons have no simple location, that "wavicles" are best regarded as both waves and particles, that in microphysics statistical probability is the closest we can come to certainty. Einstein resisted quantum theory with his saying, "God does not play dice,"[9] but apparently Heisenberg has won the argument, at least for now, with his "uncertainty principle." If these esoteric theories remain unknown to most people, the technologies related to those theories affect all the

6. E. O. Wilson, *The Diversity of Life* (New York: W. W. Norton, 1993), 29ff.

7. Freeman Dyson, "The Scientist as Rebel," *New York Times Book Review,* May 25, 1998, 31.

8. Blaise Pascal, *Pensées* (New York: Dutton, Everyman's Library, 1908), fragments 206, 348, 82.

9. "Jedenfalls bin ich 'berzeugt, dass der Alte nich w' rfelt' " (Albert Einstein, Hedwig Born, and Max Born, *Briefwechsell* [Munich: Nymphenburger Verlagshandlung, 1969], 129–30).

world. Few people can explain Einstein's famous equation, $e=mc^2$, and fewer by far know how to derive it; but its effects touch all human life. When uranium was transformed into energy in the spontaneous nuclear reactor that ran for a hundred thousand years in Africa (in what is now Gabon) two billion years ago, no human beings existed to worry about it. Today, humanly constructed nuclear reactors — don't forget bombs — influence the world's economies and political structures, to the benefit or detriment of people everywhere.

With these discoveries and activities, the human power to direct and modify natural processes increases monstrously. At the same time, the divide between living and inanimate nature becomes less absolute.

As epoch-making as the nineteenth century's discoveries of the nucleus of the atom are the discoveries of the nuclei of biological cells. Here, we enter that micronature of the three billion bits of information carried by the DNA in the hundred thousand or so genes of the human cells. A fertilized egg, described as a millionth of the size of a pinhead, begins the divisions that lead to the hundred trillion cells of an adult human body. Investigators are learning to manipulate that DNA with the aim of overcoming disastrous disease, perhaps cloning human individuals, maybe reconstituting human nature in the directions, benign or malignant, of the wielders of new powers. In this realm of science, even more than in quantum theory, the enigma of nature joins the mystery of the human self.

Human Perspectives

Within nature, I have been saying, humanity has a unique place, both privileged and limited. We are not gods. We understand human nature from a human perspective. In the mid-twentieth century, the philosopher Ralph Barton Perry invented the term "the egocentric predicament." By that he meant that human beings — each of us individually and all of us collectively — can know the world only as it is accessible to our senses (or their extension in humanly devised instruments) and our thought. We lack the keen noses of dogs, the sharp eyes of eagles, and the irrepressible skill of bacteria in mutating and multiplying.

Most of us don't want to trade places with these other forms of life; we have our advantages. But we perceive the world only as the human species can perceive it, and we organize our knowledge around human interests. There is nothing shameful in these limitations. They become shameful and silly only if we pretend they are not there, acting as though our limited understandings were somehow final and absolute. To do that is a frequent human failing, known to the Greeks as hubris, to the Hebrews as sin. The appropriate answer to it is a humility before the mysteries of self, nature, and God.

The egocentric predicament affects all our acts and thought. Think of the way we talk of environment. Among human beings, environmentalists are sensitive to the beauty of nature, the welfare of many species of life, and the needs of future generations. But the very word "environment" is egocentric; it distinguishes us from the nature outside ourselves. To the innumerable other species of life, *we* are environment, even though they do not know how to say so. We, the human species, are, temporarily, the most voracious and lethal of all beasts of prey. In terms of tenure on earth, cockroaches almost surely surpass us. Although we can sometimes best them in hand-to-hand or chemical combat, we must expect them to outlast us on earth. Maybe viruses outrank us *and* cockroaches. They are the real specialists in the arts of survival. Medical biologists warn us that we never know when they may invade us in forms that defy our best weapons of defense and counterattack.

Still, we do not envy these other beings in nature. They do not — we are virtually certain — build civilizations, write epic dramas, repent before God and their co-creatures, and envision more glorious futures.

We need not despair over the egocentric predicament. We had better beware of its limitations and deceptions. In this essay, I have already unintentionally stumbled into it. Describing macronature, I have referred to thirteen or fourteen billion years. In my attempt to stretch our awareness beyond the boundaries of human life, I used a parochially human language. Why should anybody reckon cosmic time in *years*? A year is a humanly chosen unit of time, based on one elliptical movement of the earth around the sun. It is transcultural, a measurement shared by all of us on earth, but insignificant for other planets, other suns, other galaxies. Yet, we impose it on a universe in which our planet is an infinitesimal participant. I can propose no better measurement *for us*. I only point out that, to a cosmic angel, it might be a mild joke that people reckon the age of the universe in so absurdly provincial a unit as years.

Nature and Human History

In a recent fragment of terrestrial time, human life has emerged to question nature, celebrate and lament it, and act purposefully to change it. *Homo erectus* appeared in Africa some 1.8 million years ago, then spread to much of Europe and Asia. "Modern *homo sapiens*" appeared 125,000 to 200,000 years ago and began to change irrevocably the history of nature on earth. Maybe something comparable has happened often in the multiverse. We shall never know, and perhaps our descendants will never know. But when persons interact with natural processes, we face ethical issues unknown to Big Bangs and to outward rushing or colliding galaxies. Are we somehow improving on natural processes, or are we creating a wreckage that desecrates the splendor of nature and portends our own ruin? How does the mystery of the self meet the enigma of nature?

One traditional answer is that nature is infused with purpose, either the gift of a divine Creator or an invincible immanent process. "Nature does nothing without purpose or uselessly," wrote Aristotle. In a very different context, Newton asked, "Whence is it that Nature doth nothing in vain; and whence arises all the Order and Beauty which we see in the world?" His answer was "a Being incorporeal, living, intelligent, omnipresent."[10]

But then came Charles Darwin. He was not the first to propose a hypothesis of organic evolution. However, he did it with both a comprehensiveness and a scientific attention to detail that were new. When Christians sometimes rejected Darwinism with a literal reading of Genesis, that was an unnecessary and useless controversy. Still, the Darwinian explanation of the driving force of evolution as random variation followed by natural selection was more deeply disturbing, even to Darwin.

In the concluding paragraph of *On the Origin of Species,* Darwin tried hard to give an upbeat interpretation of his own work:

> Thus, from the war of nature, from famine and death, the most exalted object which we are capable of conceiving, namely the production of the higher animals, directly follows. There

---

10. Aristotle, *Politics,* Book 1, 1256b, 2021 (many editions). Isaac Newton, *Opticks,* based on the 4th ed., London, 1730 (New York: Dover, 1952), Book 3, Part 1, question 28, p. 369.

is grandeur in this view of life, with its several powers, having been originally breathed into a few forms or into one; and that, whilst this planet has gone cycling on according to the fixed law of gravity, from so simple a beginning endless forms most beautiful and most wonderful have been, and are being evolved.[11]

Privately, Darwin made a more disturbing exclamation: "What a book a Devil's chaplain might write on the clumsy, wasteful, blundering low & horridly cruel works of nature!"[12]

A century later, Richard Dawkins, picking up the metaphor of the eighteenth-century deist William Paley and turning it against him, wrote in *The Blind Watchmaker:*

Natural selection . . . has no purpose in mind. It has no mind and no mind's eye. It does not plan for the future. It has no vision, no foresight, no sight at all. If it can be said to play the role of watchmaker in nature, it is the *blind* watchmaker.[13]

The last two centuries have aroused a host of swirling and conflicting thoughts about nature. Consider the questions of ethics. From ancient times, doctrines of natural law have affirmed ethical principles built into nature and knowable to humankind apart from any historical religious revelation. The belief, though pre-Christian in origin, was absorbed into centuries of Christian teaching and practice. But it had many definitions, many interpretations. The "nature" of natural law was rarely knowable by empirical observation of the processes of nature. More often, it was some cosmic principle of order or rationality, understood to apply to human conduct as well as to universal nature.

John Donne challenged the idea in an essay entitled "Nature Our Worst Guide," in 1633.[14] But the Romantic movement found a deep human rapport with nature. Wordsworth in 1798 found

---

11. Charles Darwin, "Recapitulation and Conclusion," in *The Origin of Species,* 1859 ed. (London: Penguin Books, 1985), 459–60.

12. Darwin, Letter to J. D. Hooker, July 13, 1856, in *The Correspondence of Charles Darwin* (Cambridge: Cambridge University Press, 1990), 6:178.

13. Richard Dawkins, *The Blind Watchmaker* (New York: W. W. Norton, 1986), 5.

14. John Donne, "Paradoxes," VIII, *The Complete Poetry and Selected Prose of John Donne* (New York: Modern Library, 1952), 285.

> In nature and the language of the sense
> The anchor of my purest thoughts, the nurse,
> The guide, the guardian of my heart, and soul
> Of all my moral being.[15]

But Tennyson in 1850, just a few years before Darwin's *Origin of Species* (1859), grieved at "Nature, red in tooth and claw."[16]

A little later, Thomas Huxley, the doughty defender of Darwinism, called himself "Darwin's bulldog." But in his famous Romanes Lecture of 1893 he argued:

> . . . the practice of that which is ethically best — what we call goodness or virtue — involves a course of conduct which, in all respects, is opposed to that which leads to success in the cosmic struggle for existence. . . . It repudiates the gladiatorial theory of existence. . . . [T]he ethical progress of society depends, not on imitating the cosmic process, still less in running away from it, but in combatting it.[17]

That is not the last work on evolution and ethics. Cooperation as well as competition is part of evolutionary survival. Both belong to the enigma of nature. Biologist Robert S. Morison has framed the issue:

> Perhaps the crucial Darwinian question for our time of crisis is whether or not man can broaden his culture, his concept of human brotherhood and his tolerance of variation so that it becomes coextensive with his gene pool.[18]

Morison affirms this without denying the cruelty and waste in the evolution of life.

Beneath the controversies about ethics were perplexing questions about the place of humankind in nature. While some Christians resisted evolution, for its apparent rejection of all natural teleology, others welcomed it. Henry Drummond in *The Descent of Man* (1894) declared that Christianity and evolution were identical. Lyman Abbott in *The Theology of an Evolutionist* (1898) rejoiced in

---

15. William Wordsworth, "Lines Composed a Few Miles above Tintern Abbey," lines 108–11.

16. Alfred, Lord Tennyson, "In Memoriam," LVI.

17. Thomas H. Huxley, *Evolution and Ethics, and Other Essays* (New York: Appleton, 1903), 81–83.

18. Robert S. Morison, "Darwinism: Foundation for an Ethical System?" *Christianity and Crisis* 20 (August 8, 1960): 122.

"Redemption by Evolution." A poem by William Herbert Carruth, popular in my youth, included the lines:

> Some call it evolution,
> And others call it God.[19]

The secular culture had similar perplexities. The poet Swinburne exulted in his place at the apex of nature:

> Glory to man in the highest! For Man is the master of things.[20]

W. S. Gilbert (of Gilbert and Sullivan fame) could have been spoofing Swinburne when a few years later he wrote:

> Darwinian Man, though well-behaved,
> At best is only a monkey shaved

and,

> Man is Nature's sole mistake![21]

Probably neither Swinburne nor Gilbert knew the pre-Darwinian hymn of Reginal Heber, who could sing of at least some locales:

> Though every prospect pleases,
> And only man is vile...[22]

The continuing argument is not likely to be settled soon.

The Industrial Revolution had more direct impact on human habits and consciousness than Darwin's science. It gave rise to the conception of nature as a hoard of materials — smugly called "raw materials" — for human use and consumption. Of course, human beings had long exploited nature as voraciously as possible with their limited abilities. But industry brought new possibilities and ambitions. People who had never heard of Francis Bacon discovered for themselves that "knowledge is power." They did not always share Bacon's belief: "God almighty first planted a garden; and, indeed, it is the

---

19. William Herbert Carruth, "Each in His Own Tongue," 1908 (in several old anthologies).

20. Algernon Charles Swinburne, "Hymn of Man," 1871 (many editions).

21. William Schwenck Gilbert, *Princess Ida,* 1884, Act 2 (many editions).

22. "Missionary Hymn," 1819 (in several old hymnals).

purest of human pleasures." Nor did they always treasure his insight: "Nature cannot be ordered about, except by obeying her."[23]

In this chaos of data and opinions, can we make any generalization about the mystery of the self and the enigma of nature? How do we relate to the nature that is our womb and our tomb? I see no unanimous judgments, no emerging consensus. Sometimes I turn to an exclamation of George Santayana that has reverberated in my memory for five decades:

> Great is this organism of mud and fire, terrible this vast, painful, glorious experiment. Why should we not look on the universe with piety? Is it not our substance? Are we made of other clay? All our possibilities lie from eternity hidden in its bosom. It is the dispenser of all our joys. We may address it without superstitious terrors; it is not wicked. It follows its own habits abstractly; it can be trusted to be true to its own word. Society is not impossible between it and us, and since it is the source of all our energies, the home of all our happiness, shall we not cling to it and praise it, seeing that it vegetates so grandly and so sadly, and that it is not for us to blame it for what, doubtless, it never knew that it did?[24]

That is not the last word. Noting the reference to the universe as an organism, I would like to nudge Santayana in the direction of Whitehead. But I find his natural piety one element in any adequate ethic of human interaction with nature. For a more robust ethic, I must turn (as Santayana did but not in the way he did) to a more specific religious heritage.

Theological Pointers

Why do I come to theology so late in this inquiry? Because it is a late arrival in the long story of human efforts to live with and cope with nature. The faith that theology seeks to understand never arises *ex nihilo*. Its origins are not *sola scriptura*. It builds upon, invades, and transforms the varieties of human experience.

---

23. Francis Bacon, "Of Heresies," 1597. "Of Gardens," 1625. *Novum Organum,* Book I, aphorism 129. All three sayings are preserved in various translations from the Latin and in various editions.

24. George Santayana, *The Life of Reason* (New York: Charles Scribner's Sons, 1905), 191.

Theology does not replace the enigma of nature with a single, coherent vision. The Christian scriptures are not a list of major premises from which believers can deduce moral rules for today's world. Nor is the Bible a grab bag of proof texts, although people use it as though it were. It expresses pervading motifs that guide thought and behavior but rarely with rigorous, consistent, prescriptive authority. In the diversity of biblical insights, Christians find guides to belief and activity. Our responses are rarely unanimous, as anybody can plainly see. From theology I expect *pensées* (Pascal) and fragments (Kierkegaard), rather than a systematic concept of the world and social policy. I encourage those who strive to weave the insights into a comprehensive understanding, but I am skeptical of their results. So I refer here to "theological pointers." The pointers are decisively important as guides in life and death. They confer on us the responsibility for discovering their significance for the mystery of the self and the enigma of nature.

We think immediately of the biblical belief in creation. Its rejection of pantheism and polytheism means that nature is not God and is not inhabited by gods. Nature is created by God. It is real — not *maya*, not a projection of shadows on the wall of Plato's cave. In the audacious refrain of Genesis 1, it is "good," yes, "very good." But good is not perfect. Lurking in the garden is the "crafty" serpent. Though God's creation, it is a tempter, a provocateur.

Although the Bible does not declare creation *ex nihilo*, Second Isaiah comes close:

> I form light and create darkness,
> I make peace and create evil.[25]

Christians today (and Jews, though others can speak more competently than I to that) rarely attribute directly to God all the acts ascribed to God in some parts of scripture. Amos asks: "Does disaster befall a city, unless the Lord has done it?" Today, even we who love Amos believe that some disasters (e.g., the devastation of cities by bombs and floods that follow deforestation) are caused by people in defiance of God. Others (e.g., eruptions of volcanoes and the tornadoes that are frequent in history) are acts of an unknowing nature

---

25. Isaiah 45:7. I am using the King James Version. The RSV and NRSV soften the saying: "I make weal and create woe." In going back to the KJV, I am not expressing a personal preference; I am following eminent Hebraists.

that is neither malicious nor benign. Nature, created by God and basically "good," has an order and disorder that stand between us and God. *Phusis,* the Greek word for nature with its inherent order, creeps into the New Testament, chiefly in the letters of Paul; the word does not appear in the gospels. At the end of the second millennium, science has explored the natural order, only partially, but sufficiently to influence any theology of nature.

Yet, biblical insights are as impressive as ever. *Homo sapiens* is one creature among others, created of the dust of the earth but bearing the divine image. Humanity, privileged above all other creatures, is granted the gift and responsibility of a limited dominion. That dominion does not extend to "the Pleiades and Orion" (Amos 5:8; cf. Job 9:9, 38:41) or even to such earthly creatures as Behemoth (Job 40:15) and Leviathan (Isa. 27:1; Pss. 74:14, 104:26; Job 41:1). Extravagant straining for power leads to destructive confusion, as at Babel.

As important as the doctrine of Creation, and more uniquely Christian, is the doctrine of Incarnation. In the famous words of William Temple, Christianity

> is the most avowedly materialistic of all the great religions.... Its own most central saying is: "The Word became flesh," where the last term was, no doubt, chosen because of its specifically materialistic association.[26]

Those who believe are bound to esteem human flesh, animal flesh, and the material world.

The biblical creation is not static. God acts in it. People act in it. Lions, wild goats, forest animals, birds, and sea creatures act in it. So do winds, clouds, fire, and springs (Ps. 104). God is capable of doing "a new thing" (Isa. 43:19). Modern theologians have sometimes implied that the biblical God acts in history, not nature. But that will not do. The exodus from Egypt is a conspicuous, certainly not the only, example of the merging of nature and history in divine activity.

The biblical ethic, in its calls for justice, constantly demands a sharing of God's gifts. The sharing extends to the family, the neighbor, the sojourner, the enemy. It extends also to future generations. If much of the New Testament portends an early day of final judgment, the Old

---

26. William Temple, *Nature, Man and God* (London: Macmillan, 1949), 478.

Testament sees providence extending to "the thousandth generation" (Deut. 5:9). Christians have tried to appropriate both accents, even when unsure just how to relate them.

All these theological pointers have their meaning for the enigma of nature and the mystery of the self. But they give rise to a major theological controversy of the twentieth century. It began with a celebration of biblical monotheism and its desacralization of nature, its denial of the many nature-spirits of animism and the nature-inhabiting gods of polytheism. Theologians rejoiced that humans, in their divinely given dominion, have the right to appropriate nature for their own ends. It is not by accident, they said, that societies influenced by the Bible have led the world in the triumphs of technology and the bending of nature to the human will. In one of the ironies of cultural history, this paean to secularization came to a peak at just the time when events forced a new ecological consciousness on humankind.

Critics quickly arose to blame religion for the reckless human exploitation of nature. Lynn White, Jr.'s, essay of 1967, "The Historical Roots of Our Ecologic Crisis," won almost instant fame. He argued that Western Christianity, "the most anthropocentric religion the world has seen," destroyed pagan animism and "made it possible to exploit nature in a mood of indifference to the feelings of natural objects." He urged a return to the faith of St. Francis of Assisi. A few years later, Arnold Toynbee, once an avowed advocate of Christianity, blamed monotheism and urged a return to a more ancient pantheism, which he claimed "was once universal."[27]

Both sides in this controversy overstate their case. René Dubos finds convincing evidence to conclude:

> All over the globe and at all times in the past, men have pillaged nature and disturbed the ecological equilibrium, usually out of ignorance, but also because they have also been more concerned with immediate advantage than with long-range goals.[28]

Modern Western society has done so more effectively because it developed greater power to do so.

---

27. Lynn White, Jr., "The Historical Roots of Our Ecologic Crisis," *Science* 155 (March 10, 1967): 1203–7 (reprinted in many anthologies). Arnold Toynbee, "The Religious Background of the Present Environmental Crisis," first published in 1972; reprinted in *Ecology and Religion in History,* ed. David and Eileen Spring (New York: Harper & Row, 1974), 137–49.

28. René Dubos, *A God Within* (New York: Charles Scribner's Sons, 1972), 161.

Before the exultant secularizers and their critics, William Temple advocated belief in "the sacramental universe": "The whole universe is the expression of [God's] will."[29] Temple's statement is the more impressive because it is not an ad hoc argument designed for the moment, but a fundamental belief. The "sacramental universe" is in tune with Eastern Orthodox belief. The Ecumenical Patriarch Bartholomeus, of Istanbul, has recently said: "The whole universe is a sacrament. The entire cosmos is a burning bush of God's uncreated energies."[30] In American Protestantism, James Nash advocates the doctrine.[31] I'm not quite persuaded. Teaching Temple's book in 1948–49, I found my students perplexed by the doctrine. Does it treat too lightly the "nasty" side of nature — its extravagant cruelty and waste? Ralph Waldo Emerson, although he adored nature far more than most people, found himself driven to ask: "Must we not suppose somewhere in the universe a slight treachery and derision?"[32]

Is infectious disease an example of that "treachery"? William H. McNeill's groundbreaking book, *Plagues and People*,[33] gives convincing evidence that infectious diseases have been major determinants of history. We have long known that in historic wars, until recently, sickness killed more soldiers than weapons. McNeill amasses evidence from around the world of the power of plagues in the history of nations and empires. In one example, he shows that smallpox was a decisive force in the European conquest of the Americas. Indeed, some Puritans in North America and some Jesuits in South America said that divine providence had used smallpox to clear the way for the newcomers — a doctrine that does nothing to vindicate God or the theological wisdom of the propounders. The devastation of bacilli and viruses, among human beings and animals, refutes any indiscriminate love of nature.

Yet, our undeniable human kinship with nature is impressive. A recent idea, pleasing to some ecologists and New Age nature devotees, is the Gaia hypothesis. Taking its name from the ancient Greek god-

---

29. William Temple, "The Sacramental Universe," in *Nature, Man and God*, 479.

30. Reported in *The Christian Century*, December 3, 1997, 118–19.

31. James Nash, *Loving Nature: Ecological Integrity and Christian Responsibility* (Nashville: Abingdon Press in cooperation with the Churches' Center for Theology and Public Policy, 1991), 112–16.

32. Ralph Waldo Emerson, "Nature," *Essays*, 2d ser., 1844 (many editions).

33. New York: Doubleday, 1977.

dess Earth, it argues that the earth is, or is very like, a living organism, regulating nature, atmosphere, and life to maintain an equilibrium. Ironically, its proposer is James Lovelock, who was part of NASA, which is often seen as an example of the human desire to master nature. Although an intriguing alternative to the concept of nature as a blind mechanism or a collection of commodities for human exploitation, it has trouble with the five great extinctions and the history of plagues. Also, it relieves human beings of responsibility, since Gaia will correct our ecological recklessness.[34]

Before the popularity of ecology, Paul Tillich, with his roots in German romanticism, objected to human "intellectual arrogance" and "a domineering attitude toward nature." But he guarded against soft idealization of nature. "Nature is not only glorious; it is also tragic. It is subject to the laws of finitude and destruction. It is suffering and sighing with us." In the sacraments, he found nature participating "in the process of salvation."[35] I wish he had given more attention to plagues and other instances where, if I am right, we have an opportunity and responsibility to do what we can to resist — and fight — hostile forces of nature.

So, I return to my theme of the enigma of nature. I must now speak more directly to the issue of human actions within and upon the processes of nature.

Human Responsibility

Within the mystery and majesty of the whole creation, Christian faith finds a modest human dominion and a responsibility to "till" and "keep" a God-given Eden (Gen. 1:26, 2:15). Human creatures have finite but expanding powers to act upon the given nature. Some uses of that power are a joyful and reverent appreciation of divine gifts. Others are a defiance and blasphemy. How can we distinguish the difference? Two examples of the question have leapt into recent prominence: ecology and genetics.

---

34. James Lovelock, *Gaia: A New Look at Life on Earth* (New York: Oxford University Press, 1979, reprinted with a new preface, 1988). Chap. 7, "Gaia and Man: The Problem of Pollution," is the chapter most criticized by ecologists.

35. "Nature Also Mourns for a Lost Good," a sermon in *The Shaking of the Foundations* (New York: Charles Scribner's Sons, 1948). The citations are from pp. 82, 81, 86.

Ecology

All living species affect their environments, sometimes in symbiosis, sometimes in destructive competition. Bees, gathering food for themselves, pollinate plants to the benefit of humankind and many other living species. Gypsy moths, also seeking food, devastate trees, with no evident advantage to anybody except gypsy moths. Other species, from the tiniest bacteria to the great whales and elephants, act upon their environments without foreseeing consequences. Inanimate processes of nature — balmy breezes and tornadoes, gentle rains and raging floods, earthquakes, volcanoes, meteorites — also affect their surroundings. The human difference is that we do so purposefully as well as unintentionally, often radically and recklessly.

Then come times of accounting. Nature strikes back. Cutting of forests leads to floods. Abuse of the soil exhausts its fertility. Pollution brings disease and death, both locally and terrestrially (as in the "hole" in the layer of protective ozone high above us). Thus, self-interest may bring an awakening of ecological consciousness. Concern for posterity — a more generous but still anthropocentric motive — may do the same.

But more than enlightened self-interest is involved. Something of primal awe before nature persists even in industrialized, high-tech society. The past destruction of the passenger pigeons and the threatened destruction of the spotted owl strike a wide public as wrong. Popular support for the Endangered Species Act has surprised politicians and industrialists. Glimmers of that sensitivity extend even to inanimate nature. The littering of Antarctica and the cluttering of "space" with debris seem somehow wrong to many people who cannot quite say why. To Christian faith they are offenses against God's creation.

This ecological sensitivity is profound, but it raises disturbing questions. Violence and destruction are frequent in nature. The prophetic vision of vegetarian lions and of wolves and lambs feeding peaceably together (Isa. 65:25) is an eschatological vision, not a legislative program. William Blake in "Songs of Innocence" marveled that God had made the little lamb; five years later in "Songs of Experience" he marveled equally at the tiger and asked, "Did he who made the Lamb make thee?"[36]

---

36. William Blake, "The Lamb," 1789; "The Tyger," 1794 (many editions).

A syndicated newspaper feature, entitled "Earthweek: A Diary of a Planet," reports each week on earthquakes, volcanic eruptions, tornadoes, droughts and floods, killing hailstorms, epidemics, and (periodically) havoc wrought by El Niño. It never runs short of materials. Some of the catastrophes are, at least in part, consequences of human activity. Most are not. Even the sturdiest faith has trouble seeing all these acts as sacraments.

Nature in its heedless destruction annihilates not only individuals but also species. As Tennyson put it,

> ... She [Nature] cries, "A thousand types are gone:
> I care for nothing, all shall go."[37]

Scientists tell us that, in the great terrestrial catastrophes of the past, something like 80–95 percent of species were destroyed, and that the recovery times ranged from ten to a hundred million years. Throughout earthly history, E. O. Wilson estimates: "Ninety-nine percent of all the species that ever lived are now extinct."[38] Other estimates run as high as 99.999 percent.

Why then should we worry if contemporary society destroys a mere 5 percent? But Wilson warns us: "The sixth great extinction spasm of geological time is upon us," differing from all the others because it comes "grace of mankind."[39] He makes a convincing case for the interrelatedness of many forms of life, for the dependence of human life on insects and microorganisms, for the unintended destruction of species by the careless elimination of their habitats.

I share Wilson's horror at the prospect he describes. I am not quite persuaded by his conclusion: "We should not knowingly allow any species or race to go extinct."[40] I think I would not mourn the extinction of mosquitoes, especially if I lived in a malarial zone, although Wilson can show me that they have an ecological value that I don't see. May I not rejoice in the virtual termination of the smallpox virus? At the moment, samples are preserved in carefully guarded laboratories, and the scheduled date for their extermination has been repeatedly deferred. But they are kept for their possible value in future experimentation — a thoroughly anthropocentric motive.

---

37. Alfred, Lord Tennyson, "In Memoriam," LVI (many editions).
38. Wilson, *The Diversity of Life,* 344.
39. Ibid., 343.
40. Ibid., 351.

Acknowledging the very great benefit of bacteria to human life, I could easily do without some: those for tuberculosis, cholera, syphilis, typhoid fever, and tetanus. So far as I can imagine, I would not miss the loss of viruses for measles, mumps, yellow fever, polio, influenza, ebola, and HIV.

A disembodied spectator might admire the ability of these life-forms to mutate and find friendly niches. Influenza and tuberculosis — super-tuberculosis is the new term — despite some human victories over them, return in new forms that baffle us. As a participant in the biosphere, not a spectator, I make my fallible but stubborn judgments: They are enemies.

James Nash, who affirms "the intrinsic value of all God-created being," nevertheless accords a primacy to the human. So he qualifies his love of nature: "even the deliberate eradication of particular species can be justified to provide vital protection for human health."[41] As examples he proposes the guinea worm and some bacteria and viruses. I agree.

May human beings rightly intervene in natural processes? Yes, we do so inevitably, simply by our existence, also by deliberate purpose. That recognition need not mute the protest against the wanton, arrogant, destructive exploitation of nature so characteristic of our civilization. The evidence mounts that these acts are, in their consequences, disastrous to human values. To Christians they are also irreverent.

Genetics[42]

Of all interventions in natural processes, medical interventions reach most intimately into selfhood. They modify not only our environment but also ourselves. They are very, very old in the human story. Historic medical treatment is partly superstition and pseudoscience. It is partly a folk wisdom that modernity disdains, then sometimes learns to appreciate. Of all medical interventions, genetic manipulation reaches most deeply into human nature. It is not like healing a broken limb or curing an infection. It goes beyond the transplants of

---

41. Nash, *Loving Nature*, 173, 189.
42. This very brief discussion of the ethics of genetics relies on my longer treatments in *The New Genetics: Challenges for Science, Faith, and Politics* (Wakefield, R.I.: Moyer Bell, 1996) and in *Human Cloning: Religious Responses,* ed. Ronald Cole-Turner (Cleveland: Pilgrim Press, 1997).

kidneys, livers, and hearts. It seeks to change the primal substance of the self — possibly even of persons through all coming generations. People greet it with both eagerness and fear.

Already, genetic interventions are producing effective drugs. Genetic testing guides men and women in decisions about parenthood. Humanity is beginning experimental therapies by genetic treatment of somatic cells to remedy inherited weaknesses or diseases. More radical are the prospects of cloning and of genetic alteration of the germ cells, initially to remove the onslaughts of diseases for generations to come, then possibly to redirect the very structure of human nature.

Ours is the first generation to face the new decisions demanded by the discoveries of DNA and its manipulation. No scriptures of any religion, no writings of ethical philosophers, no laws or constitutions of past governments have ever declared: "You shall, or shall not, mess around with DNA." Nobel laureates in biology Herman Muller and Jacques Monod not long ago declared the rearrangement of DNA to be impossible, because no surgery could slice up such minute particles. Then other scientists discovered that "chemical scissors" could do what no scalpels could do. The impossible became a reality.

The ethical challenges are stupendous. Given the history of eugenics, with its futile, prejudiced, often laughable and often vicious efforts to "improve" human heredity, we had better be wary of new efforts that may be more efficient.

Yet, we do not want to foreclose contributions to human health. Christianity has a long tradition, stemming from the gospels and extending through history, of concern for healing. And Christian faith, even though it never anticipated recent discoveries in genetics, brings some old convictions to the issues.

Again, we confront the enigma of nature. Christian faith, with its basic belief in the goodness of creation, has reason to favor those therapies that cooperate with nature. When diet and exercise prevent heart attacks, they are preferable to heart surgery. But recognition of the destructiveness of nature sometimes calls for efforts to fight natural processes. There are times to make the most strenuous effort to modify nature.

A Christian ethic might identify four big issues in genetic experimentation. The first is risk. Every day people make risk-benefit calculations. The benefits of driving a car may justify the inevitable risks — although not the risks of reckless driving. The benefits of medicine may justify risks of experimentation, but with some special warnings. Hybridizers reckon that the success of one new plant justifies the failure of hundreds that go on the compost pile. But we cannot say that about experiments on human beings. Geneticists sometimes question tampering with the evolutionary wisdom of millennia, and Christians wonder about intervening in the created order, especially if the intervention affects future generations who have no way of giving consent to risks. So, Christian faith qualifies its prejudice in favor of healing with warnings about risk. But, knowing that once risky medical procedures sometimes become routine — think of heart surgery — it will not rush to dogmatic prohibitions.

A second issue is the purposes of genetic interventions. Often our definitions of health and illness, of normality and abnormality, are social constructions. A dark skin is, in many societies, a social and economic liability. That does not commend genetic treatment to lighten skin color. What needs healing is the social prejudice, not the skin color. Past eugenic practices have often defined good and bad inheritance in ways that are now seen to be vicious and ridiculous. We had better ask whether present definitions are really better.

A third issue is justice. Who will get the benefits of new treatments? Only the wealthy? Only the residents of rich, high-tech societies? There is plenty of evidence that resources put into public health, including such elementary benefits as safe water and air, save more lives than the same resources put into costly, exotic treatments. That does not call for an end to all costly research. Sometimes work on experimental frontiers comes to benefit all humankind. Think again of the abolition of smallpox. But a theological ethic will ask of all medical practice: Whom does it benefit? What does justice require?

A fourth issue is the coming to terms with human finitude, with our essential creatureliness. It is not our privilege to overcome every obstacle, to conquer every foe. The can-do spirit is great — some of the time. It betrays us if it leads to the illusion that every problem has an answer, that the power of science can show us the meaning of life, that hope is a commodity that can be manufactured and marketed. No human conquest delivers a final answer to the mystery of the self and the enigma of nature.

Life is a precious gift. We do well to guard its health. But our lives on this planet are temporary. There are times to resist death.

But eventually, for everyone, fighting death is less important than knowing how to die.

All these issues call for a venturing ethic. They call for attention by a great variety of people — scientists, artists, theologians, workers and the unemployed, the young and the old. The church may need to go slowly in sweeping pronouncements. That takes some self-control, especially among Christians who know that the church has often been too cautious in opposing crimes of racism and oppression. Excessive caution may be cowardice. It may mean that the speed of technological forces decides major issues before ethical concerns are raised. So the churches should be insistent and impatient in questioning, but not too arrogant in judging. And they should realize that there are situations for an ethic of nuance, just as there are situations for prompt, decisive action.

A Final Word?

Do I have a final word on the mystery of the self and the enigma of nature? No. But for a helpful word I turn to Margaret Mead. The most famous anthropologist of her time, she had a professional interest in the religions of many cultures. Now and then she spoke out of her own faith.

> Was it possible that modern man might forget his relationship with the rest of the natural world to such a degree that he separated himself from his own pulse-beat, wrote poetry only in tune with machines, and was irrevocably cut off from his own heart? In their new-found preoccupation with power over the natural world, might men so forget God that they would build a barrier against the wisdom of the past that no one could penetrate?[43]

To those questions, I add the more explicitly theological declaration of H. Richard Niebuhr. Writing before the vogue of ecology, he spoke to its issues powerfully. In his "radical monotheism," he confessed that God alone is holy. His "Puritan iconoclasm" secularized all places and things, but then turned into a countermovement of the "sanctification of all things."

---

43. Margaret Mead, *Male and Female: A Study of the Sexes in a Changing World* (New York: New American Library, 1955; first published in 1949), 19.

Now every day is the day that the Lord has made; every nation is a holy people called by him into existence in its place and time and to his glory; every person is sacred, made in his image and likeness; every living thing, on earth, in the heavens, and in the waters is his creation and points in its existence toward him; the whole earth is filled with his glory; the infinity of space is his temple where all creation is summoned to silence before him.[44]

To that, almost to my regret, I have to add some warning about the hostility of enigmatic nature. But what Richard Niebuhr said is more important than what I add.

Ours is a time for an exploratory ethic, even as it is a time of emergency that requires decisive action. I have tried to suggest some pointers toward ways of believing, acting, rejoicing, grieving, and praying — all with awareness of the mystery of the self and the enigma of nature.

---

44. H. Richard Niebuhr, *Radical Monotheism and Western Culture* (New York: Harper & Brothers, 1960), 52–53.

Chapter 6

WHOLE PERSON RELIGION

Its Link to Whole Person Medicine

Rustum Roy

RUSTUM ROY's breadth of interests and achievements is exceptional, as reflected in his writings, which range from science policy and radioactive waste management, to sexual ethics and liturgies for small groups. He is Evan Pugh Professor of Solid State, Professor of Geochemistry, and Professor of Science, Technology and Society at Pennsylvania State University. A strong proponent of interdisciplinary and integrative learning, in 1976 he founded the university's interdisciplinary Materials Research Laboratory. He also was instrumental in establishing the university's geochemistry and solid state science disciplines and its Science, Technology and Society Program. Professor Roy, one of America's leading materials scientists, specializes in synthesis of new (ceramic) materials. His research is directly tied to the development of a number of totally new materials and to three major ceramic processes used worldwide. His laboratory now is the world leader in diamond and ultrahard materials synthesis and in the development of the microwave sintering process. Professor Roy's interdisciplinary work is not limited to materials science and engineering. To build a bridge between what C. P. Snow described as "Two Cultures," he was at the forefront of the Science, Technology, and Society movement, which gained widespread presence on university and college campuses and in K-12 education between 1970 and 1990. He helped to found what now is one of the oldest ecumenical house churches in the United States and served for thirty years on the board of Kirkridge, a national retreat center in the vanguard of the ecumenical movement. Professor Roy delivered the prestigious Hibbert Lectures in London, which focused on the integration of the insights of science and technology into the world's religions, and has become a well-known advocate of "radical pluralist" integration among the world's religions and cultures.

JOHN SHELBY SPONG is an "embodiment" of the prophetic tradition of the church. It should be ordinary, but it is, in fact, extraordinary in our day. That is why we celebrate his life and witness and that of

121

other prophetic voices, a few of them bishops. In the mid-1960s, I came to hear of the bishop of Woolwich, John Robinson, and pretty soon I became an admirer, friend, and kind of impresario for him at Kirkridge, on eastern campuses, and in Washington, D.C., churches. It was some years later that I met Jack Spong, our own homegrown American counterpart. There were great similarities between the two bishops, not only in the Anglican métier of their speaking and writing, which I shared, but also in their passionate concerns: *Semper reformanda* was the nature of their common vision of the church, and they tackled the task at many parallel points. Human sexuality was the one area in which I shared their concern and activism. This was a part of the human condition, we reasoned, where the church could regain credibility with the world by taking a bold Augustinian stance: "Love God and, then, do as you please." We were wrong; neither church nor world was ready for it. The traditional language of faith was another. John Robinson had even argued that "our word 'God' must go." I tried it — in a whole book on theology; it did not work. "God" is at once the cause of much of the interreligious confusion at the macro scale, and the anchor for much individual religious commitment. Petru Dumitriu, who was introduced to the Western church world by Robinson, put it well for all reformers:

> What name was I to use? "God," I murmured, "God." How else should I address Him? O Universe? O Heap? O Whole? As "Father" or "Mother"? I might as well call him "Uncle." As "Lord"? I might as well say, "Dear Sir," or "Dear Comrade." How could I say "Lord" to the air I breathed and my own lungs which breathed the air? "My child"? But He contained me, preceded me, created me. "Thou" is His name, to which "God" may be added. For "I" and "me" are no more than a pause between the immensity of the universe which is Him and the very depth of our self, which is also Him.

Jack Spong, as a bishop in the United States, had to deal with the existential need for his flock to be protected from the depredations of literalists and fundamentalists. He tried persuasively to demythologize the essence of the Christian message. And his books tackling these issues, including Virgin Birth and Resurrection, were very brave and full of scholarship and an appropriately direct style. The mainline churches owe him an enormous debt for saying so well what had long gone unsaid. Whether it worked on the faithful is not yet clear: It certainly helped those who had already "defected in place" within the church to stay.

A final note about another tie-in of my own specialty to both the bishops John: science-and-religion. I recall that after I gave the Hibbert Lectures in London, John Robinson arranged for a presentation and discussion in Cambridge of my low-church "incarnational," instead of high-church "inspirational," approach to the topic. On science and religion, I come from the "working class." I was probably the only sixty-hour-per-week working scientist who was also an activist layman involved in radical church reform for decades. My perspective ran counter to — and runs aeons away from — the "science and spirituality" miasma of Big Bangs and Hubble bubbles so popular today. Jack Spong became interested in the topic in a highly personal way. His daughter was a research physicist, and he wanted to be in deep dialogue with her. To that end, he absorbed a great deal of the "theology" of the science world and no doubt enriched a previous relationship. Again, he did it with care and real attention. We — the reforming church and the liberal community in the U.S. — will all be poorer because such an able and brave champion will not have the platform of the bishopric to raise the community's conscience. But we need not worry; it is unlikely that such a vibrant and creative spirit will go so quietly into any future.

The subject of my essay is one that could well be an area of concern for another crusade for Bishop Spong. To introduce my topic, I turn the pages of history back to the post–World War II excitement in the church about renewal and reform. I recall vividly the gatherings several times a year at Kirkridge of the young radical Protestant clergy literally ready to follow in the steps of Bonhoeffer, George Macleod, and the French worker-priests, to reform, tear down, and build anew "new forms the Church must take." The spiritual and human energy was palpable at every meeting. Perhaps its most concentrated version appeared in the Church of the Saviour in Washington, D.C., and some of that energy diffused throughout the national body of reformers. Eventually, it was also miraculously manifest in Vatican II. Reform was on a roll. But the masses were *not* ready, or perhaps only a quarter were; largely women, religious and lay. Vatican II also capped an era of intense excitement within Roman Catholic ecumenism and opened the door to genuine pan-Christian conversation and cooperation at undreamed of levels.

Two decades later, I sensed the same spiritual fervor alighting on and energizing the women's movement, both within the church and in society in general. In society in general, the political process made change possible. Within the church, it powerfully changed the women's religious communities but met with much more resistance from the male establishment on all fronts. But suddenly in the Reagan era, forward progress seemed to have stopped on all fronts. Indeed, the two PR-masters, Ronald Reagan and Pope John Paul II, used the media with incredibly powerful affect to roll back many of the liberating gains of twenty years. So, by the mid-1990s, it was hard to find a single inclusivist movement to cheer about.

This essay is about the newest group of champions to tackle the establishment to reform it. Through them, I have experienced a heartwarming replay of the messianic but sober fervor of the church-renewal "bunch." It is in the movement which I will, from the outset, term "whole person medicine (WPM)" or, even better, "whole person healing (WPH)." The terms "alternative medicine" and "complementary medicine" are better known but should be avoided because they suggest a stance *against* something. "Integrative medicine" includes allopathic and all other modalities and is much to be preferred. Champions of integrative medicine are dedicated to reforming the entire healing system. By an incredible series of coincidences, I had (over three decades ago) come to know all the leading critics and reformers: Ivan Illich, Bob Rodale, Norman Cousins. And then early in the 1990s, I came to know Deepak Chopra, Andrew Weil, Dean Ornish, Herb Benson, Bob Duggan, Patch Adams, and on and on. Lately, I have been working within Professor Andrew Weil's team in the Program in Integrative Medicine at the University of Arizona. There I have found this same spirit of altruistic fervor for changing the world for the better. I have met among the program's members many young (thirty-five, plus or minus) competent medical professionals with spiritual commitments, dedicated to service. They are the church. They are gathered in "His Name," caring for others; "Jesus" is certainly among them as he promised. It is not a coincidence, perhaps, but this time the publics — the masses — are already primed and eager for this "gospel" message. This potential tidal wave is the single most hopeful entry point for social change since World War II that I have seen, including all those mentioned above. I will elaborate on that rather strong statement in this essay.

The Whole Person

Hippocrates, iconic figure of medicine's pantheon, is certainly an appropriate one to quote in introducing a new approach to medicine. Not only did he write, "First, do no harm," but also he said, "It is more important to *know the person* that has the disease, than the disease the person has." All whole person medicine practitioners work on the second principle, and their track record on doing harm, compared to recent high-tech medical practice, shows that they do much less.[1]

Knowing a patient means knowing about her or his social life and family, environment, spiritual life and history, and mental outlook, state, and condition, in addition to all that modern diagnostic equipment can tell us about the body. No one contests that we are all, without exception, complex assemblies of three interacting "states": body, mind, and spirit — just like the three states of matter: solid, liquid, and vapor. Think of water: We all encounter the same substance in three states: ice, water, or steam. Because of another part of my particular scientific background, I sometimes like to explain the differences to fellow scientists as follows: The parallels to these conditions of *isolated body,* nearby interactions via *mind,* and long-distance-cum-long-history interactions of *spirit,* can be found in the way electrons change in common solids. Insulating, transparent solids like salt or sand have all the electrons belonging to sodium, "tightly bound" to only the sodium's core. In deeply colored crystals like gems or semiconductors, a few of the electrons are shared by one atom core and its neighbors. Finally, in metals some of the electrons move effortlessly in every direction and are shared by an infinite number. The *body* is that part of my personhood, or "self," which is most "tightly bound" to me, i.e., exclusively identified with me, not commingled with any other body. The *mind* is that part of self which interacts with my body easily and extensively all the time. It also, however, is partly "delocalized" from me. It interacts easily with other minds

---

1. Iatrogenic disease, illness caused by any medical treatment or earlier hospitalization, is one of the leading causes of hospital stays, and drug interactions are said to be the fourth leading cause of death — a fact so dramatic that the popular press just ignores it.

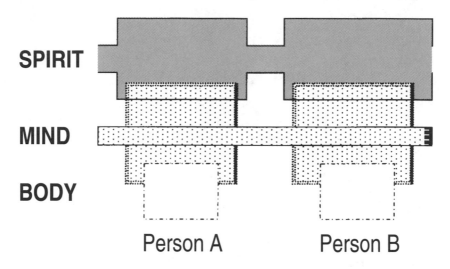

SPIRIT

MIND

BODY

Person A   Person B

This crude graphic tries to illustrate that the interactions between two "whole persons," each consisting of body, mind, and spirit, are very different in the three domains. Our bodies are largely (not, of course, entirely) separate from each other, bound by visible, measurable boundaries. But two minds can interact and influence each other and many others to an extraordinary degree. In the spirit dimension this interaction extends through time as well as space — infinitely. Thus, there are really no such entities as an individual's mind or spirit; they are always in dynamic interaction with layer upon layer of others.

---

which can instantaneously "dump" "mind" into my mind and vice versa. *Spirit* on this scale is the least tightly bound part of my self. My spirit reaches throughout time and space and is influenced by history, collective, family, and tribal memory and, much more intensely, by the spirit of my friends and community. My spirit can be influenced through my senses and beyond, through memory and beyond. It is profoundly changed by listening to a haunting Gregorian chant or by hearing of the death of a neighbor's child. An infinity of experience confirms for me that my mind can influence my body. We are all certain from common experience that human beings can and do interact through all these channels, within themselves, and across selves. Sad news can make me weep; very good news makes me jump for joy. Change the spirit with news or reflection or medicines, and it can profoundly change the body.

All of these facts about the triune nature of the self have been fully recognized in all traditional cultures for millennia. It is perhaps only in the last fifty (perhaps a hundred) years that "modern," reductionist scientific approaches took the almost unbelievable position, in practice if not in theory, that the *self* is *body* alone. If anything was felt to be wrong, it was enough to examine and treat only the body. Healing the total self could be done by "curing" whatever disease existed in the body alone. This profound and profoundly disturbing error of modern medicine is the driving force behind the dramatic changes we are *experiencing*.

Whole Person Medicine

The empirical fact is that in current medical practice, proclaiming only its scientific heritage, the physician (with exceptions, of course, who honor the older family doctor role) spends hardly two minutes talking with the patient and is totally focused on the body: the liver or breast or back — one *part* of the body (not even the whole body). Certainly, scientific medicine *at its very best* treats only a part of the person, the body. Thus, even if scientific medicine were 100 percent successful according to its own criteria, it would be a very partial solution from the viewpoint of all those who claim that the person is much more than the body alone.

The revolution that has occurred in a dozen years is due to one common denominator. The patient, the customer, has spoken: "I am *not* a body alone. I am body, plus mind, plus spirit. To be healed, I need attention to this whole person." Yet, it would be absurd to imply that a doctor treating a car accident victim or a person with a severe heart attack should start with a lengthy psycho-history. Of course there are different priorities for different situations but, in the large majority of cases, it is the reassertion of whole person status by the citizenry, who are all patients at one time or other, that has brought about the revolution.

Table 1 from the *Journal of the American Medical Association* is the quantitative proof of my assertion that a largely silent *revolution* has taken place. In 1997, the number of visits to alternative providers for the first time exceeded the number Americans made to regular physicians. That number had grown 47 percent in seven years. These are unbelievably revolutionary objective data. Any scien-

Table 1[2]
THE METEORIC RISE OF WPM
Nationally Representative Telephone Survey

	1990	1997
Use of any one of sixteen Alternative Therapies (A.T.)	33.8%	42.1%
Visiting any A.T. provider	36.3%	46.3%
Disclosed to physician	39.8%	38.5%
Paying out-of-pocket	64.0%	58.3%
Total visits to A.T.	427 million	629 million* 47% increase
Expenditures for A.T. services	$14.6 billion	$21.2 billion
TOTAL Expenditure for A.T.	N/A	$27.0 billion[†]
Out-of-pocket (for services)	N/A	$12.2 billion[‡]

* This number exceeds total visits to U.S. primary care physicians.
† Comparable to total out-of-pocket expenditures for all U.S. physician services.
‡ Exceeds total out-of-pocket for all hospitalizations.

tist would have to try to explain them. My explanation is very simple. The monopoly of allopathic medicine was broken (partially) and the people have voted with their feet and astoundingly with their pocketbooks. Can one imagine the rate of increase when (and it is no longer if, but when) *all* the insurance companies allow payments for alternative therapies? The dyed-in-the-wool conservatives of medicine, who believe literally *nulla salus* (salvation, or health) *extra ecclesiam* (outside the church, where *ecclesia* here would refer to traditional Western medicine), doubtlessly must be analyzing these data with fear and trepidation. Such data should surely make them question their basic premise that S(elf) = B(ody) and go over, formally, to S = B + M(ind) + S(pirit) and adjust the nature of their practices to conform to the reality of the wholeness of personhood.

WPM — An Old Story

Let us recall the association of religion and healing as universal in all traditional cultures. This connection of the spiritual with the bod-

2. David M. Eisenberg et al., *Journal of the American Medical Association* 280 (November 1998): 1569–75.

ily — a central tenet, e.g., in Christian Science practice — is the same bedrock that is now being rediscovered in all the contemporary "alternative" approaches. All shamans, medicine men, Kundalini adepts, qigong or Shaolin masters, whether in India, Japan, China, or the Americas, combine spiritual leadership with healing powers. These modalities did *not* disappear with the Industrial Revolution nor even up to say 1900, even though the so-called *science* of medicine was gradually developing. The theme of service through healing persisted in many religious cultures. High proportions of early Christian missionaries were doctors, continuing Jesus' ministry of healing the sick using modern medicines but including it within a wider concern for the whole person. In the United States throughout the nineteenth century, there was a genuine free market in medicine. It ran the gamut from the snake-oil dispensers and con artists on the frontier, to Mary Baker Eddy in Boston and Hahnemann's homeopathy in Philadelphia, to osteopathy, chiropractic, vibrators for sexual massage, and so on — all these flourished side by side.

But with the dawning of the twentieth century, the tide of history was turning, turning toward technology and its handmaiden, science, and derivatively high-tech medicine.

Figure 1 shows schematically how this happened. Because the new *science* dealt only with the body, it started modern medicine down the reductionist path and separated it from its natural ally and necessarily larger framework: religion. Moreover, as its reductionist nature demanded, in the fifty years before the 1970s, all of the highly successful traditional modalities, which were intrinsically wholistic — healing body, mind, and soul — were made illegal and, worse, were ridiculed in the consciousness of the culture. The triumph of life span expansion, which was due largely to prevention (from such factors as handwashings and clean water and sewer systems) and vaccination, was falsely claimed as proof of the superior efficacy of high-tech medicine. But many successful "pills" for the relief of specific symptoms did appear. Some were found by chance, some by empirical observation, some by scientific manipulation. Starting with aspirin, quinine (which was used by traditional medicine men in South Asia and brought to the West by Jesuit missionaries, hence its name Jesuit bark), Salvarsan, and eventually penicillin, there were, in fact, major discoveries that alleviated bodily pain and many acute diseases. Surgery also contributed its share of major advances, if not

The Rise of Reductionism
in Science and Medicine

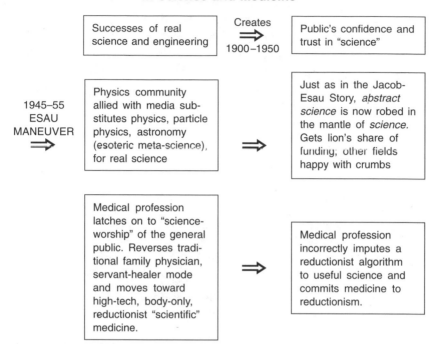

Fig. 1. The historical sequence of events that led to the dominance of American technology, especially after World War II, which was misattributed to *science* due to the clever "Esau maneuver." Science then acquired admiration and gratitude from the public and status from the Vatican for safeguarding the truth. Medicine turned away from its traditional five-thousand-year history as a healing *art* to become second-rate science. Its monopoly lasted until the 1990s, but is now crumbling.

"miracles." And soon the touchstone of the success of reductionist science had become its ability to lessen pain.

However, by the 1980s, there was trouble brewing. Discoveries of miracle drugs were rarer and rarer. The "cure" was often exaggerated. Major unexpected side effects, such as those of thalidomide, got headlines. Then the "system" of hospital-doctor-patient began to unravel. Most damaging was the feeling of millions that to their doctors they were no longer persons — body-mind-spirit, history, culture — but only bodies. Two forces were to accelerate the ultimate showdown. The first was the intrinsic connection of "cure" and "body" (only) medicine to this scientific reductionism in high-tech medicine; the second was the enormous potential for making money out of human misery when persons were at their most vulnerable.

But, *mirabile dictu,* in spite of the monopoly position enjoyed by high-tech medicine, in spite of the laying on of hands *on it alone* by the science establishment, in spite of some very real achievements and the incessant propaganda supporting it not only in TV advertising but also in TV programs about medicine, this nation's citizens began to speak and act decisively against reductionist, body-only medicine. The figures of table 1 are truly startling. Few can believe that, in 1997, more American citizens made and paid for visits to practitioners of "alternative" modalities than for visits to regular physicians, even though in 58 percent of the former cases, they had to *pay for it out-of-pocket.* Further, this cohort of adherents is more educated and has a higher income than the population as a whole. The experience in Europe is similar. The explanation is plain to see, and it is devastating news to reductionist medicine and reductionist science. The people have spoken on the basis of their own empirical research. The citizens have said, we are *not* only bodies. We are whole persons: body-mind-and-spirit. We can be "accessed," analyzed, or helped through body and/or mind and/or spirit. WPH is doing precisely that, and we know that works for us. Drawing on the world's ancient healing arts, qigong and acupuncture from China, Yoga, Ayurvedic, and massage from India, and botanicals from all over the world, and by no means excluding the enormous assets of modern scientific medicine, WPM is obviously in resonance with contemporary humans. It is in resonance with their internally coded wholism. Prayer has been given an extraordinary visibility as an agent in healing both the pray-*er* and the one prayed for. The power of belief in triggering healing is proven daily in placebo experiments and an enormous range of responses under hypnosis. There is little question that belief is the single most powerful "pill" in the world's pharmacopoeia. The impact of the victory of wholism in medicine is utterly profound because nearly everyone must deal with the choice of reductionist or wholist approaches to his or her own health. Ultimately, no scientific abstraction has any value or power over an individual. It is his or her own experience which is the judge of truth. This return to personal experience — instead of abstractions from outside — as the source of veridical judgment is the truly paradigm-changing event in global culture.

Some Extraordinary Verifications and Further Claims by Alternative Modalities

My own inquiries into the field of integrative medicine are focused on examining the data on various observations and practices in alternative modalities that directly interact with an instrument. From these, I have selected two to demonstrate the quality of scientific data that support the extraordinary claims of the "newer" modalities. I present them as I would report on very interesting developments in my field. I do not, in either case, guarantee them as verified in my own experience or experiments. The data, while outside the present paradigm, appear plausible; the scientists involved, very responsible.

ACUPUNCTURE TO HEAL VISION PROBLEMS

Empirically it should be accepted that when hundreds of millions of people have used acupuncture for thousands of years, there must be some validity to their healing practices. Yet Western medicine has consistently ridiculed acupuncture. Like Galileo's scientific critics who refused to look through the telescope, most traditional high-tech "scientific medicine" champions refuse to face the data: Are the "meridians" of acupuncture real? How can specific acupoints connect to an apparently unrelated remote part of the body? When James Reston, the *New York Times* senior editor who accompanied President Nixon on the China-opening trip in the early 1970s, had to have an appendectomy in Beijing, the operation was conducted with no chemical anesthesia, only acupuncture. Reston reported this in the *Times*. Now, decades later, some traditionalists claim that Reston fabricated the account to boost Nixon's success in China! Such dogmatism dies hard.

A more egregious case occurred very recently in the work on alternatives in a paper by Cho et al.,[3] from the University of California, Irvine group. After rejection *without review* by both *Nature* and *Science,* it appeared in the *Proceedings of the National Academy of Sciences.* Cho and his colleagues proposed to check directly on an in-

---

3. Z. H. Cho et al., "New Findings of the Correlation between Acupoints and Corresponding Brain Cortices Using Functional MRI," *Proceedings of the National Academy of Sciences* 95 (March 1998): 2670–73.

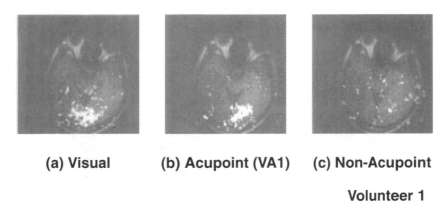

(a) Visual   (b) Acupoint (VA1)   (c) Non-Acupoint

Volunteer 1

Fig. 2. The results from Z. H. Cho et al. (see note 3), showing the lighting up of the visual cortex in the brain, caused by direct shining of a light in the patient's eyes, and the same MRI scan obtained by inserting a needle into the traditional Chinese acupoint for the visual cortex — in the right foot, little toe. Fig. 2(c) shows that if the needle is inserted even one centimeter away from the acupoint, there is no effect.

---

strument — the MRI scanner — whether a claimed acupoint actually stimulated the organs alleged to be connected to it. He asked a dozen acupuncturists to select a highly unusual acupoint. They chose the acupoint for stimulating the visual cortex. Figure 2 shows the results. When the visual cortex is stimulated by shining a light on the patient's eyes, the appropriate lobes of the brain light up in the MRI scan.

The specific acupoint for eye improvement is in the little toe of the right foot. When a needle was inserted in the acupoint, the same areas of the brain lit up (Fig. 3).

Moreover, the relationship was no accident, since when the acupoint was moved one-eighth to one-quarter of an inch, no effect was seen at all. Thus, the millennia-old data for the right choice of acupoint position for eye healing was categorically verified. But the data from acupuncture went further. The acupuncturists told the MRI operators that Yang and Yin patients might react differently. And as Fig. 4 shows, a totally unexpected feature was found: The secular variance of the MRI signals was 180 degrees phase shifted from each other for the Yin and Yang groups.

These preliminary results are arresting and will take a great deal of explaining for the radical skeptics. But what is by far the most

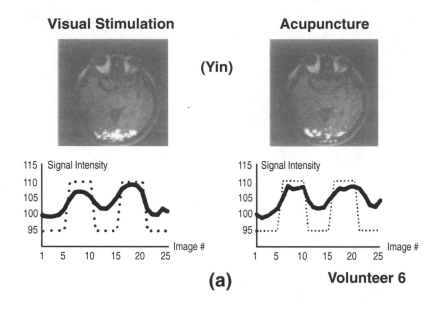

Fig. 3. The intensities of the direct visual and acupoint stimulation compared.

significant part of this study is the fact that when the authors, including very senior radiology professors of the University of California at Irvine, submitted the paper to *Science* and then to *Nature,* both journals rejected the paper *without review.* Even after Nobel laureates in medicine had reviewed and enthusiastically endorsed the paper, the journals refused to publish it. So much for the openness of establishment science to routine high-tech experimental science which in a minor way ruffles the edges of the paradigm. Certainly that also calls for an explanation.

QIGONG EXPERIMENTS IN CONDENSED MATTER SCIENCE

We turn now to a greater challenge to the paradigm in research on the changing of the atomic structure of liquids and solids and the increase in the kinetics of reactions by the chi-emissions by specific qigong masters. This research was conducted in China by senior Chinese scientists at major institutions such as Tsing-hua University and the Chinese Academy of Sciences. These high-powered physics laboratories report on the power of the chi-emission by Dr. Yan Xin,

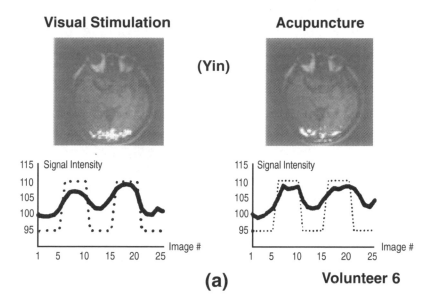

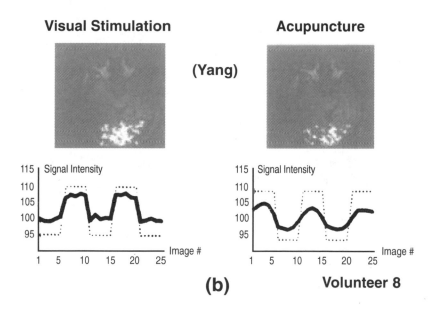

Fig. 4. Totally unsuspected information in all earlier MRI scans showing that people independently identified as Yin have the signal intensity 180 degrees out of phase with others identified as Yang, when stimulated by acupuncture.

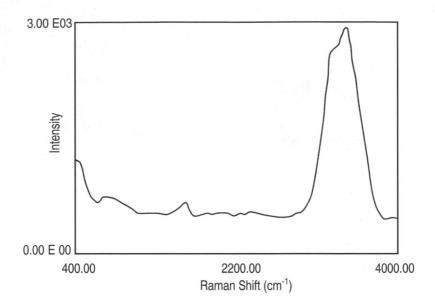

Fig. 5a. Raman spectrum of normal tap water.

widely recognized as one of the most deeply endowed qigong masters. I focus here only on one of several dozen experiments of which the results are not measured by the healing of humans, but *by modern scientific instruments*. If, in fact, Chinese "energy medicine" can heal humans, one could hypothesize that, in some way, the energy (chi) could change the body — its solids and liquids. Of course, the most important liquid in the body is water. Can a qigong master change the structure of water *as measured by an instrument?*

Figures 5a–5c show data on the Raman spectrum (a very common tool to characterize the structure of liquid water). Figure 5a shows the Raman spectrum of ordinary tap water with its broad emission at 2200 cm⁻¹. Figure 5b shows the same water after chi-emission: The peak has shifted by an enormous 1500 cm⁻¹. Figure 5c shows how the new structure decays back to the old in a couple of hours. It is also recorded that this effect involves no contact with the instrument by the healer; indeed, it can be done from a hundred meters away or even a thousand kilometers away. Obviously, I cannot certify the data's validity. Efforts are underway to repeat this experiment in my own laboratory. But dozens of similar experiments, including changing the

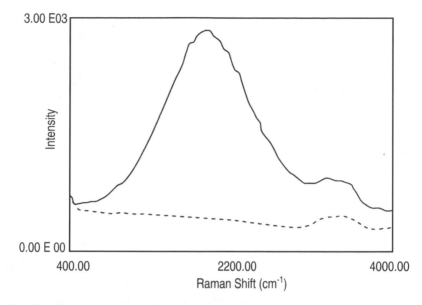

Fig. 5b. Raman spectrum of same sample of water after exposure to chi from Dr. Yan Xin. The chi can be applied at any distance, even a thousand kilometers.

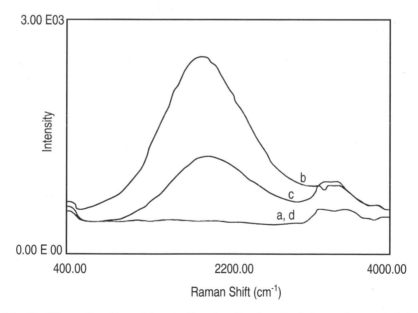

Fig. 5c. Slow relaxation of "excited" water structure back toward normal state in two to three hours.

plane of polarization in LiNbO3 crystals and bromination of hex-
ane, also are presented in this series of papers by well-established
Chinese colleagues. Every true scientist must await repetition and
confirmation, if only by the same practitioner, since it is not necessary that all practitioners be able to effect the same changes any
more than every basketball player can imitate Michael Jordan's
extraordinary feats.

In the paper and books cited on qigong studies, the interested
reader may find many fascinating reports. Only one hypothesis could
lead one to dismiss such hard data without respectful study, that is,
that a large number of well-respected Chinese professional colleagues
(some alumni of the best universities in the United States) are actively
forging data. I reject this hypothesis, and I am investigating the data
further.

I have presented only two examples of studies which claim to
"machine-verify" the plausibility of some of the contentions of traditional approaches to healing. There is an enormous range of such
fascinating examples. Especially in diagnosis, some of the records of
the capabilities of Tibetan Buddhist healers using no more than an
interview, checking of pulses, and smelling of urine are compelling.
The noninvasive nature of so many of these techniques should rec-
ommend them both on grounds of actual patient preference and on
the physicians' obedience to the "first law of Hippocrates" on doing
no harm. A fifteenth-century Middle Eastern physician gave as that
culture's goal for healing the following:

> To cure sometimes,
> To relieve often,
> To comfort always.

The Effect of the Rise of Wholism
on Science and Religion

As a senior scientist, a national-level science-policy planner, and one
simultaneously deeply involved in the U.S. religious scene, I have
had a unique vantage point to observe some of the most significant
effects of the turn to wholism and to the validity of personal experience, which are just starting to emerge. First, contrary to what

one picks up from casual observation and reading in the media, the world is turning *away* from the abstract, the disembodied, the virtual. It is, instead, redefining the real — as scanned not just by five but six senses. That sixth sense is intuition, the integration of the five senses with personal memory and consciousness. When it comes to deeply personal matters of love and life, virtual is out, real is in. High-tech is a flimsy salesword compared to high-touch. There are important reasons for this. First is the probable reality, only now being exposed to the public, of the "end of abstract (reductionist) science." That is the claim bolstered in several recent books, starting with my own *Experimenting with Truth*[4] in 1979; John Horgan, the editor of *Scientific American*, wrote the very successful *The End of Science*;[5] Jean Gimpel added *The End of the Future*[6] from Paris; Dan Sarewitz, in Washington, topped it off with *The Frontiers of Illusion*.[7] In my book, I quoted as the earliest detectors of the "End of Science" concept two very senior observers: Victor Weisskopf, head of physics at MIT and Director General of CERN, and Gunther Stent, famed biologist from Cal Tech. In the mid-1970s, Stent said: "Scientific knowledge, like our Universe, must be finite and the most significant laws of nature will soon have been discovered." He concluded "that progress as we have known it is nearing an end." In the same time frame, Weisskopf asserted,

> Very few scientists today would maintain that there are new fundamental principles to be discovered with regard to life or the other phenomena I have mentioned. Nonetheless there is today a general belief that the basic principles of the atomic world are known and no additional law or principle is necessary in order to explain the phenomena of the atomic realm, including the existence and development of life.

Science has been so successful in finding reasons and mechanisms to explain everything we do or experience that it has literally worked itself out of a job. We have all the theory we need to explain — at

---

4. Rustum Roy, *Experimenting with Truth* (Oxford: Pergamon Press, 1981).
5. John Horgan, *The End of Science* (New York: Addison-Wesley, 1996).
6. Jean Gimpel, *The End of the Future* (Westport, Conn.: Praeger, 1995).
7. David Sarewitz, *The Frontiers of Illusion* (Philadelphia, Pa.: Temple University Press, 1996).

the "body" level — everything we (99 percent of the world's citizens) experience or observe with our senses. No one claims that this "ending" applies in any way to the still unlimited opportunities for *applied* sciences and *engineering* of myriad kinds. That kind of "science" is not completed; it is not ending. The explanations and theories are saturated: observations, discoveries, and innovations are not. The proof of my assertion that no more such fundamental scientific discoveries — i.e., those which bear on *all* the neighboring and distant sciences — are likely, is empirical and obvious. The last major such fundamental scientific discovery was quantum mechanics, made seventy years ago. Since then, in spite of the fact that the world spends more money on such allegedly fundamental research in *every year* than it did in all of previous human history, nothing of comparable value has appeared. Why, then, do we expend tens of billions of dollars a year of *public funds* chasing such will-o'-the-wisps? This is the type of question the newly energized wholism-inspired public now must ask. Corporations worldwide — the private sector — have given their answer: They have simply abandoned such goal-less, curiosity-driven, reductionist science. One thousand CEOs cannot all be stupid. The theory of competitive advantage would demand that a few business leaders would break ranks, take the risks, and gain the prize. Their unanimity is a remarkable rebuke to those who insist that a nation's public funds should be devoted to this essentially futile endeavor.

Whole Person Religion

Finally, we come to the most important issue of all. While science, unknown to most of its practitioners, was a quintessentially reductionist enterprise, religion was its very opposite; quintessentially wholist — or was it? How does the new insight regarding the absolute significance of the *whole* affect our various religious worldviews? There are three separate dimensions to my answer.

First, unfortunately, a minority of fervent adherents, with their dogmas, their theories, and their abstractions, often bring obloquy on their own co-religionists. There are parallels here to the one-dimensional nature of abstract science. Many dogmatists act as though religion can be equated to theoretical *propositions* in the realm of the mind to which one must give assent. We use the term "orthodox" — literally "right dogma" — to describe what is supposed to be a standard brand of religion. Absurd, is it not? Religion, however, as even the etymology of the word shows, has much more to do with "binding" behavior, regulations, and actions, not simply with the acceptance of propositions. The Latin American liberation theologians' great contribution to Christian theology was that they stressed the equal importance of "orthopraxis" — right practice or behavior — and orthodoxy. So, true religion, whole person religion, cannot be demonstrated by its reductionist single dimension of dogma, but only in the wholist dogma-as-interpreted-in-practice. It is astonishing how the differences among religions become so much smaller using this wholist description. At the second World Parliament of Religions in Chicago in 1993, there was no new ecumenical "credo" drafted. It would be inconceivably difficult to reach such an agreement. But without too much difficulty, leaders of a hundred religious bodies agreed upon a common code of orthopraxis. Different "doxy," same "praxis." There, crystallized in a major social event, is the new hope. *The new wholist perspective avoids reductionist criteria.*

Second, while modern medicine focused only on the body, modern religion neglected the body. Although schoolboy maxims proclaim, *Mens sana* (and one could add, *et spiritus sanus*) *in corpore sano*, it is surely accurate to say that contemporary personal religion is too *disembodied.* No analogue of Hindu kundalini yoga is to be found in the West. Can one excite the spiritual to ecstasy via bodily stimulation? Here and there, new shoots of hope are appearing. The body is creeping back into religion. Several orders of Roman Catholic nuns have taken to using bodily massage as a way to bodily-mental-spiritual health. Yoga, tai chi, and qigong practices are becoming widespread throughout Western populations, although the spiritual connection is often underplayed. Sexuality and spirituality is almost as popular an organizing theme as science and spirituality.

Finally, we turn to the conundrum, manifest in the Chicago declaration mentioned above, which appears to baffle those who cannot imagine how different religions, with different, even clashing dogmas, can be part of the same whole. I dealt with this extensively in my book *Experimenting with Truth,* from which Figs. 6 and 7 are taken. The wholist approach to religion is to accept that all human approaches to ultimate transcendent questions must, *of necessity,* be limited. Each person, each culture, each tradition brings intrinsically limited per-

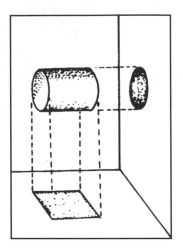 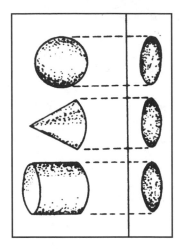

Fig. 6. Viktor Frankl's simple proof that any solid object, if viewed from only one direction, can present an inaccurate picture of the whole solid body.

spectives to dogmas about reality. (Figure 6 is Viktor Frankl's simple illustration showing how easily one can get an incorrect or partial perception of a solid by looking at it from only one direction.)[8]

Figure 7 is my own effort to show how a three-dimensional wholist religion might look from the different historical and cultural perspectives of our separate major religions.[9]

This simple exercise shows that the many different religions, whose dogmas differ, are the very proof of wholeness in a higher dimension of reality. Indeed, there is no conflict whatsoever between believers in different religions who see their religions as the accurate and true view of ultimate reality for them from their personal, historical, and geographical perspectives. The apparent conflicts arise only among those who claim — in true reductionist fashion — that their perspective is the only one, or the only true one. Among these religions, modern science stands out today as the principal *religion* belonging to this dogmatic, exclusivistic, reductionist stance. Many others, which certainly also claimed in earlier times such exclusive hegemony over

8. Viktor Frankl, in *Experimenting with Truth*, ed. Rustum Roy (Oxford: Pergamon Press, 1981), 93.

9. Rustum Roy, in ibid., 131.

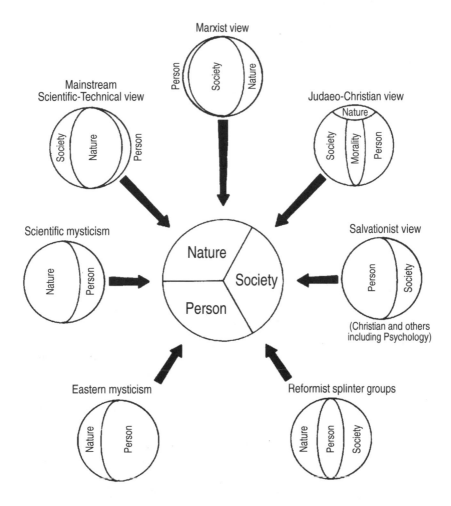

Fig. 7. The same three-dimensional sphere of reality, when viewed from different cultural perspectives, looks very different. The radical pluralist expects such differences, knowing that the reality of the whole is the same, although it appears very different to individuals from their necessarily limited and narrow perspective (see Fig. 6.)

truth and reality, have softened their stands. Some have accepted the genius of the concept of radical pluralism.

My friend Raimundo Panikkar first coined the term "radical pluralism" for this philosophical stance. It claims that reality, which must of course be totally internally consistent, can be viewed from different humans' perspectives to produce views which differ substantially from one another. The radical pluralist celebrates these differences because they reveal a richer and wider whole. What is also very important, as demonstrated at the Chicago Parliament of Religions, is that these different dogmatic views, when separately translated into praxis, are very consist with each other. In other words, when different *dogmatic stances* are translated into *practice,* the three-dimensional views converge.

Human Limitations and the Wholist Ortho-Praxis-Doxy

My final thoughts are on the very real problem faced by millions of citizens brought up in traditional, more exclusive faith structures, but now slowly moving to wholist perspectives. How does one live as a pluralist — eat, drink, work, and care about friends, other persons, and causes — aware of the many radically different viewpoints? Life is too short and our abilities too limited to simultaneously encompass even one or two religious postures and *live them out.* Moreover, the most significant quality of religion is *depth* of understanding, *depth* of commitment, *depth* of action. My own existential insight on this has come from the German terms *standbein* and *spielbein,* meaning "standing leg" and "playing leg." These refer to the fact that when we stand, we put most of our weight on one leg, the "standing leg." Then the other is free to play around, to move, even kick — that is the "playing leg"! So, a wholist person needs to deploy two religious legs in life: to build a standing leg of *depth in one tradition,* but to exercise the playing leg extensively to search out other views, other perspectives, and to increase balance and range by so doing.

Finally, the whole I allude to is seen by and made manifest only in a human person. It is, therefore, completely appropriate to call this emerging worldview "Whole *Person* Religion."

Chapter 7

CREATION SPIRITUALITY
The Deep Past and the Deep Future
of Christianity

Matthew Fox

MATTHEW FOX, a postmodern theologian, encourages enlightened treatment of ourselves, each other, and nature. He is dedicated to reviving the tradition of creation spirituality in a movement aimed at blending the wisdom of Western spirituality and the world's indigenous cultures with emerging scientific understanding and art's passionate creativity. Dr. Fox maintains that a "Theology of Spirit" was central to the earliest tradition of the Hebrew Bible and later to the mystics of medieval Europe. He teaches that a reawakening of such creation spirituality can help to revitalize religion and culture, build esteem for the insight of women, celebrate the hope of youth, and advance social and ecological justice. Cultivation of personal wholeness, planetary survival, and universal interdependence are the three primary goals Dr. Fox sets for revived creation spirituality. He holds master's degrees in philosophy and theology from Aquinas Institute and a doctorate in spirituality from the Institut Catholique de Paris. Dr. Fox is founder (1996) and president of the University of Creation Spirituality in Oakland, California, and author of twenty-three books, including *Original Blessing; A Spirituality Named Compassion; Breakthrough: Meister Eckhart's Creation Spirituality in New Translation;* and *Natural Grace* (with Rupert Sheldrake). He received the Body Mind Spirit Award of Excellence for outstanding books in print, first in 1996 for *The Reinvention of Work* and again in 1997 for *Confessions: The Making of a Post-Denominational Priest.* Among other honors, he shares with the Dalai Lama, Mother Teresa, Ernesto Cardenal, and Rosa Parks the distinction of having received the Courage of Conscience Award of the Peace Abbey of Sherborn, Mass.

IN THIS ESSAY, I wish to do three things: (1) sketch a future for Christianity based on creation spirituality principles, (2) consider the "deep past" of the twelfth-century renaissance in the Western church, and (3) hold up one example of the "deep past" in an Anglican theologian (one among many) who was deeply creation centered, namely, George Herbert.

Without an awareness of periods when our ancestors lived out an alternative Christianity, we will condemn ourselves to nostalgia or, what is worse, to living superficially and with no support from history. The purpose of holding up Herbert is to demonstrate how steeped the Anglican tradition is in creation spirituality, and this at a time — the modern era — when society as a rule wished to relegate religion to the psychological sphere.[1] This resistance on the part of Herbert (and Richard Hooker and others) demonstrates the alternative to fundamentalist and imperialistic Christianity with its accompanying colonial and patriarchal mentality — a mentality that still plays itself out in religious circles. The future ought to grow in some way out of our past; it ought to come from our ancestors — not all of it, of course, but enough of it to be able to invoke that much-abused source of revelation, "tradition." Without a sense of our "deep past," we are set up for fundamentalism or a *superficial present*.

Elements for a Deep Future among Followers of Jesus

What are some elements that will guarantee a "Deep Future" for followers of Jesus and the Christ? What will bring about an authentic renaissance in our time? What movements are afoot to usher in a healthy third millennium of Jesus followers? Where are signs of hope? I offer ten such signs of our times below.

1. Following the Historical Jesus as Set Forth in the Conclusions of the Quest for the Historical Jesus

For two hundred years, scholars have been seeking the actual words of Jesus in the early literature of Jesus followers. In our time, that effort has reached a quite significant and happy culmination. While the numbers of words and stories attributed to Jesus have been cut drastically, we, nevertheless, can begin to truly understand who this man was and what he stood for. He was a Middle Eastern sage in

---

1. Even John Locke, who was ahead of his time in so many other ways, succumbs to this privatizing of religion when he writes: "The only business of the church is the salvation of souls." And he individualizes the soul profoundly when he declares, "The care of each man's soul . . . is left entirely to every man's self." See John Horton and Susan Mendus, eds., *John Locke: A Letter concerning Toleration in Focus* (New York: Routledge, 1991), 34 and 44.

the manner of the cynic philosophers (who were not philosophers of cynicism!) who wandered about preaching, teaching, and observing. He stood on behalf of the poor and raised searching questions that were dangerous both to the Roman authorities who occupied his land against the will of his people and to some of his own Jewish tribe. He was killed because of his teachings. He questioned the suppositions in his culture regarding family and women, sexuality, economics, and political authority. His refrain about the "coming of the domain of God" was a clever but deliberate attempt to tweak the Roman Empire's presumption that it was the only domain that counted.

Another liberation that comes our way, thanks to the historical Jesus scholarship, is the clear demarcation between Paul and Jesus. Paul was a theologian. He translated his experience of the Jesus event, deriving from his mystical encounter with the Christ and from stories passed on from people who knew him (since Paul did not know him). Paul used his own vocabulary and related the Christ of whom he had gained knowledge to the issues of his cultural and religious era. Paul was a master at this, no doubt. But he made mistakes. Just three examples: his support of slavery, his negative teaching about homosexuals, and his put-down of the flesh. (Jesus did not support slavery, condemn homosexuals, or put down the flesh.) Like Paul, we, too, must theologize out of the Jesus and the Christ experience and apply the teachings therein to the issues of our time and culture. But we are no longer condemned to repeating Paul's mistakes.

2. Ushering in the Cosmic Christ and the New Cosmology

John Dominic Crossan, one of the Jesus Seminar scholars, ends his book *Jesus: A Revolutionary Biography* with the following quote from the historian Eusebius's *Life of Constantine,* which describes the Council of Nicea. Let us recall how that council, by declaring Jesus Christ the exclusive son of God, killed the Cosmic Christ Christology and distorted the teachings of the gospel, namely, that we are all God's sons and daughters.

Detachments of the bodyguard and troops surrounded the entrance of the palace with drawn swords, and through the midst of them the men of God proceeded without fear into the innermost of the Imperial apartments, in which some were the Emperor's companions at table, while others reclined on couches arranged on either side. One might have thought that a picture of Christ's Kingdom was thus shadowed forth, and a dream rather than reality.[2]

The era of dogmatic Christology had wandered far from the work and words of the historical Jesus and from the time of Christians being persecuted by an arrogant empire. The setting in which the Cosmic Christ theology was displaced by the Imperial Christology is not credible to followers of Jesus today. It has supported the builders of a Christian empire. Is this not fair warning of the price we have paid and might still pay for a Christianity that ignores the historical Jesus?

To take the historical Jesus seriously is not to ignore Christology but to deconstruct and reconstruct it around the Cosmic Christ, which is, after all, the biblically based Christology. Imperial Christology and exaggerated roles of Christ as King have been perpetrated by empire builders from Constantine to Augustine to many popes and Jerry Falwell — but we must not allow this poisoning of the Christ experience to taint all our experiences of the Christ. Indeed, Christians who do not experience the Christ cannot be Christians. Is this not the meaning of Paul's invocation of the resurrection experience? To experience the Christ is to experience the risen Christ — which always includes experiencing the wounds that he bears in his being and ours.

The creation spirituality tradition finds the Christ in nature — including our own human nature. Nature is not just the earth at this moment of evolution; it is *all of nature* in all time and space, i.e., the universe. Interestingly, this was the consciousness in the twelfth century as well. Scotus Erigena wrote that "universitas means God and creation."[3] Today's word for "universitas" is "cosmology." The work done by Thomas Berry and Brian Swimme[4] and others like Arne Wyller[5] on the new creation story from science is essential work for rediscovering the Cosmic Christ experience. It is no less significant for faith than is the work of the historical Jesus scholars.

---

2. John Dominic Crossan, *Jesus: A Revolutionary Biography* (San Francisco: HarperSanFrancisco, 1994), 201.

3. John the Scot, *De Divina Natura*, ii.1.

4. Thomas Berry and Brian Swimme, *The Universe Story* (San Francisco: HarperSanFrancisco, 1992).

5. Arne Wyller, *The Planetary Mind* (Aspen, Colo.: Macmurray & Beck, 1996).

3. Trusting Our Experience of the Cosmic Christ

Coming into the knowledge of Christ is always an experience. Just as those who met the historical Jesus had their experience of him, so those who did not had their experience of the Christ. (Paul would, of course, be in this group.) Having found more or less the words of the historical Jesus (in the Gospel of Thomas as well as in other writings), we are freed up to recognize several realities about the first century's response to the Jesus event. One is that the early followers of Jesus were tremendously *creative* and *trusted their own experience of the Christ*. The fact that they did not hesitate to put words into Jesus' mouth is not to me an embarrassment at all: It is a "Wow! What chutzpah!" What trust of their own mystical experience that they put words into Jesus' mouth that they wished he had said or presumed he had said. This hypercreativity holds for all four gospels, with John more or less taking the cake. (Six centuries later, the Celts would do the same when they composed, for example, their "I am" poems about God.)[6] Mysticism is about experience; until we learn to trust our mystical experiences as the writers of the gospels did and our Celtic ancestors did, we will not be living out of our depths as followers of the Christ.

4. Retrieving the Sacred Feminine, Creativity, and the Goddess

Protestant cultural critic Henry Adams, whose life was forever changed by his encounter with the Goddess at Chartres Cathedral in the late nineteenth century, compared the "iron horse" mentality of that century to the mentality that surrounded the "dynamo of the Virgin" that so drove the imaginations of the twelfth century. A postmodern consciousness will make room for a return of the Goddess and the Sacred Feminine in her many forms including Gaia, Mary,

---

6. From "The Black Book of Carmarthen," an ancient Welsh work, we read the following "I am" poem called simply, "God":

> I am the wind that breathes upon the sea,
> I am the wave on the ocean,
> I am the murmur of leaves rustling,
> I am the rays of the sun,
> I am the beam of the moon and stars,
> I am the power of trees growing,
> I am the bud breaking into blossom,
> I am the movement of the salmon swimming.

See Robert Van de Weyer, *Celtic Fire* (London: Darton, Longman and Todd, 1990), 92.

Love, Eros, Compassion, Divine Mother, Black Madonna, Wisdom, Sheiknah, Green Man, and more. I shall elaborate on this movement as it emerged in the twelfth century at greater length below.

Like the twelfth-century renaissance, ours will be inspired by much of the Goddess rediscovery of our time. The return of creativity understood as the true *imago dei* (or *imago deitatis*) in us all is part of this. So, too, is a reappreciation of our relation with all of nature (the return of the Green Man archetype is part of this revival);[7] the ecological struggle is a spiritual as well as a political-economic struggle in our day.

5. Deep Ecology

Our relationship with nature has been profoundly affected by anthropocentrism and the psychologizing of religion in the modern era as well as by the misuse of human imagination and creativity to serve the idols of modern technological war machines and corporations. A return to the sense of the sacredness of all our relations and of the inherent rights that beings other than the human possess will go far to heal our planet and to inspire spiritual warriors to reunderstand the prophetic call as one of interfering with ecocide, biocide, and speciescide. No religion that remains anthropocentric and preoccupied with human salvation alone will be able to lay claim in the next century to being in any way a solution rather than part of the problem of the sickness of our planet.

6. Practicing Deep Ecumenism

The return of Sophia, Lady Wisdom, and the Cosmic Christ is always a return to an attitude of universalism. Wisdom in the scriptures is not sectarian any more than she is elitist. She "calls aloud in the streets" (Prov. 1:20) and "holds sway over every people and nation" (Sir. 24:6). She "deploys her strength from one end of the earth to the other" (Wisd. 8:1) and works everywhere. She is the "designer of all" (Wisd. 8:5, 6).[8] Thus, deep ecumenism is an essential sign of our times — as it was in the twelfth and thirteenth centuries when

---

7. See William Anderson and Clive Hicks, *Green Man: The Archetype of Our Oneness with the Earth* (San Francisco: HarperCollins, 1990).

8. See Susan Cady, Marian Ronan, and Hal Taussig, *Wisdom's Feast: Sophia in Study and Celebration* (San Francisco: Harper & Row, 1986), and also Matthew Fox, *The Coming of the Cosmic Christ* (San Francisco: HarperSanFrancisco, 1989).

Islam and Christianity rubbed shoulders so closely. (People often forget how Francis of Assisi went to Arab lands to convert the sultan to Christianity. What happened? Francis converted no one; instead, he came back dancing whirling dervish dances.)

Religion's future is not in religion nor in denominationalism — yet traditions have their place so long as they are spelled with a small "t" and not a large "T." We must recover the *essences* of our various faith traditions and let the superficialities go. The essence will invariably have to do with teaching ways of living in harmony with self, others, the more-than-human, and the source of it all. The essence has to do with gratitude, awe, wonder, creativity, courage, justice, celebration, and compassion.

The work of the United Religions movement, begun by Bishop William Swing of California, is a living example of this quest for deep ecumenism, reaching into an effort to reconnect faith traditions that have been abysmally narrow and particularized for too long. All efforts *to find common ground* together (Howard Thurman's happy phrase)[9] are the heart of the matter: notice, common *ground,* not common superficialities. But to find common ground, we must be in touch with the grounding of our faith — with the mystical and prophetic charisms of our traditions. These are found more in practices such as meditation and ritual and struggle for justice than in theory or in the head.

7. Renewing Education

The forms in which we are conducting education today are not adequate. The wineskins are leaking. This is true of child *and* adult education. One would hope for a revitalization of education in our time; maybe some spiritually based schools will launch that movement. Only a reawakening to the Christ of the universe can bring the universe back to the university.

An intellectual life can combine handily with a creative/intuitive one so that the new cosmology as well as ancient ways of prayer, ritual, and ceremony can be taught in a setting that honors both right and left brain, mind and body, soul and spirit; education of *all seven chakras* — including and especially our lower ones. Clearly, this is

---

9. See Howard Thurman, *The Search for Common Ground* (Richmond, Ind.: Friends United Press, 1986).

our intention at our University of Creation Spirituality in downtown Oakland. In the twenty-three years of designing and implementing our master's program in Creation Spirituality, which is now part of the Naropa Institute in Oakland, we have learned the value of combining right and left hemispheres for learning. Our pedagogy relies heavily on artists who teach art as meditation (not how to produce objets d'art). This, combined with indigenous teachings, science, and the Western mystical and prophetic tradition, demonstrates that this kind of educational renaissance is not only possible but sustainable, and fun and serious at the same time. If Dr. Leonard Shlain's thesis is correct, that the Goddess was banished by the coming of the alphabet,[10] then there will be no authentic replacement of patriarchy's undue influence in academia without a rush of image awakening, art-as-meditation opportunities for students. This can and is being accomplished in education at UCS, at least. Rabbi Abraham Heschel has said that "education must be of the soul as well as of the mind." It is time.

8. Awakening Worship

It is also time for a renewal of worship. A new cosmology and the return of the Cosmic Christ can bring life back to worship. Worship by definition is a marrying of microcosm and macrocosm, psyche and universe. It is not for the faint of heart. Worship's purpose ought to be to enlarge our hearts ("courage," a large heart). Joy makes hearts enlarge. Then they break in grief and get even larger if the grief is dealt well with through healthy ritual and worship. Creativity follows and then compassion flows through creativity.[11]

Just as the twelfth century awakened the pent-up creativity that resulted in five hundred cathedrals being built in a 125-year period (each one dedicated to the Goddess in Christianity, Mary), so today we need not buildings called cathedrals but worship spaces and forms wherein the Goddess can return on her throne ushering in a celebration of life. The late feminist archeologist Marija Gimbutas said that the essence of the Goddess civilization was "the celebration of life."

---

10. Leonard Shlain, *The Alphabet versus the Goddess: The Conflict between Word and Image* (New York: Viking, 1998).

11. Andrew Harvey, in his new book, *Son of Man: The Mystical Path to Christ* (New York: Harmony Books, 1998), is an excellent example of someone finally combining the two strands — the prophetic energy of the historical Jesus as we know him today with the mystical dimension of the Cosmic Christ and, as Harvey explicates, the Cosmic Mary.

We can do this awakening to the celebration of life within our own tradition by deconstructing and reconstructing it with the help of today's postmodern language of multimedia, computers, techno music, deejaying, rave dancing, community building, new art forms such as rap, and by *mixing* music of many genera. The Anglican Church, with its respect for a liturgical tradition, on the one hand, but its willingness to support new forms, on the other, is particularly well situated to usher in this revolution. Reconstructed worship represents a nonviolent revolution that has seldom if ever been attempted. Now is the time, because the younger generation — one might call this the first postmodern generation — is not settling for sitting in pews to be lectured at or read to. (A Chicago priest I know tells me that if you go to a Catholic church in Chicago today, you will see no one there under forty-four years of age.) But this same young generation is staying up all night dancing trance dances at rave parties. They are eager to experience trance, i.e., transcendence. They bring much to the liturgical table with their experience at community celebration. The University of Creation Spirituality has been sponsoring Techno Cosmic Masses for three years, with the support of Bishop Swing in Oakland — and the response to them is evidence that this experience in worship is, indeed, sustainable.

9. Recovery of Our Celtic Roots

Many Westerners are totally ignorant of their Celtic heritage, which is profoundly creation-based in its spirituality when it is true to itself. I sometimes believe that the Celts are the only Westerners who understood Jesus' teachings properly. They never forgot the Cosmic Christ and never sacrificed it to empire building in the name of an imperial ("Only this Christ saves") Christianity. It is the creation-centered Celtic expression of Christianity that so influenced the development of creation theology in the West. The theology of John Erigena (also known as John the Scot) profoundly affected thinkers of medieval Europe. The settlement of Celtic missionaries along the Rhineland and into northern Italy bequeathed to us the spiritual brilliance of Hildegard of Bingen, Francis of Assisi, Thomas Aquinas, Mechthild of Magdeburg, Meister Eckhart, Nicolas of Cusa. The fact that Celtic Christianity never abandoned the Cosmic Christ, never sold its soul to empire-building Christian enterprises, never bought into St. Augustine's introspective conscience, and never fell for sexism or its body/

soul dualism or the story of how Celtic Christianity went East for its architecture and much of its theology gives us hints of how to refresh our spiritual ancestry. The profound revival happening today in Celtic awareness is a sign of our times and a very hopeful one at that.

10. Developing an Urban Spirituality

Currently, for the first time in human history, over 50 percent of our species is living in cities. All indications are that this number will swell in the next fifty years — so much so that by the mid-twenty-first century, over 80 percent of humanity will be dwelling in cities. What kind of life will people have? What kind of life will they give birth to? How can we find spirit and spirituality in our city lives now and in the future? How does the Goddess assert herself in a city context? What is the role of the artist in awakening spirit in the city and among city dwellers? What kinds of worship experiences can assist us to be better neighbors and deeper citizens? What are the unique art forms being born in our cities and how do we integrate them with our traditional liturgical practices? How do we make our cities livable, green, sustainable, and celebratory? All these issues need to be addressed in the Christian church of the future. They form the basis of a course we teach each year at the Naropa Institute's program in creation spirituality at our university in Oakland. Nature, after all, *is* the city insofar as humans are nature, and humans give birth to cities only through the gifts of nature, be they rubber trees (tires for our automobiles) or fossil remains (gasoline), steel and glass, concrete and wood — they were all nature at one time.

The purpose of education and of worship is to train people in their mysticism and their prophecy, that is, in their capacity for joy and contemplation and for struggle toward justice, compassion, and liberation. To do this is to follow Jesus anew and the best of the Christo-centric activists who followed in his footsteps over the centuries, whom we invoke as our ancestors in the communion of saints. To recover this outlook, we must reconnect to that oldest of biblical traditions, the creation spirituality tradition. This is the tradition that Jesus knew — it is the wisdom tradition of Israel — and the historical Jesus is once again understood as deriving from this tradition. It is also the tradition of the Rhineland mystics, so deeply influenced by the Celtic spiritual path.

I believe that the key to Christianity in the twenty-first century will be the letting go of the path chosen by the mainstream, imperial Christianity of sixteen centuries ago (Augustine and Constantine), which I call the fall/redemption religion, and the building of Christianity on the biblical path of creation spirituality. The former was patriarchal, dualistic, antimatter, anthropocentric, original sin–obsessed, pessimistic, empire-building, and suspicious of sexuality. Creation spirituality, which is far older than fall/redemption religion, is feminist, mystical (nondualistic), deeply ecumenical, cosmologically based, hopeful, creative, liberation-oriented and involved, and recognizing of sexuality as blessing and of sexual experience as theophanic.

To call for a return to creation spirituality is, in many ways, to call for Christianity to let go of its flirtation with and, indeed, indebtedness to fundamentalism. Because knowing something of the deep past assists us to go beyond the superficial present, I shall now examine faith in two eras when the church was creation centered: the twelfth century and the seventeenth century, focusing in this latter period on the work of George Herbert.

The Deep Past of the Twelfth-Century Renaissance

In that most dynamic of European centuries, the twelfth, a huge happening was unfolding culturally and spiritually. There was a profound coming apart, one might say a deconstruction, of the previous cultural and religious era, which was marked by stability, land-based economics, a hierarchical feudal system, monastic education and religious control, and patriarchal defensiveness that ranged from knights defending the castles to Michael, the soldier archangel, and the rocky cliff with its tides defending the monastery at Mont-Saint-Michel. All this was superseded in the twelfth and early thirteenth centuries by a renaissance that the great French historian M. D. Chenu, O.P., called "the only renaissance that succeeded in the West."[12] This renaissance, this rebirth of culture based on a spiritual vision, occurred at all levels of society and culture, including agriculture.

A warming of the climate of Europe made for an easier and longer growing season. The population increased considerably with the re-

---

12. See M. D. Chenu, *Nature, Man and Society in the Twelfth Century* (Chicago: University of Chicago Press, 1968).

sult that pressure built on the amount of land and work that the feudal system could support. The consequence was a great number of disenfranchised serfs and young people who were destined to inherit little or nothing from the manor. The crusades had emptied Europe of some of its most able knights and lords who were off fighting God knew where. One effect was that more and more women were left home to run things and make important decisions. The travel bug caught up with many a crusader and with it more and more foreign influence flowed into Europe. The intellectual life had been building for some time through Spain, where the Islamic culture had such a stronghold that the Muslims' vast (and advanced) commitment to learning and translating works from Greece, Persia, and India began finally to make itself felt in Europe via Spain.

Increasing numbers of disenfranchised youth fled from land to towns, and soon these towns grew into cities. Universities were invented with the University of Paris being the first, and, within thirty years, eighty universities had been established around Europe. This took the power and control of education away from the monastic establishment, which stayed in the countryside for the most part. Cathedrals were also established in the cities, which took the power and control of worship away from the monastic establishment that was so wrapped up in the feudal hierarchy that one chronicler of the time said "the abbots are even richer than the bishops." Cathedrals were meant to be the symbol of the rising spiritual tide of the return of the Goddess, who was recognized as the "Dame of Nature" (Alan of Lille). *Cathedra* means "throne" in Latin, and the cathedral was the throne where the Goddess sat ruling the universe with compassion and wisdom. (The modern age did its reductionist trip on this tradition by assuring us that the throne of the cathedral is reserved for a bishop — until very recently a male bishop. Thus, the Goddess lost out to anthropocentrism, patriarchy, and clericalism.) As the "Seat of Wisdom," she ruled over the university's search for truth. She was seen as the defender of the poor and powerless and the giver of life and its pleasures.

The creating of lifestyles also figured prominently in this renaissance, including the many movements of communal living which accommodated an awakening of sexual freedom and experimentation. Indeed, as the late Yale historian John Boswell demonstrated, for over 125 years, homosexuality was not condemned but allowed and confessed to by some of the most prominent bishops and abbots and even declared saints of the period.[13] Communal movements were very gender-conscious and often rotated leadership between men and women, while the members gathered to serve one another. Francis of Assisi, in many respects, borrowed the inspiration for his brotherhood from these communal movements, which he knew intimately from his travels with his merchant father.

Otto Rank has said that, if you want to know the soul of a culture, go to its architecture. An architectural renaissance was in full flowering in the twelfth century. What made this renaissance work was the influx of the Goddess as depicted in the Gothic inventions of light-dominated architecture of the time. Henry Adams's classic work, *Mont-Saint-Michel and Chartres*,[14] points out the tremendous spiritual and cultural revolution that was at stake in the move from the squat, defensive, and thick Romanesque architecture of the feudal era, such as Mont-Saint-Michel, to the light-aspiring, lofty, upreaching, nature-based (because the church pillars were like forest trees and the stained glass like light coming through the woods) Gothic invention. Clearly, the twelfth-century renaissance was nothing less than a birth of a new kind of soul: one that was more feminine and less excessively masculine, more trusting and less security-addicted, more youthful and less tired and cynical (Adams says one must become "prematurely young" to enter the twelfth century), more creative and less staid, more light-filled and less defensive, more willing to take chances than the era that preceded it.

Intellectually, the great gift of Islam, in addition to translations of Aristotle and others, was the gift of scholasticism. Scholasticism, which subsequent modern ideologies have ridiculed, was, in fact, a radical new methodology that allowed intellectual life to awaken because it substituted arguments from reason for the theological argument from *authority*. Because of this, scholasticism has rightly been called the precursor of modern science. *Sic et Non* (Yes and No) was Peter Abelard's great and influential work in the first generation at the University of Paris. The title alone well captures the intellectual

---

13. John Boswell, *Christianity, Social Tolerance, and Homosexuality* (Chicago: University of Chicago Press, 1980).

14. Henry Adams, *Mont-Saint-Michel and Chartres* (New York: Doubleday Anchor, 1959). See also R. P. Blackmur, *Henry Adams* (New York: Harcourt Brace Jovanovich, 1980).

ferment of his time and place. The human mind was beginning to be
trusted to debate and make judgments about Yes and No. Thomas
Aquinas, working out of the same scholastic methodology fifty years
later, would say that authority is the "least" important of arguments
for a case. This displacing of authority (such as the church fathers)
with reason fed the fuel in the university's fight with the monastic
theological establishment.

One of the elements in the battle of the old theological guard
against the new was the language of Christianity itself. Members of
the new movements absolutely rejected the word "Christendom," ex-
punging it from their very vocabulary. For to them, "Christendom"
represented the church's sellout to the political and economic systems that they found so oppressive. It represented the Constantinian
church, the church allied with the empire, and they would have nothing to do with it. Instead, they espoused the "apostolic life," meaning
a return to the gospels and their values as found in the life and teachings of Jesus. They returned to the historical Jesus in *praxis,* not just
in textual studies. Both the Franciscan and the Dominican movements
tapped into this spirit at their inceptions. They insisted on bypassing
centuries of Christendom's alliances with the elites of this world.[15]

I have presented this swift overview of the twelfth-century spiritual
and cultural awakening because I believe it gives us some perspective on the current ecclesial situation and the historical period in
which we find ourselves. Like our twelfth-century brothers and sisters
(Hildegard, Abelard, and Francis of Assisi, to name a few), we have
options. A strong fundamentalist wing, eager to relive the past, hung
on in the twelfth century. But pioneers like Hildegard, Abelard, and
Francis made decisions to move beyond the world of Christendom
and to ally themselves with different and younger people with visions
of hope and liberation. Just as the term "Christendom" was unacceptable to many in that era, so today many of us have trouble even with
the word "Christianity." It simply carries too much baggage with it,
not only from the past but also from current spokespersons such as the
Jerry Falwells, Pat Robertsons, and others who equate their projec-
tions with the teachings of Christ and appropriate to themselves the
exclusive title of "Christian." When one examines fall/redemption
religion, one finds fundamentalism. In many respects, the creation

---

15. See Chenu, *Nature, Man and Society in the Twelfth Century,* 202–69.

spirituality tradition is the direct opposite of fundamentalism, as the reformers of the twelfth and thirteenth centuries realized. The first sixteenth-century Anglican theologian, Richard Hooker, drawing heavily as he did on Thomas Aquinas, was far from being fundamentalist. Indeed, he took on the Puritans of his day with arguments similar to Aquinas's about nature being a source of revelation.[16]

The Deep Past in the Anglican Tradition: Creation Spirituality in the Work of George Herbert

Is there a tradition in Anglicanism of creation spirituality? Indeed, there is. I have chosen to concentrate on the writings of George Herbert (1593–1633) as a representative of the Anglican tradition. It is amazing that he accomplished both the quantity and the quality of work he did in only three years in the priesthood, while experiencing much physical pain. I find in his work deep echoes of wisdom theology and of mystics such as Hildegard of Bingen, Francis of Assisi, Thomas Aquinas, Meister Eckhart, Teresa of Avila, John of the Cross, Friedrich Nietzsche, and Ranier Maria Rilke. While other creation spirituality authors abound in the Anglican tradition, such as Richard Hooker and Thomas Traherne to mention just two, I would like to explore Herbert in some depth rather than trip only lightly through other writers. My methodology will be to ask the following question: Does George Herbert explore the Four Paths and Twenty-Six themes of creation spirituality?[17] Might these paths and themes assist us in appreciating the spiritual tradition from which he came and his own special contribution to that tradition? If these paths are clear in Herbert, then this would seem to suggest that he represents still

---

16. Hooker writes: "The light of nature is a necessary background for the understanding of Holy Scripture" (John S. Marshall, *Hooker's Polity in Modern English* [Sewanee, Tenn.: The University Press at the University of the South, 1948], 49). Since "God must be glorified in all things, ... it is their [the Puritans] error to think that the only law which God hath appointed unto man in that behalf is the sacred Scripture. By that which we work naturally, as when we breathe, sleep, move, we show forth the glory of God as natural agents do" (Richard Hooker, *Of the Laws of Ecclesiastical Polity: Preface, Book I, Book VIII* [Cambridge: Cambridge University Press, 1989], 124). Hooker equates "law" with "creation" and with wisdom (ibid., 60, 56f.). Hooker, like Aquinas and unlike fundamentalists, has a cosmology and a sense of panentheism which he calls a "mutual participation" of God in us and us in God and a "general indwelling" (Marshall, *Hooker's Polity*, 75f.).

17. See Matthew Fox, *Original Blessing: Primer in Creation Spirituality* (Santa Fe: Bear & Co., 1983).

another foundation of creation spirituality in the Anglican tradition
of spirituality.

Via Positiva (Path 1)

Under the Via Positiva, we would expect to find treatment of themes
like Dabhar, Blessing, Cosmology, Delight, Grace, Awe, Praise, Ongoing Creation, and Gratitude.[18] Herbert does indeed speak to these
topics. Regarding Dabhar, all beings as words of God, we read:

> I, who had heard of music in the spheres,
> But not of speech in stars, began to muse:
> But turning to God, whose ministers
> The stars and all things are;...[19]

He sees nature as a "book about God," as Meister Eckhart put it:

> Indeed the world's thy book,
> Where all things have their leaf assign'd:
> Yet a meek look
> Hath interlin'd.
> Thy board is full, yet humble guests
> Find nests. (274f.)

He celebrates the human as microcosm within the macrocosm and
as connected to the universe, much as Hildegard of Bingen saw it in
the twelfth century:

> For Man is ev'ry thing,
> And more: He is a tree, yet bears more fruit;...
> Man is all symmetry
> Full of proportions, one limb to another,
> And all to all the world besides:
> Each part may call the farthest, brother:
> For head with foot hath private amity,
> And both with moons and tides....
> His eyes dismount the highest star:
> He is in little all the sphere.

---

18. Ibid., 35–139.
19. John N. Wall, Jr., ed., *George Herbert: The Country Parson, The Temple* (New York:
Paulist, 1981), 263. Subsequent references from Herbert's works will be from this edition.

Herbs gladly cure our flesh; because that they
Find their acquaintance there.

For us the winds do blow,
The earth doth rest, heav'n move, and fountains flow.
Nothing we see, but means our good,
As our *delight,* or as our *treasure:*
The whole is, either our cupboard of *food,*
or Cabinet of *pleasure.*

The stars have us to bed;
Night draws the curtain, which the sun withdraws;
Music and light attend our head.
All things unto our *flesh* are kind
In their *descent* and *being;* to our *mind*
In their ascent and cause. (209f.)

Here, Herbert is writing of cosmology (his multiple references to "all things" indicates this), and he resists the introverted psychology of modern theologians like Ignatius and even Donne. He also reveals a sense of cosmology, or "the whole," when he writes: "thousands of things do thee employ / In ruling all" (283). God is the ruler of *all,* i.e., the whole.

Herbert writes of blessing when he claims that "nothing we see but means our *good,*" and when he says, "Creatures are good and have their place / Sin only, which did all deface / Thou drivest from his seat" (327). Herbert surely has a theology of original blessing when he speaks of "thy sweet original joy" that worked within his soul amid "surging griefs" (297f.). Original blessing is also present when he writes of human creation:

When God at first made man,
Having a glass of blessings standing by;
Let us (said he) pour on him all we can:
Let the world's riches, which dispersed lie,
Contract into a span.

So strength first made a way;
Then beauty flow'd, then wisdom, honor, pleasure. (284)

Like for Aquinas, nature for Herbert is not the opposite of grace; sin is. Indeed, "Nature and Grace / With Glory may attain thy Face"

(329). What an important healing of nature and grace and of human and cosmos is found in Herbert! His constant references to "all things" reveals a deep sense of "all our relations," that is, of cosmology. "Each thing is full of duty," he observes, and he ends this amazing poem on "Man" with a prayer of panentheism:[20]

> Since then, my God, thou hast
> So brave a Palace built; Oh dwell in it,
> That it may dwell with thee at last!
> Till then, afford us so much wit;
> That, as the world serves us, we may serve thee,
> And both thy servants be. (211)

He is calling on humans and the rest of creation to be God's servants. Clearly, Herbert is far beyond anthropocentrism. Panentheism is alluded to in another poem when he writes:

> Teach me, my God and King,
> In all things thee to see,
> And what I do in anything,
> To do it as for thee. (311)

God is in all things, and not only is each creature Dabhar, a word of God, but even a *song* of God making harmony together with God, as he puts it in his great poem, "Providence":

> Nothing escapes them both; all must appear,
> And be dispos'd, and dress'd, and tun'd by thee,
> Who sweetly temper'st all. If we could hear
> Thy skill and art, what music would it be!
>
> Thou art in small things great, not small in any:
> Thy even praise can neither rise, nor fall.
> Thou art in all things one, in each thing many:
> For thou art infinite in one and all. (239)

What about praise? In the same poem, Herbert names the human vocation as that of "Secretary of thy [God's] praise." Humans are here to praise:

---

20. Pantheism is the belief that all things are God. Panentheism holds that God is *in* all things and all things are *in* God.

Of all the creatures both in sea and land
Only to Man thou has made known thy ways,
And put the pen alone into his hand,
And made him Secretary of thy praise. . . .

The beasts say, Eat me: but, if beasts must teach,
The tongue is yours to eat, but mine to praise.
The trees say, Pull me: but the hand you stretch,
Is mine to write, as it is yours to raise.

Herbert sees his role as that of one who praises, for humans are "the world's high Priest":

Wherefore, most sacred Spirit, I here present
For me and all my fellows praise to thee.

He also warns that to lack praise is to commit a serious sin of omission:

He that to praise and laud thee doth refrain,
Doth not refrain unto himself alone,
But robs a thousand who would praise thee fain [gladly]
And doth commit a world of sin in one. (238)

He names tempests, sand, children, beasts, birds, fishes, flies, times, seasons, night, day, pigeons, bees, sheep, trees, springs, clouds, herbs, stars, roses, metals, poisons — "Ev'n poisons praise thee." Job and wisdom literature of the Bible, so thoroughly grounded in a panentheistic creation theology, are amply matched by Herbert's spirituality. And in the following line, I think, may lie a clue to his entire collection of poems that we know as "The Temple," and for the section in which this poem appears called "The Church." For Herbert writes, after going through so many parts of creation, how all creatures are God's work of art and together constitute God's home:

And as *thy house* is full, so I adore
Thy curious art in marshalling thy goods.
The hills with health abound; the vales with store;
the South with marble; North with furs and woods. (241)

Adoration comes from the plenty of God's house. Awe is aroused there, and when Awe withdraws, God withdraws (see 310). This amazing poem also makes a point that today's paleontologists are making: that humans discovered fire:

Nothing useth fire,
But Man alone, to show his heav'nly breed:
And only he hath fuel in desire. (241)

He continues his litany of rain, flowers, odors, thorns, pears, hedges, silks, stones — indeed, a litany to diversity itself. Lemons, milk, frogs, fish, bats, sponges, crocodiles, elephants — all get their praise.

But who can praise enough? nay, who hath any?
None can express thy works, but he that knows them.

And all praise God:

All things that are, though they have sev'ral ways,
Yet in their being join with one advise
To honor thee: and so I give thee praise
In all my other hymns, but in this twice.

Each thing that is, although in use and name
It go for one, hath many ways in store
To honor thee; and so each hymn thy fame
Extolleth many ways, yet this one more. (243)

Is this any different from Eckhart saying, "Every creature is a word of God and a book about God," or from Aquinas saying, "Revelation comes in two volumes: the Bible and Nature"? There can be no question that Herbert's is a *praise theology*, as when he writes:

Sev'n whole days, not one in seven,
I will praise thee.
In my heart, though not in heaven,
I can raise thee. (271)

And again:

Surely thy sweet and wondrous love
Shall measure all my days;
And as it never shall remove,
So neither shall my praise. (299)

All creation praises God and is a word of God:

Each Cloud distills thy praise, and doth forbid
Poets to turn it to another use.
Roses and Lilies speak thee. (333)

That God is Artist of all creatures is explicitly stated in Herbert's book *The Country Parson*, when he says: "As Creatures, he [God] must needs love them; for no perfect Artist ever yet hated his own work." And for sinners, he goes further: "As sinful, he must much more love them; because notwithstanding his infinite hate of sin, his Love overcame that hate" (108). Herbert's is a consciousness of the "book of life" (cf. 256), the idea that every creature is a word of God. Christological panentheism is found in these poems:

My doctrine tun'd by Christ, (who is not dead,
But lives in me while I do rest) (300)

Welcome sweet and sacred cheer,
Welcome dear;
With me, in me, live and dwell. (307)

This echoes the Song of Songs. God is "the great householder of the world" (70) who not only launches creation but preserves it. "For Preservation is a Creation; and more, it is a continued Creation, and a creation every moment" (107). We have here an excellent example of a theology of *continuous creation*.

Herbert's anthropology is that of the *imago dei*. In fact, for Herbert, Christ creates a double "image of God" in us. Thus, he says:

Man is God's image; but a poor man is
Christ's stamp to boot: both images regard.
God reckons for him, counts the favor his. (134)

Prayer is a return to our origins; it is breathing. "Prayer the Church's banquet, Angels' age, / God's breath in man returning to his birth" (165). Our hearts need purging just as Christ did to the temple: "Christ purg'd his temple; so must thou thy heart" (136). Here, too, we have a hint at the analogous meanings to the title of his collection of poems. The temple can mean the human heart. He also deinstitutionalizes the altar when he speaks of it as "made of a heart, and cemented with tears. . . . A H E A R T alone / Is such a stone. . . . These stones to praise thee may not cease" (139). The soul grows: "Dress and undress thy soul: mark the decay / And growth of it" (137). Herbert has a cosmic Christology wherein Incarnation and Creation come together. In echoes of the cosmic hymn in Philippians 2, Herbert talks of the "strange story" of Lord Jesus,

> as he did ride
> In his majestic robes of glory,
> Resolv'd to light; and so one day
> He did descend, undressing all the way.
>
> The stars his tire of light and rings obtain'd,
> The cloud his bow, the fire his spear,
> The sky his azure mantle gain'd.
> And when they ask'd, what he would wear;
> He smil'd and said as he did go,
> He had new clothes amaking here below. (276)

He resists dualism when he says: "sin turn'd flesh to stone" (167). Notice he does *not* say (as Augustine would) that sin turned spirit to flesh; or even spirit to stone; he is saying, in Hebraic fashion, that flesh lives and is enspirited and that sin destroys *flesh* — and in the process spirit — by rendering it cold as stone.

The Via Positiva is essentially about gratitude. About this theme Herbert writes:

> Thou that hast giv'n so much to me,
> Give one thing more, a grateful heart....
> Not thankful, when it pleaseth me;
> As if thy blessings had spare days:
> But such a heart, whose pulse may be Thy praise. (245f.)

Blessing is everywhere, and so gratitude is always. Clearly George Herbert is well versed in a rich and profound Via Positiva.

Via Negativa (Path 2)

Herbert is sensitive not just to the blessings of life but also to the suffering and struggle.[21] The Via Positiva praise becomes the path in which Rilke warns us to walk our walk of lament. Thus, the Via Negativa has a context. As Herbert puts it, "Where sin abounded, not death, but grace superabounded" (113). He does not deny either sin or suffering but puts both within the proper context of the super-abundance of grace. Herbert is sensitive to this dialectic of light and dark, blessing and suffering, of the Via Positiva and the Via Negativa:

---

21. See Fox, *Original Blessing*, 132–77.

When almost all was out, God made a stay, . . .
For if I should (said he)
Bestow this jewel also on my creature,
He would adore my gifts instead of me,
And rest in Nature, not the God of Nature:
So both should losers be.

Yet let him keep the rest,
But keep them with repining restlessness:
Let him be rich and weary, that at least,
If goodness lead him not, yet weariness
May toss him to my breast. (284f.)

This same dialectic of joy and sadness is found in his poem "Bitter-Sweet," where he speaks of his "sour-sweet days" of lamenting *and* loving:

Ah my dear angry Lord,
Since thou dost love, yet strike;
Cast down, yet help afford;
Sure I will do the like.
I will complain, yet praise;
I will bewail, approve:
And all my sour-sweet days
I will lament, and love. (297)

In "Man's Medley," he celebrates again this need on humans' part to combine the Via Positiva with the Via Negativa:

But as his [man's] joys are double;
So is his trouble.
He hath two winters, other things but one:
Both frosts and thoughts do nip,
And bite his lip;
And he of all things fears two deaths alone.

Yet ev'n the greatest griefs
May be reliefs,
Could he but take them right, and in their ways.
Happy is he, whose heart
Hath found the art
To turn his double pains to double praise. (254)

The Via Negativa actually increases our capacity for praise!

Herbert names the dark nights of the soul with laments he utters on numerous occasions:

> Why do I languish thus, drooping and dull,
> As if I were all earth?
> Oh give me quickness, that I may with mirth
> Praise thee brim-full! (236)

In his poem "Affliction II," he offers this prayer:

> Kill me not ev'ry day,
> Thou Lord of life; since thy one death for me
> Is more than all my deaths can be,
> Though I in broken pay
> Die over each hour of Methusalem's stay.
>
> If all men's tears were let
> Into one common sewer, sea, and brine;
> What were they all, compar'd to thine?
> Wherein if they were set,
> They would discolor thy most bloody sweat. (177)

Here, he sees Christ's redemption as an act of absorbing the tears of our race — Christ has suffered the sum of what all humankind has suffered. In "Affliction III," he speaks of grief and his broken heart and how God surfaced from both. He develops a kind of panentheism of the Via Negativa, the presence of God *in* darkness, suffering, and grief:

> My heart did heave, and there came forth, *Oh God!*
> By that I knew that thou wast in the grief,
> To guide and govern it to my relief,
> Making a scepter of the rod:
> Hadst thou not had thy part,
> Sure the unruly sigh had broke my heart....
>
> Thy life on earth was grief, and thou art still
> Constant unto it, making it to be
> A point of honor, now to grieve in me,
> And in thy members suffer ill. (190)

Herbert names the experience of letting go and of nothingness in his poem "An Offering":

Since my sadness
Into gladness
Lord thou dost convert,
Oh accept
What thou hast kept,
As thy due desert.

Had I many,
Had I any,
(For this heart is none)
All were thine
And none of mine:
Surely thine alone. (272)

He complains to God of his own abandonment to nothingness:

Thou tarriest, while I die,
And fall to nothing: thou dost reign,
And rule on high,
While I remain
In bitter grief: yet am I styl'd
Thy child....
Lord J E S U, hear my heart,
Which hath been broken now so long,
That ev'ry part
Hath got a tongue!...
Pluck out thy dart,
And heal my troubled breast which cries,
Which dies. (275)

In "The Collar," he also challenges himself to let go:

Forsake thy cage,
Thy rope of sands,
Which petty thoughts have made, and made to thee
Good cable, to enforce and draw,
And be thy law,
While thou didst wink and wouldst not see.
Away; take heed:
I will abroad.

All grief contains anger and Herbert's grief is no exception:

But as I rav'd and grew more fierce and wild
At every word,
Me thoughts I heard one calling, *Child:*
And I replied, *My Lord.* (278f.)

The absence of God, and even the death of God, is experienced deeply
by Herbert. Like John of the Cross and Nietzsche, he feels abandoned.
In the dark night of the soul, all lights go out, even those of the stars
and heavens. It is a cosmic darkness:

Whither, Oh, wither art thou fled,
My Lord, my Love?
My searches are my daily bread;
Yet never prove.

My knees pierce th' earth, mine eyes the sky;
And yet the sphere
And center both to me deny
That thou art there....

Where is my God? what hidden place
Conceals thee still?....

Since then my grief must be as large,
As is thy space,
Thy distance from me; see my charge,
Lord, see my case.... (286f.)

Finally, at the conclusion to his lament, he connects distance and
presence, Via Negativa and Via Positiva:

For as thy absence doth excel
All distance known:
So doth thy nearness bear the bell,
Making two one. (288)

In another prayer-poem, he pleads to God not to leave and, in the
process, names the death of God experience:

Oh what a damp and shade
Doth me invade!
No stormy night

Can so afflict or so affright,
As thy eclipsed light.

Ah Lord! do not withdraw,
Lest want of awe
Make Sin appear;
And when thou dost but shine less clear,
Say, that thou art not here. (310)

In his poem "The Cross," he returns his pain to Christ's and appropriates Christ's own words:

Ah my dear Father, ease my smart!
These contrarieties crush me: these cross actions
Do wind a rope about, and cut my heart:
And yet since these thy contradictions
Are properly a cross felt by thy Son,
With but four words, my words, *Thy will be done.* (290)

Silence is a part of the Via Negativa: "Cease, be dumb and mute," he counsels in his poem "Grief" (289).

Clearly George Herbert is well schooled in the Via Negativa.

Via Creativa (Path 3)

Herbert's theology does not cease with the crucifixion alone any more than it begins with the crucifixion. It is true to the *full* pascal mystery of life, death, and resurrection, and, therefore, he very much includes the Via Creativa, the new life that resurrection brings.[22] In his poem "The Flower" he notes how grief, too, does not last forever:

Grief melts away
Like snow in May,

As if there were no such cold thing.

Who would have thought my shrivel'd heart
Could have recover'd greenness? It was gone
Quite underground; as flowers depart
To see their mother-root, when they have blown;

---

22. See ibid., 178–249.

Where they together
All the hard weather,
Dead to the world, keep house unknown. (291)

Notice his reference to "greenness," or what Hildegard of Bingen
called "viriditas."[23] He sees the darkness as a fecund place, just as
seeds must also go into the dark to be fully born. Herbert sees the
pruning process of winter, the going underground of the Via Negativa,
as a preparation for deeper life, for a renewed Via Positiva as when
he writes:

Go birds of spring; let winter have his fee,
Let a bleak paleness chalk the door,
So all within be livelier than before. (303)

The Via Negativa assists the *within* to become enlivened.

Herbert ascribes the movement of the Via Positiva (and Via Creativa) as well as the Via Negativa to God's work, and he sees these
journeys interacting even within one hour when he says:

These are thy wonders, Lord of power,
Killing and quick'ning, bringing down to hell
And up to heaven in an hour. (291)

In the same poem, being the poet he is, he personalizes and concretizes
his own resurrection as that of being an artist:

And now in age I bud again,
After so many deaths I live and write;
I once more smell the dew and rain,
And relish versing: Oh my only light,
It cannot be
That I am he
On whom thy tempests fell all night. (292)

So great is the joy of creating that he can forget — let go of — the dark
experiences of the Via Negativa. Herbert acknowledges the deep soul-
place from which his poetry comes — as well as to whom his poetry
is gifted — in this statement on art as meditation:

---

23. See Matthew Fox, *Illuminations of Hildegard of Bingen* (Santa Fe: Bear & Co.,
1985), 30–33.

My God, the poor expressions of my Love
Which warm these lines, and serve them up to thee
Are so, as for the present, I did move
Or rather as thou movedst me. (331)

Herbert's poetry is an arena in which God acts in his life. Furthermore, his poetry is a source of joy and delight for him. Creativity is such a process. It includes play.

This on my ring,
This by my picture, in my book I write:
Whether I sing,
Or say, or dictate, this is my delight.

Invention rest,
Comparisons go play, wit use thy will:
Less than the least
Of all God's mercies, is my poesy still. (309)

In his poem "Easter Wings" Herbert prays that his resurrection will match Christ's. "With thee / Oh let me rise.... Then shall the fall further the flight in me" (157). The same theme of resurrection is sung in "The Dawning":

Awake sad heart, whom sorrow ever drowns;
Take up thine eyes, which feed on earth;
Unfold thy forehead gather'd into frowns:
Thy Savior comes, and with him mirth:
Awake, awake;...
Arise sad heart; if thou dost not withstand,
Christ's resurrection thine may be:
Do not by hanging down break from the hand,
Which as it riseth, raiseth thee:
Arise, arise. (232f.)

While the artist pursues, among other things, beauty, beauty's source is in the Godhead. The role of the artist is to bring out divine beauty. "True beauty dwells on high: ours is a flame / But borrow'd thence to light us thither. / Beauty and beauteous words should go together" (303).

Herbert sees preaching as an art form, yet the most important thing is that preaching moves people to prayer. "Resort to sermons, but to prayers most: / Praying's the end of preaching" (135). And preaching must at times yield to poetry: "A verse may find him, who a sermon flies, / And turn delight into a sacrifice" (121). In giving advice in *The Country Parson* to preachers, he tells them to pay attention to their own creative contribution, reminding them to "not so study others, as to neglect the grace of God in himself, and what the Holy Spirit teacheth him." The parson has studied diligently the fathers, schoolmen, scriptures, and later commentators, but his own work can rightly be called a "body of Divinity" that brings one authentic joy to look upon:

> Out of which he hath compiled a book, and body of Divinity, which is the storehouse of his Sermons, and which he preacheth all his Life; but diversely clothed, illustrated, and enlarged. For though the world is full of such composures, yet every man's own is fittest, readiest, and most savory to him. Besides, this being to be done in his younger and preparatory times, it is an honest joy ever after to look upon his well-spent hours. (59)

Joy accompanies the act of creativity that preaching is. "The Country Parson preacheth constantly, the pulpit is his joy and his throne." He advises telling stories which are remembered better than exhortations and speaking from the heart. "But the character of his Sermon is Holiness; he is not witty, or learned, or eloquent, but Holy. . . . Every word is heart-deep." And "there is no greater sign of holiness, than the procuring, and rejoicing in another's good" (62f.). Sermons are meant to both inform and inflame, and teaching demands that a person "discover what he is" (84f.).

Herbert himself found his art as meditation in study and preaching and poetry — but also in music. Isaac Walton reports that:

> His chiefest recreation was Musick, in which heavenly Art he was a most excellent Master, and did himself compose many *divine Hymns* and *Anthems*, which he set and sung to his *Lute* or Viol; and, though he was a lover of retiredness, yet his love to *Musick* was such, that he went usually twice every week on certain appointed days, to the *Cathedral Church* in *Salisbury*; and at his return would say, *That his time spent in Prayer, and Cathedral Musick, elevated his Soul, and was his Heaven upon Earth:* But before his return thence to *Bemerton,* he would usually sing

and play his part, at an appointed private Musick-meeting; and, to justifie this practice, he would often say, *Religion does not banish mirth, but only moderates, and sets rules to it.*[24]

On his deathbed, Herbert listed "the pleasures of my life past" as being "in beauty, in wit, in musick and pleasant conversation."[25] How telling that the pleasures he lists are all forms of creativity, of art as meditation practices.

The opposite of heeding the Via Creativa is sloth, and Herbert sees this as the primary problem in his culture. "Oh England! full of sin, but most of sloth; / . . . the most / Are gone to grass, and in the pasture lost. / This loss springs chiefly from our education" (124). In *The Country Parson,* he states:

> The great and national sin of this Land he [the parson] esteems to be Idleness; great in itself, and great in Consequence: For when men have nothing to do, then they fall to drink, to steal, to whore, to scoff, to revile, to all sorts of gamings. Come, say they, we have nothing to do, let's go to the Tavern, or to the stews, or what not.... Because idleness is twofold, the one in having no calling, the other in walking carelessly in our calling, he [the parson] first represents to everybody the necessity of a vocation. (100f.)

His theology of vocation is based on a spirituality of gift-consciousness, for as he puts it, "every gift or ability is a talent to be accounted for, and to be improved to our Master's Advantage" (101). No one is exempt from good work, for "all are either to have a Calling, or prepare for it" (101). He was not exempt from sloth himself, as he confesses:

> Indeed a slack and sleepy state of mind
> Did oft possess me, so that when I pray'd,
> Though my lips went, my heart did stay behind. (253)

Like Rilke, he has a sense that the entire cosmos is at work; only the humans are unemployed:

24. Isaac Walton, *Life of George Herbert* (1670; reprinted Oxford: Oxford University Press, 1973), 241.
25. Ibid., 253.

All things are busy; only I
Neither bring honey with the bees,
Nor flowers to make that, nor the husbandry
To water these.

I am no link of thy great chain,
But all my company is a weed.
Lord place me in thy consort; give one strain
To my poor reed. (172f.)

In his "Matins" prayer, honoring the sunlight of the new day, Herbert prays:

Teach me thy love to know;
That this new light, which now I see,
May both the work and workman show:
Then by a sunbeam I will climb to thee. (178)

He urges workers to fulfill their various tasks:

Art thou a Magistrate? then be severe:
If studious, copy fair, what time hath blurr'd;
Redeem truth from his jaws: if soldier,
Chase brave employments with a naked sword
Throughout the world. Fool not: for all may have,
If they dare try, a glorious life, or grave. (124)

Herbert is, indeed, a champion of that "glorious life" indicated by the Via Creativa and the Resurrection.

Via Transformativa (Path 4)

George Herbert has a sense of the Via Transformativa along with the previous three paths of the creation spiritual journey. The Via Transformativa is about prophecy understood as justice-making, compassion, and celebration.[26] He states that "the Parson is a lover and exciter to justice in all things, even as John the Baptist squared out to every one (even to Soldiers) what to do" (103). It is interesting that he links justice-making and the prophet's work, as in the case of John the Baptist (though he does not seem to follow up much on this category of the prophet). "Justice is the ground of Charity," he

---

26. See Fox, *Original Blessing*, 250–306.

writes (89), and charity for Herbert is what marks the parson; it is "the body of Religion":

> The Country Parson is full of Charity; it is his predominant element. For many and wonderful things are spoken of thee, thou great Virtue. To Charity is given the covering of sins (1 Pet. 4:8), and the forgiveness of sins (Matt. 6:14; Luke 7:47), the fulfilling of the Law (Rom. 13:10), the life of faith (James 2:26), the blessings of this life (Prov. 22:9; Ps. 41:2), and the reward of the next (Matt. 25:35). In brief, it is the body of Religion (John 13:35), and the top of Christian virtues (1 Cor. 13:13). Wherefore all his works relish of Charity.... So is his charity in effect a Sermon. (72f.)

Charity marks the work of the parson:

> The Country Parson owing a debt of Charity to the poor, and of Courtesy to his other parishioners, he so distinguisheth, that he keeps his money for the poor, and his table for those that are above Alms.... He chooseth rather to give the poor money, which they can better employ to their own advantage, and suitably to their needs, than so much given in meat at dinner. (71f.)

And again:

> If any neighboring village be overburdened with poor, and his own less charged, he finds some way of relieving it, and reducing the Manna, and bread of Charity to some quality, representing to his people that the Blessing of God to them ought to make them the more charitable, and not the less, lest he cast their neighbors' poverty on them also. (81)

One of his last lines was a ditty he wrote for his successor at his parsonage, and to him he advised:

> Be good to the Poor,
> As God gives thee store,
> And then, my Labor's not lost. (333)

Unfortunately, Herbert's understanding of charity is almost totally circumscribed by the notion of almsgiving and contributes very little to the idea of justice-making as the basis of love, a notion that

eighteenth-century revolutions in France and America would attempt
to rectify. His two poems on justice (214f.; 265f.) are about justification between God and humans rather than about justice among
humans. Yet, he does express a sense of injustice and an awareness of
how empire-building and religion may prove less than perfect part-
ners when he compares the American spirit to that of England in a
passage that was so prophetic that it almost prevented his book from
being published in England:

> Religion stands on tip-toe in our land,
> Ready to pass to the *American* strand....
> Then shall Religion to America flee:
> They have their times of Gospel, ev'n as we.
> My God, thou dost prepare for them a way
> By carrying first their gold from them away:
> For gold and grace did never yet agree:
> Religion always sides with poverty.
> We think we rob them, but we think amiss:
> We are more poor, and they more rich by this. (324)

Not only is Herbert capable of criticizing the empire-building of his
nation, noting how gold and grace do not get along, but also the sins
of the church, as in his poem "Church Rents and Schisms":

> Why doth my Mother blush? is she the rose,
> And shows it so? Indeed Christ's precious blood
> Gave you a color once; which when your foes
> Thought to let out, the bleeding did you good,
> And made you look much fresher than before....
> Your health and beauty both began to break.
>
> Then did your sev'rall parts unloose and start:...
> Oh Mother dear and kind,
> Where shall I get me eyes enough to weep,
> As many eyes as stars? since it is night,
> And much of Asia and Europe fast asleep,
> And ev'n all Africk. (264)

He seems to have a well-developed theological awareness of the
distinction between church and Kingdom/Queendom of God when
he warns:

Look to thy actions well;
For churches are either our heav'n or hell. (136)

He avoids a kind of religious dualism based on righteousness when he warns that not all sins are within the papal fold. Thus he says: "In the time of Popery, the Priest's *Benedicite,* and his holy water were overhighly valued; and now we are fallen to the clean contrary, even from superstition to coldness, and Atheism" (111). His preference for the Anglican Church is his preference for "the mean":

> But dearest Mother, (what those [Roman Catholicism and
>   Calvinism] miss)
> The mean thy praise and glory is,
> And long may be. (230)

The word "mean" is an important one for Herbert and, I believe, for the future of those who follow Jesus. The mendicant orders in the early thirteenth century were intended from their inception as a "mean" between the monastic state and the lay state, between exclusive contemplation or exclusive action, and the Buddhist tradition seeks a "mean" of being in the world, engaging it and being critical of it. The more I study these Anglican theologians, I believe that they likewise represent a rational or thoughtful "mean" between a Protestantism turned iconoclastic and a Catholicism turned papalalatrous. These theologians also stand within what I call elsewhere the tension between "orthodoxy" and "orthopraxis."[27]

Herbert believes that "the greatest alms" is "to teach the ignorant" (69). According to Walton, he urged fellow clergy "to restore the great and neglected duty of Catechising, on which the salvation of so many of the poor and ignorant Laypeople does depend."[28] Celebration is hinted at in his Eucharistic invitation to "taste / The church's mystical repast" (138).

George Herbert does have a Via Transformativa, although one would wish for greater development of the prophetic dimension. Given his times and century, however, his record is better than many in this regard.

We can conclude that George Herbert is profoundly creation centered, both in his chosen method for doing his priestly work — poetry,

---

27. Matthew Fox, *Confessions: The Making of a Post-Denominational Priest* (San Francisco: HarperSanFrancisco, 1996).
28. Walton, *Life of George Herbert,* 242.

music, study, preaching, writing — and in his theology. All Four Paths and numerous themes of the creation spirituality tradition are treated, with depth and originality, in his work.

Conclusion

The world that our species faces is full of hazards. Great challenges await us as we enter the twenty-first century — challenges of eco-, social, economic, racial, gender, and gender-preference justice. As regards eco-justice alone, Lester Brown of the Worldwatch Institute says we have only twelve years to change our ways as a species or the planet will not be able to sustain the damage we are doing to it. Changing our ways is a spiritual task — it is *metanoia,* a transformation that is heart-deep and structure-deep. It will take a spiritual awakening, a deep renaissance, to bring this change about. Healthy religion, that is, spirituality, is a necessary leaven to that change. As sociologist Robert Bellah puts it, "Culture is the key to revolution; religion is the key to culture."[29]

But cosmology, art, and spirituality are the key to religion. Whether we have the faith to reinvent religion and culture by way of cosmology, art, and spirituality will be the test of those who claim to follow in the footsteps of Jesus the Christ in the third millennium, as it was in the first and second. Our prayer must be that we will opt for the creation spiritual ways of some of our ancestors — the historical Jesus included — over the ways that built empires and ravaged earth and her creation so arrogantly.

29. Robert Bellah, *The Broken Covenant* (New York: Seabury, 1975), 162.

Chapter 8

CAN BISHOPS TELL THE TRUTH AS THEY SEE IT?

Krister Stendahl

KRISTER STENDAHL, holding a newly earned Th.D. degree from Uppsala University in Sweden, arrived at Harvard Divinity School in 1954, where he remained on the faculty for thirty years, eleven of them as dean. Leaving Harvard in 1984, he became bishop of the Church of Sweden in Stockholm. Upon his retirement, he returned to Cambridge and served as chaplain to Harvard Divinity School and as Myra and Robert Kraft and Jacob Hiatt Distinguished Professor of Christian Studies at Brandeis University. Bishop Stendahl's writings have addressed various issues of theology, history, and the arts of ministry, as well as contemporary problems in church and society. Explaining why Jews and women have been a significant focus of his biblical and theological work, he has said: "The Christian Bible includes sayings that have caused much pain both to Jews and to women. Thus I have felt called to seek forms of interpretation which can counteract such undesirable side effects of my Holy Scriptures." The bishop's published work includes *The School of St. Matthew; The Bible and the Role of Women; Holy Week; Paul among Jews and Gentiles; Meanings* — a collection of essays celebrating diversity within the Bible as an asset to the faith and to ecumenical Christianity — and *Energy for Life* and *Final Account,* both giving further consideration to this theme.

I BECAME A BISHOP late in life, after having been a professor of biblical studies for decades. So it happened now and then when I addressed this or that question — often on the basis of my understanding of the scriptures — that people said: "You could say that when you were a professor, but you cannot say it now when you are a bishop." I was inclined to answer that I did not accept that kind of ecclesial schizophrenia. Was I too defensive? I did and do want to be accountable — but how, and ultimately to whom?

181

After all, as a bishop, I had been elected — by the clergy of the diocese and an equal number of lay people. My understanding of the scriptures and the Christian tradition was in the public domain both by my writings and various media coverage. Those who had elected me knew what they were getting. Furthermore — actually, even more — it was important for me to believe that it really *took* when I was consecrated a bishop by the laying on of hands and prayers for the Spirit. That should set me free from constantly having double vision: What do I think, and what should I think and say as a bishop? I had to trust my calling and those who had called me.

At least in the Church of Sweden, the bishop goes last when we process into the church, but first when we go down the aisle on our way out into the world. This quaint symbolism suggests leadership in facing the future, the unknown, the world as it is — for better or for worse. So, what should be the role of bishops in the tending of traditions? As an old biblical scholar, I am perhaps extra aware of the long history of interpretation by which the scriptures have come alive and engendered life through the centuries. It makes me acutely conscious of the need for new interpretations which keep tradition alive. For tradition is a means both of continuity and of change. Tradition is the term for organic change. Both dimensions of the tradition are mutually stimulating and necessary. That is what makes the scriptures what the Episcopal Prayer Book calls "the true and lively word." Faithful interpretation is "faith filled" interpretation.

It would be sad if our bishops were not actively and creatively engaged in that tending of the tradition. Spiritual leadership should not be degraded into administrative supervision of the status quo, or — even worse — into discouraging everything that disturbs the so-called peace of the churches. The leadership of bishops functions not so much by overt actions as it does by what and whom they encourage and whom and what they discourage. There are two distinct styles of reaction to new suggestions. Either we tend to ask with a mental frown: "Why should we?" Or we say: "Why not? Let's try it!" Admittedly, there are suggestions that should be seriously questioned, but it is good to test from time to time which style of reacting has become the dominating pattern. I like the word the French came to use for the role of chaplains: *animateur* — one who animates.

Does all this sound irresponsible? I am afraid it does to some. But the future of the church and its present health need renewal so badly that our caution — not least the bishops' form thereof — must be trumped by Paul's advice in the oldest of all the New Testament writings: "Quench not the Spirit, do not despise prophecyings" (1 Thess. 5:19). That must be so, not least when it is often stressed that one of the roles of bishops is to be the sign and the guarantors of the unity of the church. However, the long history of the church and contemporary experience make it abundantly clear that few things can stifle the Spirit more effectively than the unity argument or its echoes in the form of "let us not rock the boat," or in more condescending pastoral words, "our people are not ready for it yet."

Perhaps we should turn to the apostle Paul's reflection on unity and diversity. It was in Corinth he was forced to think creatively about the subject, for there he was in the minority. He could not expect to be obeyed as when writing to the Galatians: "If anyone — even an angel — is preaching to you a gospel contrary to that which you received (from me), let him be accursed" (Gal. 1:8). Basta! He cannot afford such single-mindedness in Corinth. He has to become ecumenical. He has a new vision of how diversity can become an asset rather than a liability or a sign of weakness. He reminds the Corinthians that the various theologies of various teachers should not be seen as competing philosophies. Such an understanding he calls "carnal" (1 Cor. 3:1, 3), what the New English Bible in its wordiness renders "on the merely natural plane"; I would say "secular." In his eagerness, he then mixes the metaphors as he urges the Corinthians to allow for variety of teachers and teachings and "not to judge before time," leaving the judgment to God. He is actually subjectively sure to have the right theology, but "I am not thereby justified" (4:4), and as to those who teach wrong, their work will come to nought, but they themselves will be saved (3:15), a quite generous attitude in the perspective of church history.

Paul returns to the theme of diversity and unity in those famous chapters (1 Cor. 12–13) about the one body and the many members with their distinct functions, the one Spirit and the many gifts, themes that find their climax in his Ode to Love. Here, love is not measured by how peaceful and warm it feels but by how much diversity it can comprehend. For love is, as he says, "not seeking its own," but it is hungry for that which is different. (That wonderful insight is easily lost in the moralizing of many translations that say that "love is not selfish" [13:5].)

We need so to celebrate unity in Christ and in the Spirit that the "secular" hunger for unity — which often is a desire for power and the capacity to manipulate — does not repress the Spirit and make us afraid of prophets. From feminist theologians, I have learned to turn the well-worn sentence around and ask: How much diversity do we need — and how much unity can we afford? All that, in order not to oppress some and thereby impoverish us all.

The issue of unity and diversity of conviction came to a critical test in our Council of Bishops during my time in Sweden when ethically relevant legislation was pending. As is or was the procedure in Sweden, the government requested the archbishop, "after hearing the Council of Bishops," to comment on proposed legislation about same-sex partnership. A majority among us were unwilling to consider celibacy the only lifestyle for gays and lesbians. But could the council go public by saying that in much we were of one mind, but on some matters we were of different convictions? Should not the church speak with one voice? Should we try clever and innocuous language and avoid points of disagreements? The final report did openly state both our agreements and disagreements — which created a new respect for the bishops. Truthfulness gave more credibility than a watered-down consensus statement out of episcopal collegiality.

It should not be hard to figure out why I offer these reflections in honor of Bishop Spong and his ministry. By so doing, it also seems appropriate for me to share with him and others outside my own tradition a memorandum that I submitted in 1994 to the Evangelical Lutheran Church in America, especially to its bishops. Those paragraphs which follow may serve as an elaboration of how I think of an answer to the question that gave the title to this article. It does so on a subject where there is no hiding for bishops — as Jack Spong knows better than most.

MEMORANDUM ON OUR BIBLE
AND OUR SEXUALITY

TO: The Evangelical Lutheran Church in America
FROM: Krister Stendahl
February 28, 1994

Our Bible

Space for Allowing Some Questions to Remain Open

Churches — and not least their bishops — are tempted to think that, unless we take clear and unified stands, the authority of the church and the faithfulness to the scriptures will suffer loss. Paul knew that temptation. But in Corinth he learned that such an attitude comes out of a secular — he calls it "carnal" (1 Cor. 3:1, 3) — way of thinking about the church on the model of competition between schools of philosophy. In that third chapter, he casts about for other images — architectural and agricultural — to make his point: While I am convinced of being right in my views, that does not settle the matter — let us work side by side in full conviction (cf. Rom. 14:5), leaving the judgment to God. "Do not judge before time" (1 Cor. 4:1–5). Such an attitude may strike the world as unwise or dangerously open-minded, but there it is.

Space for Opinions and Advice

Churches are not very good at maintaining the distinction between commandments and advice or opinions. Also here Paul is a good guide (1 Cor. 7). He takes care to distinguish between what he sees as the Word of the Lord and the words of Paul (vv. 10 and 12). It is here that he gives his own opinion, instead of pressing a word of scripture — as can always be done — to yield an answer with scriptural authority (v. 25). And he ends this section by saying about his personal opinions, "and I *think* that I *too* have the Spirit of God." He does not say "I know." It should be of great interest to the church that this attitude of Paul's is found in the only section where he deals explicitly and extensively with matters of sexuality. In Romans 1, his comments are part of his general picture of Gentile, i.e., Graeco-Roman depravity, and in 1 Corinthians 6, we have a kindred list of vices, also including idolatry. My point is this: Let us not rush into a mood and language of authority but relearn Paul's: On this one, I have no Word from the Lord — but my tentative advice is . . .

Toward the Ethics of Character

Perhaps we should also recall that the truly devout Bible-reading Christians of Lutheran piety did not read the scriptures so much in the anxious decision-making mode, seeking divine answers to preconceived questions. Rather, they read attentively and extensively — the Bible was their whole library, their whole literature. They were shaped by the whole story, the whole Bible as it entered their subconsciousness and formed their thinking and sensitivities. For them, the Bible played more into what is called the ethics of character than the ethics of decision-making. We should be aware of the ways in which the ethics of decision-making stifles spirituality and forces right/wrong dichotomies on situations that may not allow for such, while the ethics of character often comes closer to both reality and biblical modes of evaluation.

Our Sexuality

Where Are We Now?

While Christians usually — and correctly — criticize the world for its excessive and exploitative preoccupation with sex, it seems that the churches have themselves become mesmerized by questions of sexuality. Few issues seem to be more polarizing or consume more energy in hierarchies and assemblies. It is time to remember that the sixth commandment is only one of ten, and that originally the words "You shall not commit adultery" were to protect men from having other men stealing their wife or wives, as is obvious to anyone who knows the Old Testament stories. Which reminds us that, in both Judaism and Christianity, sexual ethics has evolved and will evolve out of the sacred interplay of scripture, tradition, and human experience and understanding, both scientific and sociopsychological. So it has been with our cosmology, with our understanding of slavery, and — except in the United States — with the death penalty. The church and the scriptures live by interpretation, not by repristination. Faithful interpretation is faithfilled creativity.

Fidelity and Mutuality .

To cut a long story short, I think the two foci of a Christian teaching on responsible sexuality are *fidelity* and *mutuality*. While the church traditionally has been forceful in teaching fidelity, the church's record on mutuality has been weak, indeed. Even the very emphasis on fidelity — not to speak about premarital virginity — was in actuality applied more forcefully to women than to men. As a Bible reader, I note with interest that the mutuality theme breaks through in Paul's chapter on sexuality when he counsels mutual consent and balances the patriarchal pattern of the husband's ownership of the wife's body with: "and likewise the husband does not rule over his own body, but the wife does" (1 Cor. 7:4–5) — a statement remarkable in its time.

As the churches assess their teaching about sexuality, it would be reasonable to expect that Item One on the agenda should be a radical repentance for the dehumanizing neglect of mutuality as one of the two cornerstones of our sexuality, a cornerstone that became a stumbling block.

On Procreation

Allow me one more observation about 1 Corinthians 7. The theme of procreation is not part of Paul's reasoning about sexuality, nor is it anywhere in the New Testament. There is no reference to the commandment to multiply and fill the earth (Gen. 1:28; the King James Version translates with ecological foresight and/or influenced by the Latin Vulgate: *re*-plenish, i.e., optimal, not unlimited growth). This is worth noting since in both the Old Testament and in Platonic and much of the Christian tradition, procreation is by far the decisive regulating principle for sexual ethics. The absence of the procreation criterion for ethics in Paul and in the New Testament is usually explained by the expectation of the end of the world being at hand, "for the form of this world is passing away" (1 Cor. 7:31). That sounds reasonable enough but not quite convincing because, for example, Paul's reasoning about marriage and celibacy is motivated not only by his eschatology but also by other motifs (1 Cor. 7:32). Nor is abortion condemned or even dealt with, although it was practiced and well known in the cultures surrounding the churches of the New Testament. Also, here one may ask whether the eschatological urgency gives a sufficient explanation to this silence.

Whatever the reason for the New Testament absence of references
to procreation as the only legitimation for sex, it strikes me as interesting that in contemporary reflections on sexual ethics, the arguments
from procreation have lost much of their force. There are many reasons for this: insistence on optimal rather than maximal population
growth, on sustainable ecology, on the health of women and families,
etc. Even if the Roman Catholic hierarchy does not allow safe contraceptives, their acceptance of rhythm methods is a recognition of sex
as an expression of love and communion beyond mere procreation.

The Challenge for Our Generation

It could be argued that this lessening of the bond between sex and
procreation is the central force in what often is called the sexual revolution. While contraception is not a new phenomenon to humanity,
highly safe and user-friendly contraceptives have given families, and
especially women, a new power over their lives and careers. This con-
stitutes a quantum jump in the human condition, and thus calls for a
radical reassessment of sexual ethics. If procreation is not a primary
factor, moral arguments must find new grounding in those principles
of fidelity and mutuality. If sexual ethics is not driven by fear of un-
wanted pregnancies, then the possibility of a more humane morality
of love can emerge. *That* is the challenge for the churches of our time,
a time of much promise for renewal.

Imagine that this, our generation, is blessed by being around at a
time when a hitherto mostly silenced half of humankind enters into
the arena where the perceptions of the world are shaped, and where
theology and ethics are interpreted, tested, critiqued, and created.
This glorious liberation of women is bound to open up new insight,
new imagination, new understanding for us all.

Homosexuality: Gays and Lesbians

We all must handle our sexuality responsibly. For Christians, that
means sexuality must be expressed according to the principles of fidelity and mutuality. Such responsibility applies equally to those who
have come to know themselves as homosexual — a term of relatively
recent coinage.

German psychologists in the 1890s seem to have invented the term,
and it soon came into English, although it did not make the *Oxford
English Dictionary* until its Supplement in the 1930s. If known at the

time of the fascicle on H, it may not have made it anyway since it is a
bastard formation that Oxford dons may have found offensive (Greek
homo = same, not Latin *homo* = man, plus Latin *sexus* = gender).

There is power in terminology, and the very word "homosexuality"
has both positive and negative impacts. On the negative side, it defines
people by their sexual orientation, and it overlooks probable internal
differences between gays and lesbians. It tends to make the sexual
aspect of these persons' lives far more dominant than is reasonable.
After all, gays and lesbians have to get up in the morning and go to
work, etc., as all people do. The term tends to make us blind to the
fact that sexuality is only one part of life and love — thus playing into
the hands of the very "sexification" of society which the churches
claim to oppose.

On the positive side, the word expresses well sexual *orientation,*
not just acts. Thus, it helps the awareness that there are persons who
have always known themselves as erotically inclined toward their
own gender, i.e., a homosexual orientation. Christian homosexuals
witness convincingly that they have never "exchanged natural relations for unnatural" (Rom. 1:26–27), to quote Paul's reference to
what we now call homosexuality. Actually, recent studies have made
it plausible that, when Paul here speaks of "nature," he does not think
of biology or anatomy, but about the supposed hierarchy of male
and female which was threatened by lesbians. In the Graeco-Roman
world, homosexual acts between free men were actually frowned
upon but were accepted when involving slaves or minors — for then
the hierarchy was preserved.

The pastoral question, then, is how to respond to those who witness to the church and before God that they have "changed nothing"
and that they would lie before the Lord if they confessed as sinful
their love's orientation. It seems clear to me that our answer must be
one in support of their search for a responsible sexuality of mutuality
and fidelity. It must be a holy duty for the church to give that support
at the very center of its life and structure, i.e., in its ministry and its
sacraments. If any persons need the church's blessing it is certainly
gays or lesbians who pledge themselves to a life together in fidelity
and mutuality.

There are persons who have *always* known themselves to be homosexual, and we know that such has *always* been the case. Churches
sometimes behave as if the question were a new one which a permis-

sive society has now dumped in their bosom. The only thing that is new is that some persons have had the courage to come out in the open. I began my ministry where and when homosexual acts were criminal and where, consequently, threats, blackmail, and fears of detection were rampant. Hence, I cannot imagine any valid — let alone Christian — defense for secrecy. As a Swedish hymn has it, "Only in openness have I a future." The church must express its gratitude and give its support to those who have found in themselves the strength to break out of societies' and the church's conspiracy of silence.

The Obligatory and the Gift

It strikes me as of great significance that exactly in matters pertaining to marriage, divorce, and celibacy, both the gospel material and Paul's teaching include a — perhaps surprising — caveat, a warning against what Jesus elsewhere speaks of as "they bind heavy burdens, hard to bear, and lay them on people's shoulders, but they themselves will not move them with their finger" (Matt. 23:4).

When Jesus, in Matthew's gospel, restores the original intention of marriage, without the divorce that Moses was forced to allow for, Matthew has the disciples say, "If such is the case of a man with his wife, it is not expedient to marry." Jesus' answer is: "Not all can receive this word, but only those to whom it is given" (Matt. 19:10–11). And the text continues with the famous words about celibacy for the sake of the Kingdom of Heaven — thereby breaking the dominance of procreation as governing sexual behavior. Here comes that same caveat: You cannot make it obligatory, or in Jesus' words, "The one who is able to receive it, let him receive it" (v. 12).

Also in Paul, who was much given to laying down the rules without ifs and buts, we find the same note when he witnesses to his preference for a celibate life for the Lord: "I wish that all were as I myself am. *But* each has his own special gift from God, one of one kind and one of another" (1 Cor. 7:7).

For us Lutherans, it should not be strange to listen to that note. The miseries and moral distortions of an obligatory celibacy was not an insignificant factor in Luther's work for reforming the church. Thus, it cannot be right, biblical, Christian, or Lutheran to lay the obligation of celibacy on gays and lesbians as the only option for their sexuality — or perhaps we should rather say, for their love.

Chapter 9

REFLECTIONS ON
THE CHURCH AND THE CITY

Paul Moore, Jr.

PAUL MOORE, JR., was installed in September 1972 as the thirteenth bishop
of New York in the Episcopal Church. He began his ministry in the Chelsea
area of New York City, then moved to Grace Church (Van Vorst) in Jersey
City, New Jersey, in the same diocese in which John Shelby Spong later
became diocesan bishop. In 1957, Paul Moore was called to be dean of
Christ Church Cathedral in Indianapolis, a position he left when he was
elected to the episcopate in 1963. Bishop Moore currently serves on the
National Board of the NAACP Legal Defense Fund and chairs its "Committee of 100." He has been senior fellow of the Yale Corporation as well
as trustee of the General Theological Seminary, Berkeley Divinity School,
Bard College, and Trinity School. He is active in the Institute for Committee Empowerment of the Community Service Society and is a member of
the Board of Human Rights Watch. He also serves on the Advisory Committee of the Anglican Observer at the United Nations. Following a visit to
East Timor in 1989, the bishop and his late wife were staunch activists for
human rights there. A tireless worker on behalf of human rights globally,
the bishop convened an international and interfaith conference on religion
and human rights in 1994. Another of his special interests is the plight of
America's cities. Bishop Moore is the author of *The Church Reclaims the
City,* a study of church urban work, and *Take a Bishop like Me.* He has
served as president of the national Church and City Conference, whose
clergy members seek to enhance the work of the church in downtown and
metropolitan areas.

S TAND IN TIMES SQUARE at midnight as the great ball descends and
the new millennium begins. The multicolored neon lights, the roar
of the great crowd, the explosions of fireworks erupt at the heart
of the city, signaling the joy and the fright of the years to come.
You bump against a teenager, whose spikes of orange hair crown
a pale, nervous face. A large black woman pushes you. "Excuse me,"

191

she shouts through a broad smile. A man in bib overalls, unshaven, clutching a garbage bag, struggles to pass you. A young woman in a flaming red dress hangs onto her man in his three-piece suit. Wedged nearby are two wailing children in blue snowsuits, clinging to their mother for dear life. The huge TV screen facing you above counts down the final seconds of the millennium. You are in the center of *the* twentieth-century city. What awaits you — an apocalypse or anti-climactic business as usual? What is going on inside of you — a broken heart, a rush of anticipation, or cynical disgust for the frenzy?

The Church and the City: Different Things to Different People

To speak of the church and the city in the next millennium, I first ask what church, what city, and from whose point of view? Heraclitus, an early Greek philosopher, said you cannot step into the same stream. Likewise, one day to the next, you cannot live in the same city, or, for that matter, attend the same church, for the city and the church are dynamic, ever-shifting groups of thousands of individuals, who themselves are in constant change in body, mind, and soul.

It is now Sunday and you go to church to find out what the preacher has to say about the quirk of the calendar which has come to represent the vast reaches, the cosmic revolution of what we call time. On this same day, the skinny boy with the orange hair goes to a storefront in the East Village, where New Age mysteries take him to the presence of another world. The smiling black woman attends a stately Baptist church in Harlem. The white uniform of the Ushers' Guild, which always enhances her sense of being a child of God, today makes her feel like an archangel awaiting the Final Trump. The words she hears from the pulpit begin by solemnly repeating the horrors of racism across the past thousand years, then build, decibel by decibel, to pro-claim the glorious future of the children of God, who will march to their deserved glory in the centuries ahead. The well-dressed couple go to St. Thomas', Fifth Avenue, to hear Handel's *Messiah,* sung with the heavenly voices of the boys' choir, testament to the ancient beau-ties of the Anglican heritage. The sermon reaches beyond the weekly fare of examining liturgical texts as they help us in our daily lives and, instead, sets forth an exquisite vision of the City of God. The homeless man, still clutching the garbage bag which contains a loaf of bread, a change of socks, and a ragged sweater, finds a dark corner of the Cathedral of St. John the Divine, where he shivers through the long liturgy, waiting for the soup kitchen to open. The service, in all its reverence, unexpectedly touches him and he stumbles up to the altar to receive a bit of bread and a sip of wine. The children in the blue snowsuits go to Sunday School in their cozy suburban church in New Jersey, while their mother, upstairs, having had her millennial experience in Times Square, relaxes for a blissful hour of quiet in familiar surroundings, silently asking God to give her strength for the next week. And so it is that each seeks what he or she calls God.

Ordinary spiritual moments, like those just described, comprise the more obvious and visible activities of the Church of God in the city. Through them, the Spirit we call holy, flows invisibly. No one knows how much or how little these encounters will penetrate the lives of these few citizens. Indeed, a thousand pages would not be enough to describe the action of grace on human lives in only one small part of a city, in only one day. But through faith and reason, we have come to understand that the Body of Christ moves forward, even toward the next thousand years.

The Allure of the City

I grew up in the country. At night, I heard the wind in the trees, the call of an owl, the occasional barking of a dog. In the long afternoons, I rode my bicycle through the countryside or fished for sunfish in the pond nearby. There were cows, chickens, dogs, and horses. The smells were good: fresh mown grass, cow manure, roses. I loved the rolling hills and woods, the stone walls, the great elms with nests of Baltimore orioles swinging from their boughs. The land was sweet, and I felt a part of it.

But every month or so, my family would go to the city. Lying in bed on the top floor of my grandmother's house, I heard different noises: the deep humming of the traffic, the occasional siren, a shout from the street below. It was scary but wonderful. On some level, I came to love and stand in awe of the city.

The word "city" has a resonance, conveying more than a densely crowded area. It radiates the mystical aura of thousands of cities throughout thousands of years: Cairo, Babylon, Nineveh, Timbuktu, Athens, Rome, Byzantium, Florence, Paris, London, Calcutta, Peking,

Tokyo, Johannesburg, San Francisco, New York — and, shining
above all for those who have been immersed in scripture, Jerusalem. As is often said, the Bible begins in a garden, Eden, and ends
in a city, heavenly Jerusalem. Yet, the Bible is ambivalent about the
city. It speaks of the heavenly Jerusalem but also of the wickedness
of Sodom, Gomorrah, and Babylon.

The Church's Discomfort with City Surroundings

Even though Christianity was born in urban settings, the church
somehow has been suspicious of urban values. The American imagination has pictured rural life as more wholesome than urban life.
This may be due to the influence of the Romantic movement — of
Rousseau and his image of the noble savage. Or it may have to do
with the westward movement of our ancestors from the cities of Europe and, later, from the cities of the eastern seaboard of the United
States to the vast, unspoiled beauty of the frontier. Another possibility
for Christians' attraction to rural settings is that the happiest years in
the life of Jesus were spent in the countryside, before he confronted
Jerusalem for the last time.

A romantic view of nature fueled the explosion to the suburbs after
World War II and deeply influenced the life of the church. When I began my ministry right after the war, mainline churches were following
their people to the suburbs. Sensing the threat to the church's integrity
in this migration, Gibson Winter wrote *The Suburban Captivity of the
Church*. But some of us aggressively championed urban ministry. We
believed the church should stay in the inner city and minister to those
who were there, whatever their religious background, rather than
following others to the suburbs where new churches would be built.

Ambivalence toward urban life underlies the problems of the
church in the city. This is not just a cultural issue but a symptom
of our wavering about the prophetic strain in theology and, indeed,
about the Incarnation itself. City crowding is distasteful to those who
ultimately regard religion as the conversation of the alone with the
alone. The Protestant tradition of individual responsibility leans toward the country, whereas the catholic emphasis on the corporate
nature of life in the Episcopal Church feels more at home in the city.
These are sweeping generalizations, of course. Nevertheless, they illustrate that there are issues we face in urban mission that lie beneath

the surface, and, if we are not clear about this mission, these unseen forces can hinder effective ministry.

Identifying the Mission: Continuing Jesus' Ministry

I was taught in the Marine Corps that, before making a plan of attack, an officer had to be clear about the mission of the operation. He had to decide his troops were going to take the hill before he planned how to take the hill. Similarly, we must be clear about the church's mission in the city before speaking of implementing plans for ministry. Is the church's mission in the city just to survive? To provide a chaplaincy to church members? To arrange inexpensive cultural events? To run charities? Or is it more than any of these?

Episcopalians believe the church is the Body of Christ. From this article of faith stems our understanding of our mission in the city. "The Word was made flesh and dwelt among us." The mission of this Word, which we have come to describe as the second person of the Trinity, was anticipated long before the birth of Jesus, most vividly in Isaiah 61:1–4:

> The Spirit of the Lord God is upon me, because the Lord has anointed me; he has sent me to bring good news to the oppressed, to bind up the broken-hearted, to proclaim liberty to the captives, and release to the prisoners, to proclaim the year of the Lord's favor, and the day of vengeance of our God; to comfort all who mourn; to provide for those who mourn in Zion — to give them a garland instead of ashes, the oil of gladness instead of mourning, the mantle of praise instead of a faint spirit. They will be called oaks of righteousness, the planting of the Lord, to display his glory. They shall build up the ancient ruins, they shall raise the former devastation, they shall repair the ruined cities, the devastation of many generations.

This was the text Jesus used for his first sermon in Nazareth. Matthew describes Jesus in another text from Isaiah (Isa. 42:1–7 and Matt. 12:18):

> Here is my servant, whom I uphold, my chosen, in whom my soul delights; I have put my spirit upon him; he will bring forth justice to the nations...a bruised reed he will not break...he

will faithfully bring forth justice. He will not grow faint or be crushed, until he has established justice in the earth; and the coastlands wait for his teaching. I have given you as a covenant to the people, a light to the nations, to open the eyes that are blind, to bring out the prisoners from the dungeon, from the prison those who sit in darkness.

We can never know how the redeeming of the world is being accomplished through the Incarnation, for this redeeming occurs across the world, outside as well as inside the church. However, Christians represent this embodiment in the institution of the church. Therefore, our mission is to continue the ministry of Christ, as he described it in his first sermon at Nazareth. If we are to carry out a ministry imaging Christ, we are to love each individual who comes our way.

Ministry to Individuals

I once visited a dying woman who was unconscious when I entered the room. There she lay, this formerly fastidious lady, her hair now a tangle, her skin blotchy, her body smells mixing with the sickly odors of disinfectant. I recalled her attending the eight o'clock Eucharist each Sunday, carrying her own prayer book, quietly reverent in following the liturgy. She would greet me politely at the door and go on her way. I called on her from time to time in her modest apartment. A few antiques and silver picture frames spoke of her past genteel life.

On her death bed, however, she was a wretched piece of human flesh, beyond pride, beyond style, even beyond consciousness. After I made a silent prayer to our Lord, I approached the bed and said, "Mrs. Patterson." No response. I spoke louder, "Mrs. Patterson!" Still no response. Despite her unconscious state, I began the prayers for Holy Communion: "Almighty God, unto whom all hearts are open, all desires known, and from whom no secrets are hid." I glanced up when I came to the Our Father, and sensed that she was listening and even moving her lips slightly. I took the Host and placed it on her lips. As I did so, her hands stretched forth, one palm covering the other, as if she were at the altar rail. Her eyes opened. She consumed the wafer, and her hands returned to her sides. She looked up at me with the touch of a smile on her lips, closed her eyes, and went back to sleep. She died that night.

Thus does the ancient rite of Communion of the Sick convey a delicate, soul-touching love that penetrates even unconsciousness. Lying behind this particular ministry of love was a readiness on the gentle lady's part to receive it, built upon a lifetime of quiet reverence, a childhood in the church, and her family of old-fashioned Episcopalians who had weathered the confusions and hurts of existence by constant devotion, nurtured by the Book of Common Prayer.

Ministry to Groups Who Suffer

Christians are to bring love to powerless, suffering people. I knew another traditional churchperson in Poughkeepsie who had listened over the years to the Sermon on the Mount and to the parable of the Last Judgement: "I was hungry and you gave me food." This man had chanted the Magnificat at Evensongs: "He has filled the hungry with good things and the rich he has sent empty away."

When the gentleman retired, he read an article in the newspaper about migrant laborers in the fertile valleys west of the Hudson River. One day he drove over to see them and was horrified that they and their families were living in barracks, being paid little, and subsisting without proper medical care. These laborers had no security, adequate sanitation, or home to return to. The Poughkeepsie resident started a program for migrant workers and their families, and within ten years, a vigorous, well-funded ecumenical ministry supported them. Now, the needs of the migrants have been brought before the government as well as the church. Who knows how or why particular biblical passages motivated an ordinary Episcopalian to be the channel of love that brought a glimpse of the Kingdom to Ulster County.

The migrant program was not just a social service project. I visited there one summer evening and celebrated the Eucharist on an old picnic table. The migrant families gathered around, dressed in their tattered best. The setting sun bathed the scene in golden light as the Lord's Supper was served to the least of these, and to his sisters, children, and brethren. This ministry of love grew out of one layman's long hours in the presence of God and out of a heart made ready to respond.

Ministry to Prisoners

Christians are to bring light to those in prison and working for their freedom. Several years ago, a friend of mine, a Presbyterian minister, was talking to the chaplain of Sing Sing, the state prison in Ossining,

New York. This friend, the Reverend George "Bill" Webber, was the dean of the New York Theological Seminary. The chaplain said, "Bill, why don't you start a seminary at Sing Sing?"

Years later, Bill asked me to attend one of his classes there and address the inmates who were veterans of the armed services. After extensive screening and security checks, I reached the dreary, windowless room where Bill's seminary class met. I am always a bit apprehensive about entering an alien situation, but these men put me at ease with warm greetings and ready conversation.

One inmate was serving a life sentence for a murder of passion years ago; another was a doctor who had been imprisoned for many years, convicted of giving his wife an overdose of drugs; another was a youngster who had committed an armed robbery of a store to feed his habit. Because of the political climate, there was little hope of their being released on parole. They complained there was no purpose in being a good inmate when one could not earn parole, regardless of how outstanding his behavior. Others spoke of conditions that dehumanized them. But the prisoners were warm and affectionate men, not bitter. I felt at home with them.

Later, in the auditorium, a first-class jazz band played for us. "The Star Spangled Banner" was sung as everyone stood at attention. I spoke to a most responsive gathering. On leaving, most of the men gave me a warm hug and I went home filled with hope and love. My associates and I had gone to minister to the inmates, but they ministered to us in the strange chemistry of the Kingdom because, although they spoke of having no anticipation of early release, their spirits seemed filled with expectation.

Concern for Peace and Justice

Christians are to fight against injustice, wherever it occurs in the world. By sheer chance, my wife, Brenda, and I were asked in 1989 to visit East Timor, a tiny nation which had been under military occupation since 1975. In that year, Indonesia, with the approval of President Ford and Henry Kissinger, illegally invaded East Timor, killing and otherwise causing the death of some two hundred thousand people of a population of seven hundred thousand. This slaughter was accomplished by illegally using weapons from the United States. Following our first visit, my wife and I kept in touch with Carlos Ximenes Belo, the courageous Roman Catholic bishop who was awarded the Nobel peace prize. The years have dragged on with massacres, torturing, and other horrors. We and others have tried to bring pressure through our government and the United Nations for a peaceful and just solution.

On our last visit in 1997, Brenda and I had an extraordinary experience, which showed me, once more, the mysterious interweaving of suffering, love, and beauty in the life of the Kingdom. Bishop Belo had planned a pilgrimage for all the youth of East Timor. We accompanied him to the foot of Mt. Remaliu, the highest peak on the island, where the young people were to place a statue of the Virgin Mary. On the long drive from the coast, we passed trucks, buses, motorcycles, even people walking to the foot of the mountain. There, in the sunset of this jungle valley, thousands of young Timorese celebrated the Eucharist with their bishops. The fading, golden light, the solemn faces of the young people, the brilliant white altar cloth, and a palpable presence of the Holy Spirit became a vision of the Kingdom breaking through that troubled land.

After the service, the people began the climb to the peak of Mt. Remaliu. They slept under the stars and, the next day, celebrated another Mass halfway up the mountain. At the conclusion of the service, as the bishop took off his vestments, a young man rushed up to him with an expression of terror across his face, crying, "They have murdered one of our brothers! They murdered him, stabbed him with a knife!" Apparently, an unstable man, some say in the pay of the Indonesian military, had killed one of the Boy Scouts who was monitoring the event. The crowd then turned on the assassin and killed him. The bishop's dream of a moment of faith, peace, and joy for his beloved young people was shattered.

The courageous youth were resisting Indonesian military occupation. Some had lost their brothers in a massacre a few years before. All of them had lost at least one relative in the long struggle. The bishop had hoped to instill a peaceful, nonviolent approach to their courage through the beauty of the pilgrimage. He called off the attempt and returned home, battered once more by the cruelty of Indonesian forces.

As I write, a referendum on whether East Timor will become independent or gain autonomy within Indonesia is scheduled for early August 1999. Although this seems like progress, the Indonesians continue to arm militia who are pro-Indonesian, and the tension on the island is high. Many proindependence supporters are in hiding be-

cause they are the targets of violence and must be convinced it is safe
enough to return to register to vote in the referendum and campaign
for East Timor's sovereignty.

Despite political violence, there is hope of eventual peace. A net-
work around the globe exists, from the Nobel Committee in Oslo, to
other Nobel laureates throughout the world, to hundreds of organizations across the world's many churches — all of whom continue to
support Bishop Belo's struggle. Since the bishop has led his church
to stand courageously with the struggling people, the number of
Christians in East Timor has grown from about 40 percent of the
population to 90 percent, a clear response to the prophetic leadership of Bishop Belo for justice and peace. It is a cliché to say that the
church grows with the blood of martyrs, but it seems that this is so
in East Timor. And certainly it has been so elsewhere, as in Uganda.
This dynamic, in a lesser degree, is true for the church in the city,
when it is willing to sacrifice for its people.

Preserving the Integrity of Worship
and Spreading the Blessings of the Eucharist

We Christians are to express our love of God in worship. Our Lord
not only went aside from time to time for solitary prayer but also
took part in the worship of the synagogue and temple. Jesus was so
passionate in his devotion to the liturgy and to the corporate worship
of his people that his anger flared at the corruption in the temple.
In a rare fit of rage, he overthrew the tables of the money-changers.
This act so infuriated the temple authorities that they began to plot
his death.

One of the marks of a faithful church is a like passion for the
integrity of corporate worship. This is no easy task because of the
variety of cultures and classes in the average American city. Liturgy
must be incarnate in the culture where it is carried out. Jesus lived
among a homogeneous first-century people. They were familiar with
the Hebrew scriptures, and observed the great festivals of the Jewish calendar — Chanukah, Passover, Tabernacles — each setting forth
the people's relation to Yahweh. However, religious communities in
American cities exist among people of many backgrounds, languages,
customs, and ways of thinking about themselves. There is further di-
vision between persons of great wealth and power and those who
live in abject poverty. Yet, the Episcopal Church is a Catholic church,

with a universal character to which any human being will be drawn if the incarnation of the Word wears the flesh, speaks the language, and offers a love which can be understood.

LANGUAGE

Thus, central to the relation of the church to the communities it serves is the translation of the liturgy into the native languages of the people. In the Diocese of New York, for instance, liturgies are presented in English, Spanish, French, Chinese, Japanese, Korean, and Haitian. The music, also, should be indigenous, as well as the style of liturgy. Great divergence is common, for example, between the formal rites of Fifth and Park Avenue churches, and the relaxed, flexible, more informal services of some inner-city parishes. But even in the inner city, subcultures collide, as in New York between Latino and West Indian groups and among generations.

THE EUCHARIST

The Eucharist itself sets forth archetypal images and patterns, according to the most basic of human experiences — listening, eating, kissing, loving, offering, suffering, dying, rising from death, healing, and being strengthened for combat. Thus, a Eucharist can transform any human event, whether it be the joy or the sorrow of the individual, the community, or the nation.

The Eucharist is the heartbeat of the church, feeding all the members of the Body as the heart pumps blood into the brain, feet, legs, and loins. I have seen the Eucharist bring a sense of victory and peace at the time of Martin Luther King's death, fill a cathedral with the glory of Easter, give courage to soldiers, civil rights workers, and persecuted minorities as they faced possible death, and give peace to the dying and to those who were left behind in grief. The gift of the Eucharist, like the gift of Jesus Christ, must penetrate every aspect of a Christian community, so that the parish acts out its whole life in the rhythm of it. Rings of grace should radiate from the altar, through the people of God, out into the life of the city.

Abbé Michonneau, who was part of the postwar worker-priest movement of France, spoke of paraliturgies, giving a foretaste of later experiences of the Eucharist through different means — street processions with music, banners, and candles, or demonstrations against injustice, where a crude cross was carried — all calling attention to why the people were there and from whence they had come. The style of these paraliturgies must fit the style of the neighborhood, just as demonstrations, which are, in a sense, themselves paraliturgies, must fit the style of those taking part.

I recall a stylized celebrity picketing of the South African Consulate to which well-known political figures came. One had to call ahead for a reservation so that there would be sufficient room in one of the several police wagons to be taken comfortably to jail! I also have seen demonstrations of the poor and the homeless straggling along a back street. Each of these, if motivated by the cause of justice or peace, is a liturgy and extends the reach of the Eucharist far beyond the walls of the church.

The Eucharist is the bedrock of Christian spirituality, for it prevents the individual from becoming self-absorbed and from using prayer only for personal welfare. Participating in the Eucharist is something one does whether or not one is thinking clearly, one's faith is strong, one is under stress or deeply troubled. And through the Eucharist, God's love is spread.

PRACTICING PERSONAL SPIRITUALITY: THE IMPORTANCE OF PRAYER

Christians are to be a people of personal devotion. Some interesting observations have been made over the years about the life of prayer in the city. I believe prayer to be particularly important in the hyperactive urban environment not only because of its prophetic dimension but also because it is an action and the heart of the Christian community of love.

Jesus often turned aside for personal prayer. So must we. In the city, Christians should learn to pray for a few minutes each morning, even when walking or riding to work, to visualize the day which lies ahead and dedicate it to the Lord. Then, from time to time, when one has a moment, God's presence can be sensed. In the subway, a city dweller can pray for some of the individuals passed by, especially if they seem to be in pain. One can become aware of the Lord's presence in them. People also can look up once in a while to the sky and thank God for the beautiful blue of it. These so-called arrow prayers can keep an individual in touch with existence beyond one's egocentric sphere and transform the day. Whenever one can, one should stop in an empty church for a few minutes of peace, and, as he or she is able, several times a week, meditate on a passage of scripture. These are obvious and, perhaps to some, even banal suggestions.

One can go far deeper, however, and explore some of the ancient ascetical practices as they apply to prayer in the city. The experience of urban loneliness and despair has been compared to the Dark Night of the Soul, a salient experience of St. John of the Cross and St. Teresa of Avila. They found that, in enduring darkness, loneliness, and despair, they were far closer to our Lord when the darkness lifted.

One can work through the spirituality of Jean-Pierre de Caussade and his Sacrament of the Moment, whereby the guilt of the past and the anxiety of the future fade away before the reality of the present moment. The past does not exist anymore; the future has yet to be. There is only the present, the Sacrament of the Moment, in which is contained the full grace of God.

Expanding the experience of prayer, one also can practice Francis de Sales's suggestion of taking a "nosegay" from the garden of one's morning meditation and carrying it during the day as a reminder of time with the Lord. This can be an image, a saying, or a feeling.

Preserving the integrity of worship, expanding it, and building an appreciation of the rewards of devotion help to enhance harmony in the community. The more individuals living in the conscious presence of God, the more effective the church will be in its mission to the city, and the more alert Christians will be to the outcroppings of the Kingdom.

TEACHING THE WORD OF GOD AND ACTING IN HIS IMAGE

Christians must be teachers of the Word, as Jesus himself was a teacher. He taught simply, in parables or stories, and most effectively by acting out the power of God's love. Without Jesus' actions, his words now would not be remembered. He taught the love of God not just by saying, "God loves you," but by touching the sores of the leper. He did not just say, "Feed the hungry"; he fed the five thousand. He did not just urge his followers to take care of one another; he washed the disciples' feet. Nor did he just say people are one family; he spoke over the bread and wine at the Last Supper, saying, "This is my body, this is my blood," and then offered his own body to be broken and his own blood to be poured out the next day on the cross. Jesus did not just promise resurrection; he died and, in some mysterious way, was seen to have risen from the dead.

Trying to imitate in daily life what Jesus was, said, and did is not to belittle formal instruction, Bible classes, preparation for confirmation, and so forth. But teaching and preaching have little impact if the lessons are not acted out in the life of the parish and diocese.

Living out the Eucharistic rhythm of sinning and being forgiven, falling sick and being healed, dying and rising, is the nature of the life of the church as it tries to be the Body of Christ. However, fulfilling this vocation in a modern Western city seems to require a complicated institutional base and confronts enormous obstacles not unlike the obstacles which brought Jesus to the cross.

Overcoming Barriers to Ministry

One of the most frustrating aspects of carrying out the mission of the church is the array of obstacles which confront ministry. Sometimes it feels like struggling through a jungle, blinded by undergrowth, tripped up by roots, and ensnared by vines. Often clergy cannot identify what it is that is blocking progress and seeping the vitality of the institution.

Correcting Misunderstanding of the Church's Charge

One major hindrance to mission is a misunderstanding of the church's purpose. A majority of churchgoers think of the church as a place to find peace of mind, to be strengthened, or to be healed. And so it is. But this peace, this strengthening, this healing is given to us so that we may carry out Christ's mission of compassion, justice, and peace more effectively. The church should function as both a command post and an aid station in the struggle of the Kingdom.

Opening the Church's Closed Doors

Most persons see the church as a place to bless the major events of life: baptism, confirmation, marriage, and burial. Many parishes, especially large and prosperous ones, look down with institutional disdain on nonchurchgoers' seeking such services. However, with imagination and perseverance, these events can become a means of communicating the realities of the faith. If two young people who do not belong to the church come to be married, they should be welcomed, for their vulnerable state may make them open to a new understanding of the church. The same is true for those bewildered by a death in the family.

Years ago, two of my friends wanted to be married in a church. One was a widow, the other had been divorced for a long time. The rector told them the parish had rules about counseling divorced persons who wished to be married because counseling took up clergy time. Therefore, he said, he never married divorced persons unless they were members of the parish. My friends, both lifelong, if lapsed, Episcopalians, were deeply hurt. Luckily, I found a more open parish which welcomed them warmly and married them. The couple became members of the parish. In the course of time, I gave last rites to the husband, which meant the world to him and to his wife. The point is that even an unexpected or unconventional motivation for choosing a church wedding or funeral can be used as an opportunity.

In a modern city, there are thousands who are ready to become Christians but who never have been exposed to the faith in a way that has reached them. Clergy must be alert to those moments which may happen only a few times in persons' lives — the moments when they are ready to be touched by the love and word of God.

Preventing the Church's Strength from Being Sapped

Those who come to church only to be consoled and who are upset when they hear a message that is controversial are a constant drain on a parish priest and on the evangelical dynamic of a congregation. Some can be brought around by patient persuasion, but others finally leave. Clergy must be ready to let them go. This is a hard lesson. But if a priest agonizes too long over someone who simply will not listen, who is not willing to stay in the parish even when slightly uncomfortable, the priest can undermine his or her vitality and the morale of the community. I experienced this once in a parish I had. After two years of worry, sleeplessness, and frustration, I decided to go forward with more progressive lay leadership and let the dissidents go. The result was like a resurrection.

Counteracting Theological Ignorance

Another barrier to the church for people is an intellectual one. I do not agree with all of Bishop Spong's writings, but it is most important to have voices like his heard. No, you do not have to believe the snake talked, in the Christmas story as history, or in Noah's ark. Yes, there are many ways to understand the Resurrection beyond whether an angel rolled away the stone. If the image of Jesus walking on water turns one off, so be it. This individual still can be a Christian. Unfortunately, many persons have no understanding of the Christian faith beyond what they were taught as youngsters in Sunday School.

I often hesitate to use the word "God" in my sermons because I do not know what image that word summons up in the imagination of the people in the pews. I become angry when I hear someone say at a funeral, "It must have been God's will that little Johnny was run over. He was such a sweet child, but God wanted him in heaven." Wrong! There is so much misunderstanding in the popular mind about the Christian faith, it is a wonder persons of average intelligence attend church.

More writers like Bishop Spong should clear the way for skeptics to approach the faith seriously, and parish priests should dare venture into the areas he has explored in their own sermons. What are the essentials of the Christian faith? What are the unessentials? What is true history, and what, instead, is truth-conveying myth? Such clarifications would enable decent, sensitive, intelligent people to approach the church with more intellectual honesty. Historically, the Anglican Church has been a leader in modernizing theology. Anglicans must continue this tradition not only in the groves of academe but also in parish teaching and in sermons. Just because some people are not college graduates does not mean they do not have intellectual problems with the faith.

Rebirth in Old Structures

Another complicated obstacle to the mission of the church is the old age of the buildings where people gather. There are those who say the buildings can be eliminated — that the church should return to the early days when Christians met in each other's homes, when the church was people, not buildings. Now these great and handsome monuments to the glory of God stand throughout the city, most of them over a hundred years old. Millions of dollars are spent keeping them up, yet sometimes a mere handful of worshipers occupy their cavernous depths on a Sunday morning. These structures are problematic for a struggling church, but a stubborn loyalty to the past glory days and to the ancestors who built these churches in better times keeps them going. Tear them down, some say. Let the dead bury the dead. Let us get on with it! One needs, after all, only to look at the growth of the Pentecostals meeting in homes, garages, or storefronts to see that structures are not central to propagating the faith. Thus, critics argue the masonry relics of another day are no longer needed.

But there is another way of looking at these old places. Perhaps they are not millstones but rather anchors which keep us in the city. I have seen churches torn down, merged, and the money put to mission in the same community. But without the building, the mission disappears over the years, and there is one less presence in the inner city.

Even if a church remains standing, sometimes secular forces complicate the task of members' maintaining their structure in keeping with their desired ministry. Officials or special interest groups often are interested in a building as a landmark or example of an architectural style long gone and, thus, prevent a congregation from renovating in an economical fashion.

Neighborhoods in a modern city change rapidly. The church I served in Jersey City, an old Gothic beauty, once was the pride of "the carriage trade." When we took over, with the help of outside assistance the parish became a model of urban mission. Later, it almost died. Now, thanks to the foresight of Bishop Spong and others and the leadership of the new rector and his people, the church has been renovated, the parish house repaired, and some of the neighborhood gentrified. The church, for the first time in over fifty years, is a self-supporting parish. My philosophy as bishop was to hang on to such old places (with a few exceptions), even if they were barely surviving, put them on the back burner, and wait for the imaginative leadership of a young priest or a demographic change in the neighborhood to revive them.

Surpassing Parochialism (with the Support of the Diocese)

Parochialism is another perennial problem. It has its roots in a lack of understanding of the nature of a Catholic church. Historically, the diocese has been the basic unit of the church. There is an ancient saying, *Ubi episcopos, ibi ecclesia* (Where the bishop is, there the church is).

But apart from history or ecclesiology, the diocese as the primary unit of the church makes sense. This organizational structure enables parishes in wealthy neighborhoods, or with large endowments through no effort of the present congregation, to assist parishes in poor neighborhoods. Thriving parishes *should* want to help their less fortunate neighbors. If assistance to less prosperous parishes is arranged through democratic processes and planning at the diocesan level, an equitable distribution of resources can be made and long-range goals established.

However, rich parishes usually resent their resources going to the diocese, over which they have no direct control. They would rather give money to churches, which, for whatever reason, are attractive to them. But this puts a receiving congregation in the embarrassing position of having to beg for assistance, woo the grants committee of a wealthy church, and conduct its programs according to the whims of the donor church. The reason for such a relationship, advocates say, is that a direct, personal relationship between congregations can develop closer ties among the churches' people. There is some truth to this. Notwithstanding the pluses, the downside is that a charismatic priest, who can dramatize his or her work, will attract more support. And when such a priest leaves, the donor parish may lose interest.

In fact, both methods of funding are useful. A progressive "tax" on parishes furnishes the diocese with the necessary resources to keep the needy parishes functioning. Yet, there is still opportunity for prosperous parishes to fund special discrete programs over and above the bread and butter of a poor parish's budget. This is obviously a complicated process and highly ideological and political. It really comes down to the issue of *control* and, underneath that, the age-old conflict between charity and justice. Charity makes the donor feel good but is humiliating to the recipient. Justice empowers the poorer person or institution and may make the richer one resentful. This tension often is manifest in illogical outlooks and patterns of behavior. People would rather give money to a private hospital than pay more taxes to support the rights of every person to have decent medical care. Prominent men and women will stay up all night helping at a church-run shelter for the homeless, but they will not use their influence to lobby for better housing policies.

It is necessary to think of the diocese simply as a unit of the church that facilitates the flow of resources. Funneling mission funds through the diocese eliminates the poor parishes' humiliation of begging. Through properly structured block grants to areas of the diocese, parishes in need can work out with one another an equitable distribution of resources.

Planning for urban mission cannot be done by putting pins in a map of the city where no parishes exist. I prefer viewing the church from an organic perspective: A bishop waters the plants that show signs of growth, prunes dead wood in those places that are withering, and allows some places to lie fallow. Old churches, like old stumps in the forest, can lie dormant for years and then begin to sprout with new life. Thus, old buildings, while presently a liability, may be a long-term asset to the life of the church.

There is no easy answer to parochialism. It is a built-in human trait. But church leaders who see the pragmatic and ethical good sense of breaking out of parochialism for the good of the wider church need to keep emphasizing common life across parish boundaries.

I have been speaking of mission in terms of the parish, but some of the most effective ministries of service and social action — which are unaffected by parochialism — are carried out by church institutions. In New York, the Episcopal Mission Society and the Seamen's Church Institute are venerable institutions which carry on ministries of great scope with prisoners, children, addicts, homeless, and retarded persons. Seamen's Church Institute not only gives pastoral care and training to seamen but also has initiated a vigorous program for seamen's rights. Another variation from conventional ministry can be launched by cathedrals, especially if they are not hampered by a conservative vestry.

Major Concerns the Church Must Address on Local, National, and International Levels

In order to maintain its integrity, the church must address ongoing challenges to the principles of peace, justice, and compassion, the marks of the Kingdom.

Conquering Bigotry

One of the most debilitating and enduring of these threats is racism. Thousands of volumes have been written on the subject, thousands of organizations have fought against it, millions of sermons have been preached about it, and yet this virus persists.

In the mid-1960s, Malcolm Boyd, an activist white priest who went on freedom rides in the early sixties and worked unceasingly for racial justice, preached a sermon to a huge interracial service at the National Cathedral in Washington. (He had just been fired from his job as chaplain at Wayne State University for saying on television that Jesus had a penis, as a way of emphasizing the Incarnation.) I knew he was greatly agitated when he ascended the great marble pulpit, and I was somewhat anxious about what he might say. At the climax to his peroration, he said words to this effect: "The only thing that will end discrimination in the work place, the only thing that will end discrimination in schools, in housing, in churches — is intermarriage!" The congregation was stunned. If he had said, again, that Jesus had a penis, I think the older white members of the congregation would have been less shocked. But, in truth, I think he was right in his analysis.

Perhaps Boyd was not literally right; certainly education, equal justice, affirmative action, and so forth, are critically important. But intermarriage is a symbol of the heart of the problem. Until people are one flesh — until physical separation is eliminated — there will be racism because, without this melding, people will continue to divide themselves as "we" and "they." I do not mean, of course, that all marriages should be interracial but that it would be welcomed to have enough intermarriage to blur racial lines so that skin color would not cause any more comment or antagonism than does hair color.

This may be an old-fashioned idea, but it is based on the sometimes bitter experience of many years. Although laws have improved and more African-Americans are in positions of leadership and affluence in the United States than ever before, I believe there is more social separation of the races now than there was thirty years ago. There also is more anger and despair among poor blacks than there was then. Legal discrimination has changed to an even more difficult kind: economic discrimination and segregation.

The downside of integration is the dilution of ethnic pride in the courageous heritages of the African peoples. However, this need not be so. I am writing this essay on St. Patrick's Day, which indicates, to put it mildly, that integration does not weaken the glories of a particular heritage.

Intermarriage symbolizes the one flesh we share as human beings, the equality of worth in creation, and the flesh of all humanity which Christ took on. I remember the joy with which blacks and whites embraced each other during the early civil rights movement. The breaking of the barrier was exhilarating. Holding hands during the singing of freedom songs, especially "We Shall Overcome," was a kind of liturgy, a "Kiss of Peace."

The church perhaps is the only institution which can further such an intimate association — fleshly contact by which the demon of racism can be exorcised. Yet, the cliché that eleven o'clock Sunday morning is the most segregated hour in the week is still true after all these years of struggle. This is embarrassing and humiliating for the church.

Seeking solutions can be awkward and condescending on both sides. But I do believe it is absolutely necessary to encourage contact at every level. I often wonder why the artistic community is so far ahead of the church in this regard. The easy mixing in the world of music, be it jazz or opera, does not seem to weaken the power of black culture. Indeed, American music and art have been invigorated by black conventions. If anything, African-American music gives distinctive sound to the music of our country.

Whatever programs, events, or movements unfold as the years go on, we must continue to say, "The Word was made flesh (all flesh — black flesh, brown flesh, yellow flesh, red flesh, white flesh) and dwelt among us. And we beheld his glory."

Regrettably, racism underlies not only our economic and social structure but also our foreign policy. Consciously or unconsciously, leaders in Washington have let loose armed might against people of other races and ethnic groups more than against white people. I cite Vietnam, Nicaragua, Guatemala, Chile, El Salvador, and East Timor. The fear of Communism was often cited in these conflicts and certainly commercial motives were involved, but I still feel deeply that the carelessness with which our representatives directly or indirectly caused the death of millions of innocent people had to do with whites devaluing others as human beings because of their races. For instance, during World War II, I remember being brainwashed into thinking that the Japanese were somehow less than human because they were Asians.

Because of the emotional chasms among the races, because of unfamiliarity with the others' ways, fear and paranoia are engendered and, as a result, strange reactions occur.

Improving the Penal System: Identifying the Sources of Crime and Fostering Rehabilitation

The correctional system in the United States is a flagrant symptom of racism. Some two million persons go through the system a year. In New York State, 80 percent of these are minorities. There is a subtle interweaving between racism in the culture and the fact that at least 35 percent of the inmates are imprisoned on drug-related charges. Whether it be in foreign policy or in domestic, our reaction to crime, addiction, or revolution is use of force, most frequently by white people against persons of color.

If a fraction of the funds used in building prisons and in attempting to eliminate the source of drugs in third-world nations by quasi-military means were spent in an intensive drug rehabilitation and prevention program within and without the prisons, the results would be far more effective and much less expensive. Furthermore, the causes underlying drug use, such as hopelessness on the part of young people in the ghettoes because they see no future for themselves, also need to be addressed with more vigor. However, humane approaches to these problems and to the human suffering caused by them are labeled as "liberal" or "bleeding heart" and are politically unpopular. The use of force and the infliction of punishment seem the ways to win elections. The return of capital punishment is other evidence of legalized violence.

How should drug-related crimes be prevented? A popular answer is, "Lock 'em up and throw away the key," however expensive and ineffective that policy may be. How should drug imports be stopped? The answer for some has been, "Bomb them out of existence." After several years of this policy, it has become clear that it does not work, as admitted recently even by Barry McCaffrey, the "czar" of the national drug program.

The techniques of correction and the strategy of U.S. armed forces are not within the expertise of the church. However, the resort to force and violence as a solution to foreign and domestic problems is a mind-set against which the church must struggle.

I do not know what has turned the mood of America away from rational and humane solutions to domestic and foreign social problems. A few years ago, the phrase "compassion fatigue" was coined. I think it is true that people in our country tire easily of anything which is not a quick fix. However, any objective study of society shows that healing the wounds of three hundred years cannot occur overnight. The War on Poverty did not fail; it was terminated before it had a chance to succeed. Generations of families living in poverty cannot be turned around in a few years.

There is a need to dig deeper than catch phrases such as "compassion fatigue" to understand America's failure to approach solutions to crime with greater compassion. Human beings have within them the ability to act nobly or cruelly and the willingness to make sacrifices or to conduct themselves selfishly. Recent leadership in our nation has pandered to the selfish, the greedy, the violent, the cruel streak in human nature. In this vein, prison construction is not driven by correctional philosophy. Rather, it is influenced by the political advantages to the rural regions where prisons are built, even though erecting them so far away from the cities where the inmates' families live has a negative effect on prisoners' morale and rehabilitation.

This leads me to another subtle change in the public's attitude toward incarceration. In the 1950s, I served on the board of what then was called the New York Prison Association. The philosophy behind the correctional system at that time was rehabilitation, or *correction*. Now, the strategy is prevention of crime through punishment. Underneath this motivation lies revenge and fear. And underneath the fear is prejudice born of racial separation and economic discrimination.

A change in the American policy of increased prisons, mandatory sentencing, and neglect of minority opportunity is economically feasible. It costs more to keep one man in prison than to send him to Harvard. An increase in the quality and number of probation and parole officers and a massive increase in drug treatment are cheaper than building and sustaining prisons. For Christians, the main objective should not be creating economic wealth; rather, it must remain building social justice and decency.

We often read of programs which succeed brilliantly because an institution or a group of individuals has taken the trouble to care for young persons and to give them a sense of worth. This "treatment" is time-consuming and often frustrating, but I have seen it work time and again. The public sector could provide such programs if people chose to have it do so not only in the area of correctional systems but also regarding other challenges to society such as the current shortfalls in education. No one should be surprised that so many students in the New York school system fail, when one looks at the size of classes and the disintegration of buildings.

Recognizing Global Economics as a Contributor to Poverty

Beyond the matters described above is an even more serious long-term problem, economic globalization. The disastrous results of global

corporate power are evident in this country, as corporations lay off
American workers for cheaper labor overseas.

Another result of exploitative globalization is the tangle of problems symbolized by third-world debt, engendered by greed-inspired
high-risk loans made by major world banks. There are signs that some
corporate leaders are beginning to realize the dangers of such imbalance. Economic disruption, widespread social chaos, and terrorism
will occur if the present course continues to be followed. Thousands
will suffer from violence, starvation, or disease.

I have had little success working with businessmen to persuade
them to face the results of inopportune business policies on local,
national, or international levels. (My only small success was in the
1960s, when business communities saw their cities go up in flames
and, consequently, cooperated out of fear with programs for black
economic development.) The church feels more comfortable subsidiz-
ing a small staff in Washington to affect legislation than confronting
churchpersons who are leaders in corporate America. Nevertheless,
church leaders have an obligation to do so on the highest level.

I would like to see the presiding bishop of the Episcopal Church in
the United States, together with the leaders of other denominations
and faith groups, meet with the CEOs of major corporations to confront the realities faced by the disadvantaged members of society. If
churches and business communities backed programs together, they
would be effective. And, if corporate leaders cooperated in supporting
such ventures, they would not have to fear their competitors' gaining
an advantage.

A Summary on the Church and Social Problems

Concerns like those discussed above in a cursory fashion are an appropriate part of any analysis of the church in the city. If the underlying
causes of human suffering are not addressed, local charitable and
social-action programs are like putting one's fingers in a dike. Given
its wealth, there is no need for the United States to allow its most
vulnerable citizens to suffer unnecessarily. Furthermore, many residents, both legal and illegal, have families in developing countries.
Callous foreign policy toward such places directly affects those for
whom clergy are pastorally responsible.

Some solutions are complicated and long-term. But others are obvious and simple, such as providing affordable housing, improving

schools, remaking the correctional system, feeding the hungry, and giving more attention to the young. These are rather simple solutions to domestic problems if the political will and the pocketbooks of the people are behind them.

Far more difficult is how to effect change in the global economy so that it assists all the people of the world rather than just widening the gap between rich and poor. Economic exploitation by western European nations and Americans over the centuries is one of the reasons for the chaos which seems to be enveloping sub-Saharan Africa, for the volatility of the financial markets in Asia, and for the grinding poverty of many Latin American nations. On some level, perhaps an unconscious one, the rise of terrorism grows out of resentment against long-term economic injustices. This resentment often cloaks itself in religious loyalties. Persons suffering from social dislocation often find relief in the emotional outlet of violent religious fundamentalism.

Sooner or later the dangers of the imbalance between rich and poor will be recognized more broadly, but still it is extremely unlikely that global corporations will make a concerted attempt to redress these inequalities on their own. Nor is it likely that the governments of powerful nations will have the political will to act, since corporations have growing power over them. It must be remembered, however, that history often gives us surprises, bad as well as good ones.

Thus, the church must continue to point out the suffering caused by economic disparities and the danger of rising resentment in third-world nations. The voices for reform may be weak but must speak out, for sometimes an unlikely chain of events can affect history. For instance, Michael Harrington, sitting at the feet of Dorothy Day in a Catholic Worker storefront on the lower east side of Manhattan, was inspired to write a book called *The Other America*. President Kennedy read it and conceived the "War on Poverty," which had an enormous national impact as it was carried out under President Johnson.

Understanding the Doctrine of Separation of Church and State

It is the mission of the church to discern the causes of human suffering, to speak out clearly against them, and to do all in its power to redress unjust structures. The results of these efforts may seem minimal; sometimes an activist may never know the impact on a person which made a great difference. Regardless of whether the church influences the world, it must, by bearing witness, reflect the true image of Christ.

Some object to the church becoming involved in politics, stating that this contravenes the principle of separation of church and state. Quite the contrary. The doctrine of separation exists not only to protect religion from interference by the state but also to give the church the freedom to judge the state. It is often said that one of the causes of the Russian Revolution was the silence of the state-controlled church concerning the oppression of the poor, and that one of the underlying elements in the rise of Nazism was the acquiescence of Germany's Christian churches to Hitler.

I believe strongly that the church should speak out on issues but should not become officially involved in partisan politics. It is up to churches to point out injustices and, when possible, to suggest solutions. It is up to Christian and non-Christian individuals to decide what political party is most likely to address the pressing issues.

Sensible Evangelism in Multicultural and Multigenerational Contexts

The church, as an instrument of redemption, should always seek to grow. However, evangelism can be hurtful to the image of the Body of Christ if it is selfishly motivated. If people are drawn to the church for solace only, for social status, or for emotional spiritual thrills, they are not being drawn to Christ as he is — the crucified and risen Christ. Anglo-Catholics may be attracted by the aesthetics of a solemn high Mass; evangelicals may be caught up in the uplift they get from the latest group dynamic. Indeed, many persons join the church for egocentric reasons but, once a part of it, learn the deeper purposes of the faith. This requires that a parish live out the gospel in its daily life by being a community of love to which people come to be loved, healed, comforted, and taught.

Soon, however, parishioners must be sent out from the parish to minister to the poor and suffering and to struggle for peace and justice. Hundreds of such parishes exercise ministries of outreach by feeding the hungry, housing the homeless, caring for the sick in mind or body, nurturing children, and working for social justice. It is a sign of hope that so many such programs exist. These parishes draw people to them for the right reasons. As noted, I once experienced the loss of church members who disapproved of a progressive program but gained others who became vigorous parts of the parish's life and were fulfilled by its social ministry.

Often, the church works with public funds to accomplish its purpose. This is a delicate relationship because being the recipient of government help can blunt the church's willingness to criticize city hall. Another danger is to be a parish which is simply a social agency. I have seen many such churches ailing with what I call the "doughnut syndrome" — running many programs paid for by others but having few members at the core of the parish.

There are various methods of evangelism in the city, but they all require constant vigilance and energy. At the center, the parish must be a loving community not only in the atmosphere within the parish but also in its role in the community.

Building Membership

A small parish committee needs to exist which has evangelism as its primary objective. Simple measures often are very successful, like asking each parishioner to bring a friend to church, having a few parishioners on the lookout for newcomers at the coffee hour, and using baptisms, weddings, and funerals as opportunities to reach families on a level of intimacy that is possible at such times. I am often surprised that such simple measures do not exist in many places where there are complaints about shrinking attendance. Another technique for attracting and retaining new members is to give newcomers jobs to do and the opportunity to provide leadership. Too often the old guard say they want new people yet resent their taking over some of the functions of the parish.

The Liturgy and Sermon

The quality of the liturgy and the preaching makes all the difference. A television producer may spend hundreds of hours on a thirty-second commercial, but some clergy take only a few minutes with the organist and let it go at that. The priest, with the help of some lay persons, should examine carefully what newcomers experience from the moment they enter the church to the moment they drive away.

Many factors contribute to a satisfactory experience at church, but an inspiring sermon is the most important. People stay away after a few boring sermons. Sermons should never be read. If the priest writes out the sermon, which is often helpful, he or she should preach as if preaching from notes — always preaching to the people and making eye contact. A sermon is not a lecture; it is a homily which should motivate listeners or cause them to reflect, and, therefore, it should have emotional content. It is painful but helpful to have two or three loyal lay persons give the rector candid feedback from time to time.

A warm welcome, quiet before the service begins, variety to the liturgy, good lighting, dignified but not pompous movement, suitable timing, music that always includes at least two familiar hymns, appropriate informality during announcements and the Kiss of Peace, and care that a sense of the holy is present during the canon are additional ways to augment the service. It is also helpful for a priest to instruct lay readers carefully so that they may be heard in the back pews. Appropriate arrangements for the coffee hour are a cordial way to end a Sunday gathering, but persons never should be pressured to participate. There are those who wish to be anonymous. These are some obvious measures clergy and lay members can take to make the Sunday service one which a newcomer will wish to revisit.

The experience of attending church needs to be interesting, inspiring, exciting even, but never boring. However, in the attempt at avoiding dullness, clergy should be careful not to go to another extreme. Episcopalians certainly are not the only Christians who like familiarity as well as variety. The liturgy should be a careful mixture of both.

Addressing Multiculturalism

Evangelism to people of varying cultures and languages poses a special problem. After much discussion over the years in the Diocese of New York, it was determined that the more independence Latino congregations attained, the more successful they were. It also was found essential for them to have Latino clergy. The shortage of Latino clergy was addressed by the establishment of the Instituto Hispano Pastoral, which trained Latino men and women for lay and ordained ministry. Unfortunately, the organization was terminated after I retired because of a lack of funding. Yet, the Hispanic people of New York and many other American cities provide by far the most fruitful opportunity for Christian evangelism.

The Caliber of Clergy and the Sticky Issue of Tenure

Finally, it is the quality of the clergy that is the most important element in parish vitality and growth. Against all demographic indicators and confounding economic pessimism, I have seen so-called "dead" parishes come to life with the advent of a new priest. I have witnessed this in St. Bartholomew's, a large upper-east-side parish in New York. I have seen it in borderline parishes in the inner city, such as Good Shepherd in the Bronx. And I have seen it in small-town parishes, such as Calvary, in Stonington, Connecticut, and in rural areas in the Catskills.

If it is true that the growth and vitality of a parish, at least in the Episcopalian institutional ethos, depend so much on the priest, what can be done to give rise to more effective leadership among clergy? Recruitment is one answer. Rather than waiting for men and women to present themselves for ordination, there should be a conscious effort to seek young men and women who are leaders and to cultivate them in such a way as to inspire vocations to the ordained ministry. The clergy are becoming much older as a group. We need younger men and women who are likely to be more innovative. Emphasis on lay leadership is needed, and it is essential that lay leaders stand by their priest. But I have yet to see a parish prosper, however dedicated its laity, unless the rector is effective.

This brings us to the issue of tenure, a thorny issue which has been discussed for years not only in the church but on college campuses. I believe that tenure is an institution whose time is past. It arose in a stable society in which freedom of the pulpit needed to be safeguarded. Today, there are volatile social movements, especially in the city, and there is a fast-changing culture which separates generations far more than ever before. (Slow-moving traffic tends to be bumper to bumper; traffic going sixty miles an hour leaves large spaces between cars. So it is with fast-changing culture and its impact on generational separation.)

It is increasingly difficult for the clergy to find employment if they are over fifty years old — this is a problem that cannot be ignored. Changing the tradition of tenure will take courage and the willingness of clergy to risk their security. This is not an easy choice, especially for clergy with families. If a responsible national committee of the Episcopal Church addressed the problem in all its aspects, some unforeseen solutions might arise. For instance, I used to imagine (but never carried out) an idea of changing clergy who had been in a parish over fifteen years with another priest of equal longevity and in a relatively similar situation. This would not create miracles, but at least a fresh start might lift the morale of one who had been preaching to the same congregation, year after year. A review of theological education would be part of such a survey for change.

Resourcefulness versus Immobilization

Energy, commitment, and imagination can deal with almost any problem. Without such commitment, the church idles and dies. After fifty years in the ministry and thirty-five years as a bishop, I realize the intractability of many problems and the inertia and apathy of any old institution. But, even if we do nothing, the fast-changing times will alter the church. If we take initiative and truly open our minds and hearts to the Holy Spirit, we can use the times as a source of energy and ride the waves of change like surfers. I like the image of a surfer, paddling quietly a few hundred yards off-shore, waiting for his wave to come. He sees it, turns toward the beach, and paddles faster and faster until he catches the wave. He stands up and soars to the beach. Another surfer sits with his back to the sea, does not see the wave coming, and is wiped out.

A Brief Word on Sexuality

So much has been written about sexuality that I hesitate to bring it up. But, since gay rights has been one of Bishop Spong's principal issues, I would like to comment, without belaboring all the pros and cons. My own conversion, as it were, came in dealing with the question, "Is honesty a bar to ordination?" I knew there were many gay priests who were not open about their sexual preferences, nor was there any reason they should be. Everyone has a right to privacy. However, when one woman who was open about her sexual orientation applied for postulancy, the Standing Committee and I, after long deliberations, decided to ordain her. Since then, an increasing number of openly gay and lesbian clergy have ministered in the Diocese of New York with great effectiveness and have been accepted by parishes from the North Bronx to Staten Island, *because they were good priests.*

Unlike Bishop Spong, I did not think it necessary to seek a resolution from our diocesan convention to ordain homosexuals, because the prerogative of choosing ordinands lies with a bishop and a diocese's standing committee. I realize there are parts of the world which are not ready for this step, and parts of the United States as well. Problems of acceptance characterized the civil rights movement, too. But since the right to discern vocation lies with a diocese's bishop and its ministries commission and standing committee, I think each diocese should make its own decision.

As with women's ordination, the practice of ordaining homosexuals will be accepted as the years unfold. No church in a major metropolitan environment in the United States today can afford to reject gay and lesbian persons.

Cooperation and Understanding among Faiths

Ecumenism is such a complicated issue that I am reluctant to deal with it in a short space. But one cannot think of the Kingdom of God and ignore that the church is composed of all baptized Christians. One cannot think of the Kingdom and ignore God's chosen people, the Jews. One cannot seek a religious solution for peace and ignore the Muslims. Nor can one have a sound understanding of creation or the Incarnation and ignore any human being.

Ecumenism can go from the insipid banalities of Brotherhood Week or prayer breakfasts to the amazing ecumenism in action of the civil rights movement. My firm belief is that true ecumenism is healthiest when it consists of persons working together for justice and peace. High-level theological discussions are important to the goal of institutional unity, intercommunion, the breakdown of prejudice, and the economics of over-churched small communities.

However, I have grave reservations about institutional amalgamation of churches which have vibrant doctrinal emphases and vital histories that nourish their roots. For instance, I would go along with intercommunion between Episcopalians and Lutherans, but their union would weaken the social activism of the Episcopal Church, such as it is, and the ecclesiastical roots of each church. The end product of mergers might well be a boring lowest common denominator, like that which has failed on college campuses over the years.

But the Lord commands us to be one. On a theological level, we are indeed one: "There is one Body and one Spirit.... One Lord, one Faith, one Baptism." I believe we should strive for intercommunion, but eschew institutional unity. The church need not follow corporations with larger and larger mergers. Churches are most effective in their particularity of time and space. As Jesus was incarnated in a particular time and place, in a particular human being, Christians need to foster the Incarnation of their separate churches in all of their particularities — geography, history, liturgy (or lack of it), music, and architecture. Thus incarnated, the Christ is a vivid image for his people, not a stained-glass Jesus with curly blond hair and blue eyes.

Having said all the above, I feel strongly about the need of churches and other faith groups to work together on issues of justice on the neighborhood, municipal, state, national, and international levels. Such mighty coalitions are necessary to confront the demonic trends of our society.

Many models of such cooperation have proven effective. In my own ministry, I have always been dependent on an intimate ecumenical fellowship of persons with the same values. In Jersey City, a coalition and I fought city hall; in Indianapolis, another allied group and I struggled against a pervasive conservatism, the extreme of which was the John Birch Society, founded across the street from where my wife and I lived; in Washington, an alliance and I fought Congress for home rule and local needs; in New York, blocs formed to protest against police abuses, the destruction of the South Bronx, prejudice against people with AIDS, and homelessness. Each of these ecumenical groups was structured differently, but what they had in common was a fierce commitment. More sophisticated arrangements exist, such as the Industrial Areas Foundation, which forms the basis of realistic urban efforts across the country.

National and international groupings also can be persuasive, although they vary in structure and long-range effectiveness. Some are formal, like the National and World Council of Churches, and some are ad hoc, like many movements in the 1960s. It is important to differentiate between a movement and an institution. The former is more vigorous, but less stable; the latter is long lasting but always tending to the stultification of bureaucracy.

The effectiveness of coalitions, in part, is based on a solid understanding of the dynamics of community organization. The temptation is to enlist powerful people to serve who can provide access to political clout and funding. However, I have found that the more powerful the committee's membership the less radical and, therefore, the less vigorous its program will be. An organization influenced by powerful financial or other celebrities will be less likely to confront the real source of a problem, which may be the very bank to which a member belongs or the very politician to whom a powerful organization member has access.

To sum up, I am leery of ecumenical mergers. But I am vehement about the need for ecumenical and interfaith cooperation on social issues, and I feel it is important to include secular groups, whenever feasible, in working for the Kingdom.

Conclusion

I conclude these remarks on Christianity at the birth of the twenty-first century by quoting from the charge I gave to the Diocese of New York in my retirement sermon:

> I charge you to be a Catholic church in love with freedom. I charge you to exercise your freedom by having courage. We have been made timid by great dangers: our lives are threatened on the streets by crime and drugs; our whole world can be destroyed by a nuclear war. But this is not a time to be timid; this is a time to be brave. I charge you to be Catholic, universal, open to all people. I charge you to be free in your mind to push forward the boundaries of theology, to liberate your thinking from the dusty metaphysics of the past to a new dynamic of the gospel, so that the vigor of its love invades the issues of the day. I charge you to face without flinching the approaching crises in our cities and our land. Dare to look on reality and stare it down by transforming it, whether homelessness, crack, AIDS, or a school system in deep trouble. No way, they say, can such problems be solved. No way, I say, can they remain unsolved.
>
> But how can I help? Start small. Get to know a homeless person. When you see a bad law coming up, write your Congressman. If you are young and brave, go to El Salvador. Whatever it is, do it at the behest of Christ, because one act of courageous love, however small, leads to another. When

men and women act together with courage, the power of goodness grows.

You are messengers of God's truth, clothed with the beauty of God. Take hope, be strong, be brave, be free, be open, be loving, and hold up the glory of the Heavenly City. Without a vision, the people perish. See that vision yourselves; remove the scales from your eyes so that you can see the Heavenly City so clearly that you will never cease until you have built Jerusalem in our land.

INDEX